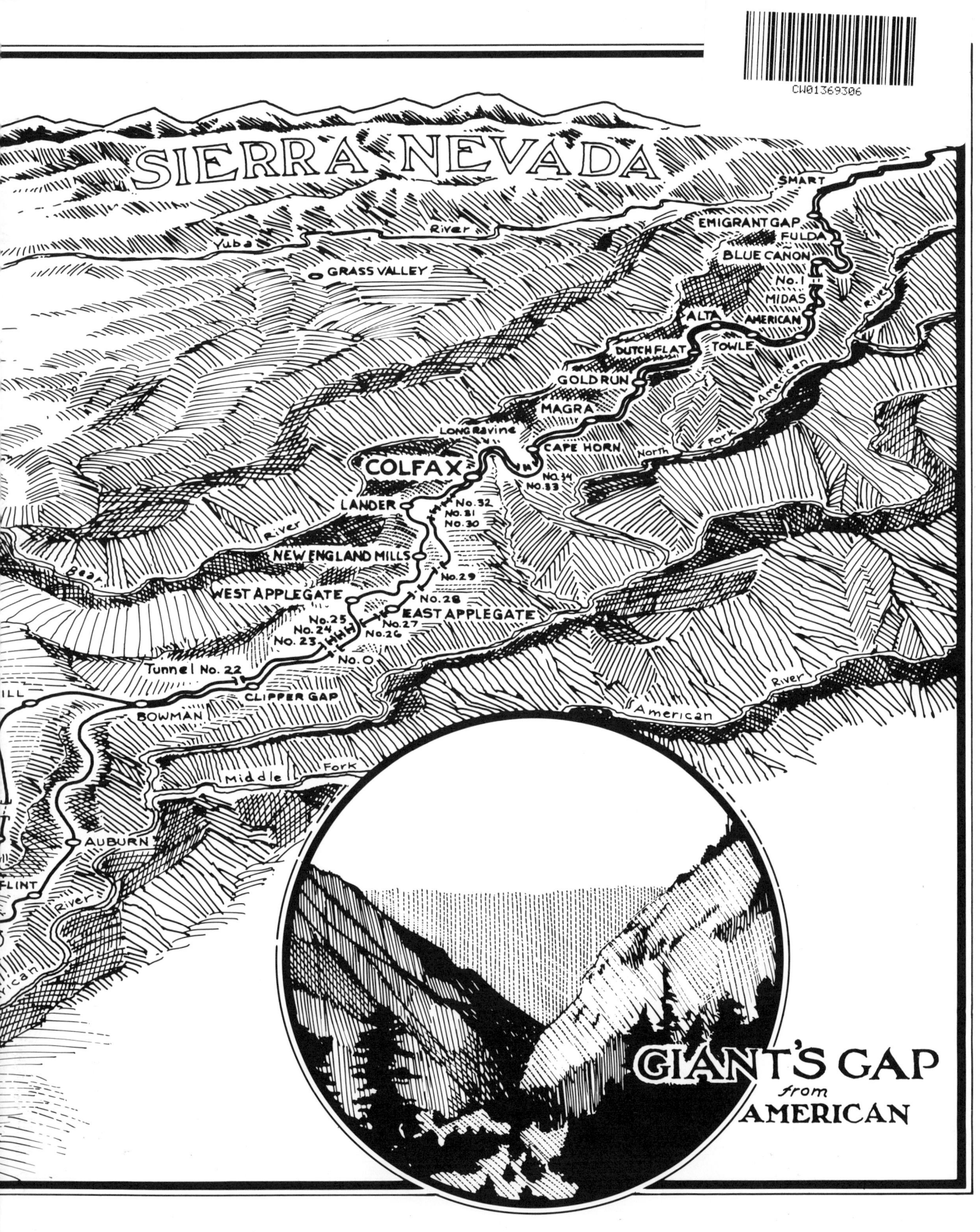

DONNER PASS

Southern Pacific's Sierra Crossing

John R. Signor

Golden West Books

San Marino, California • 91118-8250

DONNER PASS
Southern Pacific's Sierra Crossing

Copyright © 1985 by John R. Signor
All Rights Reserved
Published by Golden West Books
San Marino, California 91108 U.S.A.
Library of Congress Catalog Card No. 85-22001
I.S.B.N. No. 0-87095-094-0

Library of Congress Cataloging-in-Publication Data
Signor, John R.
　Donner Pass: Southern Pacific's Sierra crossing.
　Bibliography: p.
　Includes index.
　　1. Southern Pacific Company — History. 2. Donner Pass — History. I. Title. II. Title: Southern Pacific's Sierra crossing.
TF25.S68S52　1985　　385'.09794'37　　85-22001
ISBN 0-87095-094-0

First Printing — November 1985
Second Printing — January 1988
Third Printing — March 1997
Fourth printing — April 1999
Fifth Printing — February 2003

NOTE TO THE READER

Along the rails of the Southern Pacific System, many station and location names are of Spanish origin. On the route over Donner Pass, Blue Canon and Strong's Canon employ the Spanish word for canyon which in cañon. The Spanish language employs an accent over the letter "ñ." Southern Pacific station name boards and location signs, for some unknown reason, do not feature the Spanish accent. The text of this book does respect the proper use of this accent.

TITLE PAGE ILLUSTRATION

The *S.F. Overland,* running late due to storm conditions on the Salt Lake Division, rolls down through Yuba Pass on a wintry afternoon in the 1950's. A rotary snowplow, working the No. 2 track, pauses momentarily in its labors while the varnish slips by. Original oil painting is by John R. Signor.

Golden West Books
P.O. Box 80250 • San Marino, California • 91118-8250

To
Gerald Martin Best
1895-1985

Pioneer Southern Pacific O-gauge prototype modeler, chronicler of locomotive data and rosters of motive power, locomotive photographer, and author-historian of Southern Pacific topics and books.

Acknowledgments

The gathering together of information, spanning over a century of Southern Pacific operation in the high Sierra, could not have been accomplished without drawing on the resources and experiences of many.

Giving of their time and knowledge, employees of the Southern Pacific organization provided the core of material for this volume. Everyone was most eager to preserve and record their railroad heritage, especially at this time in history when, through merger, the Espee is rapidly changing.

I am deeply appreciative to Messrs., R.E. Buike, L.D. Farrar, A.C. Fox, R.B. Hoppe, W.F. Loomis, and J.C. Root, all from the headquarters office in San Francisco, who provided their generous support for this project.

From the division offices at Sacramento, I am grateful to the following people. They are the Ivanusich brothers (Joe and John), K.A. Moore, Rose P. Swanson, M.L. Wells and Blanche Wallner. Each one led me to many important details presented in this story.

Personal experiences and observations on the Mountain were gleaned from A.R. Aske, Rich Bowler, Manuel and Isabel Bravo, T.F. Custer, Dan Gaylian, Homer Jackson, Lawrence Kearny, A.G. Lutz, Jim Mahon, D.T. McDermott, W.R. McGee, Henry Midkiff, R.A. Miller, Sr., G.E. Nester, Johnny O'Kane, J.G. Pomykata, Roscoe C. Rasmussen, R.L. Schapp, Steve Wagner and W.G. Willits. All of these fine people were based out of Roseville at one time or another.

Also to A.C. Phelps of Auburn; Bill and Kay Fisher of Colfax; Sandi Strawn of Norden; Dennis Beeghly of Sparks; R.A. Miller, Jr., and Wes Ridgeway of Dunsmuir; and J.D. Schmid of West Oakland.

I am grateful, from the public sector, for the assistance rendered by Virginia Renner of the Huntington Library in San Marino; Sarah Timby of the Stanford University Special Collections; Conrad Pfeiffer of the Roseville Public Library; Walter P. Gray III of the California State Railroad Museum; Richard Markley of the Tahoe National Forest; John Creasor of the University of California at Berkeley; Jerry Harmon of the Shasta National Forest; David P. Morgan, editor of *Trains Magazine;* and also, to Roger Titus of the Donner Memorial State Park. Additional data was provided by Richard Tower of San Francisco.

It has been an enjoyable pleasure to examine the incredible wealth of photographs which surfaced during the course of researching this book about the Mountain. The task of singling out the best print to fit a particular layout has been difficult, as the Southern Pacific had vast archives yielding many important illustrations. I also wish to thank the many men who stood along the tracks on the Mountain waiting for a particular train to steam or growl by. I acknowledge, with gratitude, the following individuals who provided photographs from their own cameras or from their collections. They are A.R. Aske, R.R. Aszman, Dennis Beeghley, Ted Benson, Gerald M. Best, Manuel Bravo, R.E. Buike, S.R. Bush, Dr. Robert J. Church, "Duke" Davis, Dick Dorn, Donald Duke, Guy L. Dunscomb, Jim Evans, Bill Fisher, G.N. Flanders, Chuck Fox, James H. Harrison, D.T. McDermott, A.S. Menke, Bob Miller, Jr., Clint Nestell, J.F. Orem, Bruce Petty, A.C. Phelps, W.S. Pringle, T.O. Repp, Doug Richter, John Shaw, Dave Stanley, Richard Steinheimer, Roger Titus, W.C. Whittaker, Ted Wurm, Ken Yeo, Tim Zukas, and Mr. and Mrs. Roger Zwanzinger. Special camera work and processing of prints was undertaken by Stan Kistler, Guy L. Dunscomb, Richard Steinheimer, and Fred Schneider III.

Lastly, I would like to acknowledge the efforts of L.D. Farrar, Alan Aske, Dennis Beeghley, Jerry Harmon, Donald Duke, Vernice Dagosta, and my wife Julie for reading the manuscript for factual, as well as, spelling and grammatical errors.

— JAMES H. HARRISON COLLECTION

Table of Contents

Introduction 9

1 - Construction and Early Operation 1860-1899 11

2 - The Harriman Influence 1900-1929 51

3 - The Modern Steam Era 1930-1955 145

4 - Contemporary Operations 1956-1985 211

Epilogue 275

Appendix 276

    A - Mountain Passenger Trains 1899-1984 276

    B - Seasonal Snowfall at Summit 1878-1926, Norden 1926-1985 279

    C - Selected Timetables 280

Bibliography 287

Index 288

— RICHARD STEINHEIMER

Introduction

Lean back in your chair and get ready to enjoy the most authoritative and complete book on Donner Pass railroading you or I will probably ever read.

John Signor, researcher, writer, artist and Southern Pacific conductor from Dunsmuir, California, brings us the full story of rail operations over the West's first mountain mainline.

This story begins with surveyor Theodore D. Judah and the four Sacramento businessmen who took Judah's plan for a Pacific Railroad and actually pushed the rails of the Central Pacific Railroad over the "impossible" 7,000-foot Sierra Nevada summit. In fact, during the construction, if it had not been for the heavy snows of the last three winters, the Central Pacific could have met the rails of the Union Pacific at Laramie or Cheyenne. With men of lesser drive and courage, it could have been Truckee or Reno.

As it was, the 1869 meeting of the rails at Promontory, Utah, transformed California from and island of mining and farming, 15,000 miles away by sea by way of Cape Horn, to a state fully involved in the political, economic and social life of the Union.

For all the wealth and power gained by the "Big Four," their reputations would always rest firmly on their conquest of Donner Pass despite the universal doubt and ridicule by those not involved with the project.

One hundred and twenty years later, the old Central Pacific route is still the ultimate proving ground for the men and machines of the Southern Pacific, as it was for the diligent Chinese laborers and their Irish foremen in the harsh days of construction.

Here's where men proved they had the *right stuff*...men like Charles Crocker, the tough-fisted construction boss; and his right hand man, James Strobridge, who carried on his work but with only one eye, lost due to an earlier blasting accident. Donald J. Russell helped lead the double-tracking program of the 1920's, later rising in the ranks of the Southern Pacific to the presidency. Sacramento Division Superintendent Bill Hack took to the Sierra with flangers, rotary plows, cab-forwards and 2-8-0's in the tremendous winter of 1937-38, keeping the pass open despite an 805-inch snow season at Norden.

Giants still roam the mountain. Regional maintenance of way manager Jim Mahon's forceful management of snowfighting is probably worth two rotary snowplows, anytime.

In this book, *Donner Pass*, you'll see how operations on "The Hill" evolved from the early 4-4-0 steam power to the generations of cab-forwards that gave enginemen a great advantage in the tight tunnels and in the nearly 40 miles of snowsheds that once roofed-in most of the railroad between Blue Cañon and Truckee. Also, the arrival of the first diesels, and the generations to follow.

Accompanying the text are incredible pictures taken by Southern Pacific and outside photographers showing the many trains, stations and facilities that once were a part of Sierra railroading. Locations unfamiliar today, such as Champion, Donner, Strong's Canyon, Stanford, Summit and Cascade, all have their unique stories revealed to those of our generation who are more familiar with everything demolished along the rights-of-way, bulldozed depots, remote CTC operations, and motive power that hardly varies from railroad to railroad.

It's the richness of research and pictorial content of *Donner Pass* that places this book on a par with the finest pictorial histories produced anywhere in the U.S.A.

As railroad enthusiasts, and as employees, we owe a debt of gratitude to John Signor and his publisher, Donald Duke, of Golden West Books. Their collaboration and the many contributions of Southern Pacific employees and fans has created a book worthy of this great mountain railroad.

Richard Steinheimer
Sacramento, California
July 1, 1985

**A Central Pacific engine heads out the 12-mile tangent east of the American River Bridge. It was in the immediate vicinity of Arcade Creek that President Lincoln, in a controversial decision, established the foot of the Sierra Nevada mountains. —
ALFRED HART, SOUTHERN PACIFIC COLLECTION**

1
Construction and Early Operation 1860-1899

From a strategic vantage point near Donner Summit one can trace for several miles, the Southern Pacific's double-tracked right-of-way over the high Sierra. Now and then a modern 100-car train drawn by powerful diesel locomotives snakes into view, threading the tunnels, curves and sheds, and then disappears from sight. As of this writing, trains have been rolling over this portion of the legendary "Overland Route" for nearly 120 years with few serious interruptions. In an age where freeways are hammered through locations that the most optimistic surveyor of a century ago would have considered even a wagon road as sheer folly, it is easy to lose sight of the engineering achievement that this railroad represents. The formidable geology of the Sierra Nevada is one of the principal topographic features of the entire western United States. This massive granitic block forms an unbroken range of mountains extending 360 miles along the eastern border of the state of California, and divides the watersheds of the Great Basin and the Pacific slope. The western face, riddled with steep and narrow box-like canyons, is 50 to 60 miles broad with a gradual rise of only two to six percent. The eastern face, in contrast, rises abruptly from the bordering valleys; 4,000 feet or more in the north to 7,000 feet or more in the south along the Owens Valley. The summits, many enveloped in glaciers, increase gradually from 6,000 to 8,000 feet in altitude in the Feather River country to about 10,000 feet west of Lake Tahoe. Twelve peaks exceeding 14,000 feet are prominent in the south. That a railroad, built largely by hand with primitive tools and techniques, was able to surmount such an imposing barrier is amazing enough. The fact that, with certain minor modifications, it continues to adequately meet the needs of modern operation is extraordinary and a credit to its designers and builders.

The recorded history of these mountains began precisely on April 2, 1772, when missionary Pedro Font, while traveling with a band of soldiers in the San Joaquin Valley, mentioned in his diary about lofty peaks to the east and termed them "Una Gran Sierra Nevada" -a great snowy range. Spanish occupants of the coastal hills thought of them as "terra incognita," distant and foreboding and a barrier to invasion from the east, although later events proved otherwise.

The first white men to provide a definite account of travel across the Sierra were a party of trappers led by Jedediah Smith who, having entered California by a southern route in 1826, attempted to leave the following year. Traveling northward in the San Joaquin Valley, Smith made attempts to cross the Sierra at the Kings and American rivers only to be turned back by heavy snow, but a successful crossing was finally made by following the Stanislaus River to its source. The divide was crossed not far from present day Ebbetts Pass. Joseph Walker and his party passed over the mountains a few years later between the Merced and Tuolumne rivers. Colonel John C. Fremont and his band of soldiers, with Kit Carson as guide, crossed the Sierra with great difficulty during the late winter of 1844 at an elevation of 8,573 feet by way of, what was subsequently named, Carson Pass. Fremont was soon followed by others traveling the central "Overland Route" to California.

The notch in the Sierra through which the rails of Southern Pacific's Mountain Subdivision, of the Sacramento Division, today surmount the Sierra, had not up to this point been utilized. This distinction was to go to Elisha Stevens and his party of emigrants. Traveling west in the Humboldt Sink during the summer of 1844, the party encountered an old Paiute chief who led them west following the present Truckee River. With some difficulty, Stevens and his party crossed the mountains during the winter of 1844-45 above what later became Donner Lake. This breech of the Sierra, at an elevation of 7,135 feet, might well have been called Steven's Pass were it not for the tragedies which befell another group of emigrants traveling the same route during the autumn of 1846.

Freighting by wagon and team over Donner Pass increased noticeably as the mines of Nevada burst onto the scene. — R.A. MILLER JR. COLLECTION

A group of emigrants, having gathered in Missouri and led by George Donner, started west in the spring of 1846. But an untried detour in Utah cost them several weeks delay and reaching what is now Donner Lake, on October 31, 1846, the party found the summit obscured by snow. Some remained at the lake while another party set out on horseback for Sutter's Fort seeking help. Late in December, with no rescue in sight, a group of 15 of those left behind attempted the pass on crude snowshoes. It was this group, known as the party of forlorn hope, that resorted to cannibalism. Eighteen men died of starvation and exposure while two men and five women reached safety. Of the 81 who reached Donner Lake that fateful season, 36 died at its shores or while attempting the summit.

These isolated parties were the pioneers in a westward movement which, following one single event, expanded from a trickle to a flood. On a cold January morning in 1848, James Marshall scooped up some gold from an excavation near John Sutter's flour mill at the settlement of Colma and the Gold Rush was on. "Never before in history," writes historian Carl Wheat, "had men so rapidly overun so vast an unoccupied territory." Within 18 months, the American population in California soared from 2,000 to over 53,000 individuals. The majority of these fortune seekers came by sea around Cape Horn but many undertook the long journey overland. The preponderance of these followed the Donner Pass route into the state. By 1849, Lt. George H. Derby, of the Topographical Engineers, was reporting that an average of 100 wagons and 200 emigrants were using this well-beaten path over the mountains each day.

This great migration served to further the cause which would bind the west coast to the rest of the nation by rail. Some agitation for a Pacific Railroad had been voiced as early as 1836. By 1850, the Pacific Railroad was a regular order of business before Congress. In 1853, Congress directed Secretary of War Jefferson Davis to "ascertain the most practical and economical route for a railroad from the Mississippi River to the Pacific Ocean." Davis responded by dispatching five columns of Army Engineers whose reports filled twelve large volumes with maps, narrative and pictures. After three years of reconnaissance, their work was largely completed and today many of the routes that they recommended have developed into the mainlines of major western transcontinental railroads. Even the mainline of the Union Pacific and Central Pacific closely follows the Pacific Railroad survey from Council Bluffs, Nebraska, to the Sierra Nevada mountains. The surveyors found the barrier of the Sierra so great, that they recommended two routes west which

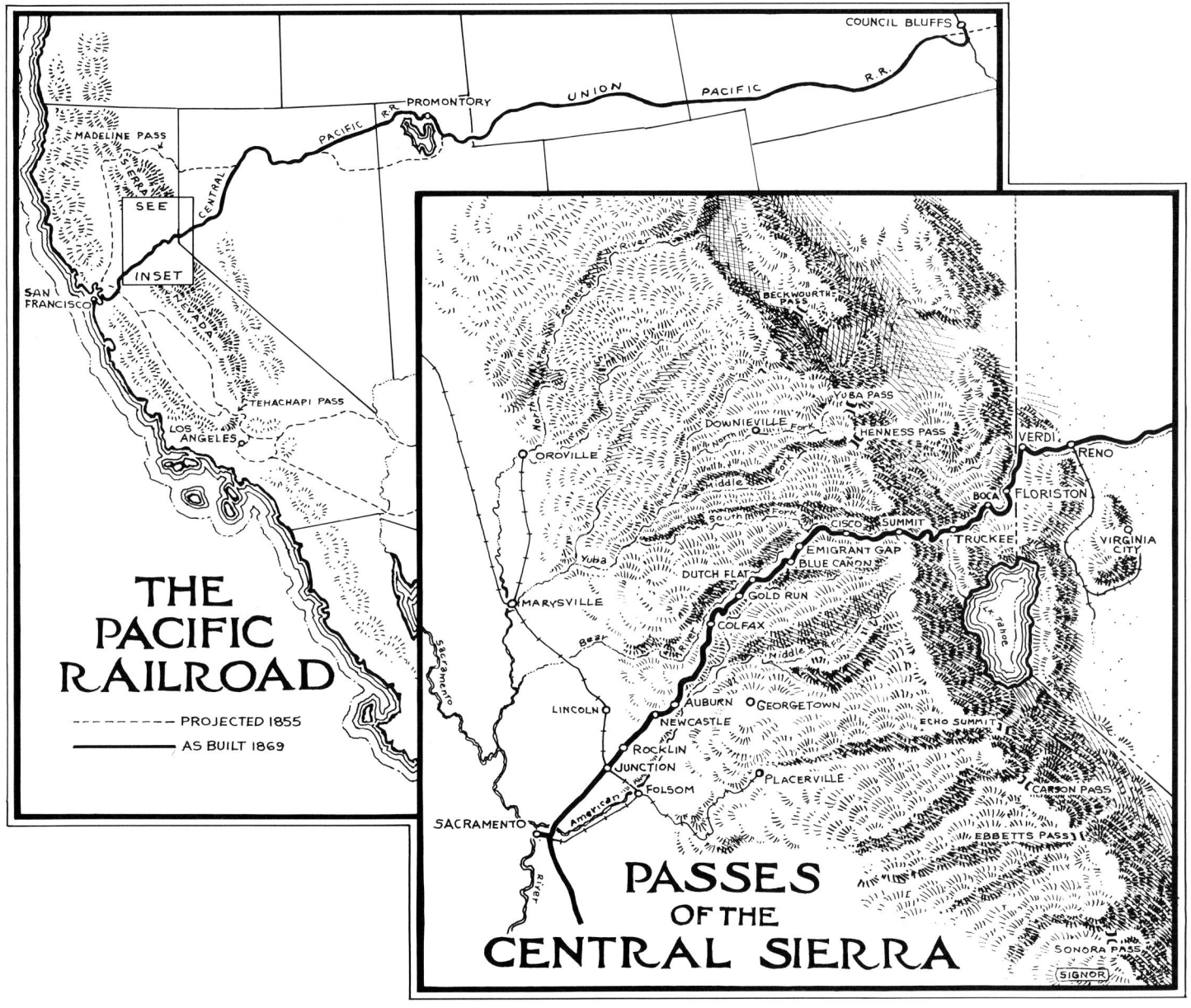

circumvented the range entirely; one through Tehachapi Pass in southern California and another threading the canyons north of Mt. Lassen.

While the Army was at work mapping the west, a young civil engineer named Theodore Dehone Judah came to California during May 1854, as the chief engineer for California's first rail venture, the Sacramento Valley Railroad. It was Judah's concentrated enthusiasm for the Pacific Railroad which ultimately led to its construction and the conquering of the Sierra Nevada by rail.

The idea of a Pacific Railroad was a popular one on the coast and railroad conventions were held at San Francisco in 1853, 1854, 1857 and 1859 to urge Congress, by resolution, to act on the matter. It was at the 1859 convention that Judah was selected to represent the group in the nation's capital. Judah had prior experience in Washington, was enthusiastic and knew the Sierra as well as anyone.

Following the completion of the Sacramento Valley Railroad in 1856, Judah was engaged in surveying the Sierra for passes suitable for a wagon road. While a passage for wagons was the immediate goal, a railroad grade was uppermost in his mind.

The railroad convention advocated the adoption of the Noble Pass route for the Pacific Railroad. This projected course, surveyed by the Army in 1855, entered California at the 41st parallel, crossing what is now the Madeline Plains in eastern Modoc County. It then followed the drainage of the Pitt River past Shasta City and into the

Theodore Dehone Judah, whose concentrated enthusiasm for the Pacific Railroad ultimately led to the conquering of the Sierra Nevada mountains by rail. — DONALD DUKE COLLECTION

upper reaches of the Sacramento Valley near present day Redding. Judah studied this route carefully as he did the so-called Henness Pass route. Henness Pass was north of Donner Summit about 20 miles and was achieved by diverging from the regular Donner route at Verdi. By taking this pass, a comparatively easy crossing of the Sierra could be made by following Dog Valley and the Little Truckee River to the headwaters of the Yuba River. From there, the route moved south to Downieville. Armed with this information and a good deal of optimism, Judah lobbied long and hard in Congress for the Pacific Railroad.

Returning from Washington during the spring of 1860, Judah once again journeyed into the mountains. At that time, Daniel W. "Doc" Strong, a Dutch Flat druggist, was seeking a road over the Sierra by which some of the emigrants could travel and thus, be diverted through his settlement. He was aware of Judah's search and wrote him of a new route he had stumbled upon. Discarding a conventional river canyon location, Strong discovered a route which followed an unbroken ridge between the south fork of the Yuba and Bear rivers and the north fork of the American River.

Judah responded promptly and, with Strong's aid, enough money was raised in Dutch Flat to pay for the cost of an investigation. This examination brought out that Strong's route for a railroad was feasible, shorter and more direct than any previously offered and fully 150 miles shorter than the survey of the Army. In August 1860, Judah returned to Dutch Flat with a definite location for the Pacific Railroad over the Sierra Nevada. On November 1st of that year, a circular was published, detailing his plans and inviting subscriptions for "The Central Pacific Railroad to California."

Judah journeyed to San Francisco seeking capital for his venture but there were few takers. Men of means were only interested in the quick return which could be generated in a frontier economy. Judah's project would take years to return a profit and besides, no one seriously believed that a railroad could successfully breach the Sierra. A subsequent meeting in Sacramento proved even more disheartening.

It was at a second meeting in Sacramento, held in a room above a hardware store at 54 K Street, that the tide began to turn. About a dozen men were present and among them were four merchants; Leland Stanford, a wholesale grocer; Charles Crocker, a dry goods dealer; Mark Hopkins and Collis Huntington, proprietors of the hardware store downstairs. It was these four men who would undertake the project, amass great wealth from it, and ultimately cast long shadows over the affairs of men in the west as the legendary and formidable "Big Four."

As a result of his previous disappointments, Judah toned down his presentation from the idealistic "Pacific Railroad" to stress the more immediate short term features of the idea — how to expand business, stifle the competition and how to capture the Nevada mine traffic then rushing to the Washoe. Nothing was decided at this meeting but at Huntington's request, Judah was invited to recount his plans in more detail to a smaller group of just the four. As a result of these private conversations, Huntington said he would be willing to pay his share for a proper survey but would promise nothing more until the results of the survey were analyzed, and the others agreed. Judah left at once for the mountains and made barometrical observations of three routes; one through El Dorado County by way of Georgetown; another by way of Dutch Flat; a third by way of Henness Pass. The Noble Pass route, which entered California at the 41st parrallel, had by now been discounted as the possibilities of a more central route seemed reasonably certain.

Field parties were organized in the spring of 1861, and a thorough survey of the Dutch Flat route demonstrated that the difficulties of the course could be avoided or overcome for railroad purposes and that a grade no greater than 105 feet to the mile could be developed. With satisfactory reports from Judah, Huntington and his associates incorporated the Central Pacific Railroad Company of California on June 28, 1861. Stanford, who had just been elected Governor of California, was selected as president of the corporation, Huntington as vice-president, Hopkins as treasurer and Judah as chief engineer. Crocker became the major construction contractor.

After filing the report on his surveys, Judah sailed for New York on October 10, 1861. His objective was to do all in his power to secure, through Congress, the passage of a Pacific Railroad bill which would recognize the Central Pacific Railroad of California as the organization to build the western end of the transcontinental road. In line with this, he was to secure as much government aid as possible.

That spring (April 12, 1861), war had broken out between the Union and Confederate forces and Judah found that Congress was more receptive to the Pacific Railroad than before as it had now become a war measure. His drive was a key element in a series of motions which led to the Pacific Railroad Bill passing in the House during May 1862. It was passed by the Senate the following day and on July 1, 1862, President Lincoln affixed his signature to the document.

The Pacific Railroad Bill provided for the construction of a railroad and telegraph line from the Missouri River to the Pacific Ocean. The Central Pacific was charged with building eastward over the mountains to the boundary of California. This provision was ultimately lifted to allow the Central Pacific to continue eastward until it met the Union Pacific, the company authorized to build west from the Missouri. Considerable aid was granted, including a 400 foot wide right-of-way through all public lands with provisions for station and terminal grounds, ten and ultimately 20 alternate sections per mile, and a large cash subsidy. This amounted to, in United States bonds, $16,000 per

Collis P. Huntington

Mark Hopkins

Leland Stanford

Charles Crocker

— ALL DONALD DUKE COLLECTION

Four Howe truss bridges and several hundred feet of trestle were required to span the American River. — SOUTHERN PACIFIC COLLECTION

A view of the original Dry Creek bridge, 17 miles east of Sacramento. This bucolic scene, long gone, is now in the heart of the busy Roseville yards. — SOUTHERN PACIFIC COLLECTION

Work is underway in 1864 on the elaborate Newcastle trestle which was 528 feet long and 66 feet high. — SOUTHERN PACIFIC COLLECTION

mile in flat territory and $48,000 to the mile for the 150 miles east of the western base of the Sierra Nevada mountains. All of this aid, however, was contingent on the successful completion and approval of the first 40 miles of track.

Surveying parties remained in the field during the fall of 1862, restudying alternative routes. At this time, serious attention was directed towards the Feather River Canyon. Judah, Huntington and three others went so far as to hike down the middle fork of the Feather River. This route proved to be an extremely crooked one with angles of every variety. Judah estimated that between 30 and 40 tunnels, with much rock work, would be required. This route, adopted much later by the Western Pacific Railroad, was ruled out as too difficult and costly to pursue.

Meanwhile, the government's offer was formally accepted and at last, on January 8, 1863, construction on the Central Pacific Railroad began at Front and K streets in downtown Sacramento. No sooner was it evident that the "Big Four" actually intended to build a railroad over the Sierra, when the most tremendous opposition to the enterprise developed in California.

All those with vested interests, including the steam navigation companies, clipper ship owners, express and telegraph companies and toll road operators, joined the chorus of discord. Sacramento Valley Railroad's L.L. Robinson scoffed that "a railway across the Semmering Alps, from Vienna to Trieste, is a bagatelle as compared with the projected line via Dutch Flat." The contention that the four merchants, widely known for their shrewdness and an ability to turn a quick profit, were actually planning to build the western half of a transcontinental railroad, was not taken seriously. Despite this antagonism, the first 18 miles of road through the streets of Sacramento, across the American River and on to Junction (now Roseville) was finished February 29, 1864. However, due to delays in rail shipments, it was not until April 26th that the railroad was in operation to this point. Here a connection was made with the California Central Railroad, a modest pike projected north from Folsom towards Marysville.

Placer County now joined those opposed to the Central Pacific. The completion of the line would ruin a wagon road already in place over the mountains, in which the county had a large vested interest. As the rails slowly inched their way toward the mountains, a pamphlet was issued August 18, 1864, entitled "The Dutch Flat Swindle," alleging that no rails would be laid beyond Dutch Flat. Its authors also predicted that the route over the Sierra, designed to monopolize the California-Nevada trade, would never be completed beyond a wagon road. Some credence was

The roots of the Central Pacific were firmly planted in the California State capital on the banks of the Sacramento River. The Arcade station appears on the east bank. — JAMES H. HARRISON COLLECTION

lent to this allegation as the "Big Four" had indeed organized the Dutch Flat & Donner Lake Wagon Road Company to extend an already existing partially completed road from Virginia City west to meet the railhead. After two seasons, however, the road was no longer of service as an adjunct to the Central Pacific and was given to the counties through which it passed.

Even Judah had reason to complain. He saw the first 40 miles of the railroad as a part of a great transcontinental route which would one day bind the nation together. Judah wanted to build for the ages. But the "Big Four" were only interested in building the first 40 mile section to the degree of quality required for government inspection, in order to become eligible for the federal aid.

A decision of great importance had been made by President Lincoln concerning the government money. The Pacific Railroad Bill, in its original form, provided for a 300 percent increase in the amount of loan bonds available per mile once construction crews reached the western base of the Sierra. The increase in aid, wisely granted by Congress out of deference to rugged mountain construction, was to apply to the 150 miles encountered east of that point. Just exactly where

This modest riverfront shack served as the railroad's first passenger station, division headquarters, supply base and executive offices. — DONALD DUKE COLLECTION

Three Central Pacific Ten-Wheelers, heavily ladened with wood, pause for the camera at Rocklin (ABOVE) while in helper service during the 1880's. Contemporary accounts held that each engine consumed 16 cords of wood on the 82-mile run from Rocklin to the Summit. — DONALD DUKE COLLECTION

Shown at the left, Bloomer Cut, an 800-foot long by 85-foot deep slot in the foothills below Auburn, dwarfed a westbound Central Pacific locomotive. — ALFRED HART, SOUTHERN PACIFIC COLLECTION (BELOW) Central Pacific's 880-foot Long Ravine Trestle towers 113 feet above the Nevada County Narrow-Gauge Railway line en route to Grass Valley. — SOUTHERN PACIFIC COLLECTION

the base of the Sierra began was a serious bone of contention. The Department of the Interior suggested that it should begin at the end of the first 50 mile section. The California Supreme Court was of the opinion that it began 31 miles east of Sacramento where there was an appreciable rise in gradient. Huntington and his associates, however, summoned the professional advice of Josiah W. Whitney, California State Geologist, E.F. Beale, U.S. Surveyor General of California and J.F. Houghton, California Surveyor General, who all concurred that the western base of the Sierra actually commenced at Arcade Creek, 7.18 miles east of Sacramento. This was demonstrated by the character of the rock and, although not perceptible to the eye, a regular and continuous ascent. This evidence was then presented to President Lincoln by Aaron Sargent. Lincoln moved quickly to establish the new location making the Central Pacific eligible for more than $700,000 in bonds. "Here is a case," said Sargent, "in which Abraham's faith has moved mountains."

Judah questioned the ethics of the "Big Four" in this maneuver and in refusing to endorse their position on the matter, he widened an already growing rift with Huntington, The showdown came in mid-1863. Determined to buy the "Big Four" out, Judah sailed for the east via Panama on October 3, 1863, reportedly to meet with investors, "men of known public spirit," who would, without other designs, take the Pacific Railroad to a successful completion. Catching yellow fever aboard ship, Judah passed from the scene November 2nd. For a time his assistant, L.M. Clement, continued his work but at the next board meeting the associates advanced Samuel Sherry Montague to the position of Chief Engineer.

Despite these upsets and controversies, track was laid to Rocklin by March 10, 1864. A week later an excursion was run to the site with an estimated two-thirds of the California State Legislature, their families and friends aboard. On March 15, 1864, three carloads of granite, weighing 30 tons, were shipped from Rocklin's Brigham's quarries destined for San Francisco — reportedly the first freight to pass over the new road. By December of that year, the first Federal aid had been earned and it could not have come at a better time.

Extremely heavy grading was encountered at Bloomer divide on what is now the No. 1 track below Auburn. Work was begun there late in 1864, blasting a cut more than 800 feet long to a maximum depth of 85 feet through a formation of cemented boulders. Every foot had to be cleared with black powder, but the construction crews prevailed and trains were first run into Auburn on May 13, 1865. The steep sides of this rocky cut stand today just as the builders left them. The cement that dulled drills and broke picks so long ago shows no more signs of disintegration than if the cut had been carved out of solid granite.

With more money available, the work force in the mountains was increased. By April 1865, it had swollen to 1,200; by June 2,000 and before July there were over 4,000 men at work. It was during this period that the first Chinese were put to work on the construction of the Central Pacific. Railroad labor was uncertain and expensive, and many of California's laborers were also miners. Mining was more to their liking than the discipline of railroad work and when they "hired out" it was usually for the sole purpose of getting a "stake" in order to go prospecting for gold. During the White Pine excitement which occurred in the mountains of central Nevada, almost 2,000 laborers were shipped across the Sierra by the builders of the Central Pacific before they were able to get 100 men to stay on the job. Most signed on just to get transportation over the mountains.

It was Charles Crocker who conceived the idea to employ Chinese. James Harvey Strobridge, his superintendent of construction, was skeptical of the plan, but gave in after a series of trials clearly demonstrated their worth. Crocker argued that a race capable of building the Great Wall of China could certainly be useful in railroad construction. Before the Central Pacific was completed, and the race across Nevada against the Union Pacific was in full swing, Crocker boasted of nearly 12,000 on the payroll. Although this was an exaggeration calculated to strike fear among the opposition, and their true numbers will probably never be known, it was substantial, amounting to, perhaps, as many as 9,000.

The railroad was now deep in the heart of the gold country. The first gold strike at Auburn had occurred exactly 20 years earlier. Known as Rich Dry Diggins at the time, Auburn was now a sizeable community, but the spirit of '49 hung over the town and surrounding vicinity. James Marshall's famous discovery had occurred at Colma, only a dozen or so miles southeast of the town and for the next 30 miles the Central Pacific right-of-way wound upgrade through the gold-bearing foothills. Rails reached Clipper Gap on June 10, 1865, and trains were first run into Illinoistown, 55 miles from Sacramento, on September 4th. This settlement, now in the immediate vicinity of Colfax, served as the gateway for the rich Nevada City-Grass Valley district, second only to the Mother Lode itself as a source of vein gold in California.

Grading above Colfax began August 1, 1865, and before the end of the year two-thirds of the work between there and Dutch Flat, a distance of

Master photographer Carleton Emmons Watkins captured this westbound freight train on a glass plate negative as it rounded Cape Horn in the 1880's. The grade was steep in this section and the train's descent was controlled by brakemen riding the car tops (LEFT) and whose principal duty was to apply and release the primitive staff brakes, a method not always successful. There is record of at least two trains which, speeding out of control, plummeted over the edge to the valley of the north fork of the American River 2,000 feet below. — BOTH DONALD DUKE COLLECTION

13 miles, had been completed. One-half mile below Dutch Flat station, the grade rested on tertiary gold-bearing gravel. This portion of the ground, essential for railroad location, was jealously guarded by Central Pacific agents from attack by local miners. As late as 1916, its value was placed at $8.00 a cubic yard.

The grade up to this point had been realized without too much rockwork. It had been the original plan to bridge the deeper ravines and gaps between Colfax and Newcastle with timber structures, but wherever possible earthen embankments were built. In a stretch of 25 miles of track over broken country, the only wooden structures were the Newcastle trestle (86 feet high and 528 feet long), a smaller structure near Auburn (30 feet high and 416 feet long), several hundred feet of trestle and two 40 foot spans a Lovell's Gap, one near Clipper Gap (50 feet high and 450 feet long), and one trestle of four bents at Lower Illinoistown Gap.

At Cape Horn, a promontory overlooking the gorge of the north fork of the American River, five miles above Colfax by rail, the Chinese met their first great challenge. Lowered over the cliff in "bosun's chairs," the Chinese did preliminary rock cutting while suspended 2,500 feet above the river. The battle with the Sierra was now being waged in earnest. Increases in the work force made it possible to extend the line of constuction to the very summit. Camps were erected at all the tunnels and heavy grading points. In the next 50 miles up and over the summit, the builders contemplated drilling 16 tunnels through the granite ridges of the high Sierra. With mountain construction in high gear, more than 500 kegs of powder a day were being consumed. There were as many as 30 vessels at sea simultaneously, all loaded with supplies from eastern manufacturers destined for the Central Pacific.

Work had begun at the east and west portals of the 1,659 foot summit tunnel in August 1865 and in early 1866 it was decided to pursue the work from four faces. In order to begin work from the center, it was necessary to sink a shaft through rock so hard that seven inches was all the progress that could be made in a day. It was December 19, 1866, before the shaft was deep enough to begin the laterals.

The winter of 1865-66 was a harsh one. Snow in the mountains stopped work on the tunnels and heavy rains made the wagon roads below the snow line impassable. The clay soils of the foothills were reduced to a mire that made staging impossible. One stage got stuck in the mud and was left stranded in the streets of Gold Run for six weeks. The end of track was cut back to Colfax and those parties wishing to continue over the mountains had to resort to a saddle train.

With the spring thaw, railroad work was resumed in early 1866. During that summer, three shifts of men were kept at work day and night on the approaches to the tunnels, while tracklaying continued at lower elevations. Trains were operated to Secret Town in May. Dutch Flat was reached by the end of June and Alta on July 15th. By November 29, 1866, through cars were operated to Cisco and the builders were working hard against the granite barriers blocking the last 12 miles to the summit. Seven tunnels were planned in the space of two miles from the summit to Tunnel No. 13.

The formation, through which these were bored, was so hard that explosives shot out of the holes like a charge from a cannon without disturbing the solidity of the surrounding rock. The builders had no precedents to guide them in the use of powder and very often a great deal more was used to do the work than was necessary. There were many instances where the too wasteful use of black powder upset the plans of the engineering department and sent a goodly number of Celestials to their graves. J.H. Strobridge, himself, lost an eye in a blast at Bloomer cut. A nitroglycerin factory was established near the summit tunnel but its use was abandoned after a major mishap. Crocker ordered the workers to bury the stuff.

The winter of 1866-67 was more severe. There were 44 separate storms, some of which deposited as much as 10 feet of snow. The total snowfall was 40 feet and at Summit the pack averaged 18 feet on the level. The snow came early and stayed late. During that bleak winter the railroad was barely kept open to Alta and the remaining 21 miles to Cisco was abandoned to the elements until March 19, 1867. At that time there was still 15 feet of snow in the Summit Valley.

The builders were determined not to let the huge undertaking stagnate as they had the previous season. Work on the tunnels went on, even though it was necessary to dig snow tunnels up to 200 feet long in order to keep the entrances open. There were many snowslides that winter with entire camps carried away and the bodies of the men not recovered until the following summer. Track and grading work near the summit was out of the question under such conditions so Crocker reponded by sending the force not engaged in tunnel work to the Truckee River canyon where lighter snowfall made grading possible. In an heroic effort, teamsters hauled a locomotive, 40 cars and enough material for 40 miles of track over twisting mountain roads to Coburn's Station (Truckee) to begin work on the east side of the range. It was June 1867, before these forces were brought back to the summit.

Emigrant Gap, almost one vertical mile above San Francisco, was the point where the Central Pacific moved from the American River side of the ridge to the Yuba River side. — ALFRED HART, SOUTHERN PACIFIC COLLECTION

On August 30, 1867, the summit tunnel was holed-through, although two more months went by before the first locomotive was able to pass through. By the time winter set in again, the rails were two miles east of the new station at Summit. Most of the grade was ready for the track layers between this point and Coburn's Station but it was decided to wait until spring to complete this section. A large force of men continued to make progress, however, in the Truckee River canyon. Grading was comparably light and only two tunnels were required; No. 14 through hard material west of present day Floriston, and No. 15 between Mystic and the state line. A Central Pacific locomotive first nosed across the state line into Nevada on December 13, 1867.

The seven mile gap in the line was completed just west of Coburn's Station on June 18, 1868, and the next day the first through train entered the settlement. Originally called Gray's Station, then Coburn's for the proprietor of a local stage stop, the place was eventually christened Truckee after the railroad was established. Stages connected at Truckee for such isolated points as Randolph, Sierraville, Sierra City, Downieville, Jamison City, Eureka Mills and Loyalton.

On May 4, 1868, the rails had reached the end of track on the north bank of the Truckee River, 14 miles east of the California-Nevada line. At this spot, an auction was held for town lots and, on May 9th, Reno sprouted into existence. From the very outset, Reno was the transfer point for freight and passenger traffic destined for Virginia City and the Washoe, and as such, grew rapidly. Tracklaying continued eastward and Wadsworth Nevada, was reached on July 22, 1868. Here division yards and repair shops were erected.

It had taken a total of five and one-half years to build the 188 miles from Sacramento to Wadsworth, but with the rail "pipeline" to the coast in place, construction escalated to a fever pitch. The next 501 miles, built eastward to a junction with the Union Pacific, took but nine months to complete. From 20,000 to 25,000 men and from 5,000 to 6,000 teams were employed and between five and six hundred tons of material were used daily.

The Central Pacific and Union Pacific forces established a definite junction point in the barren wind-swept country north of the Great Salt Lake and on May 10, 1869, at a tent town called Promontory, Utah Territory, 690 miles from Sacramento and 1,086 miles from Omaha, the rails of the Pacific Railroad were officially united.

During October of the previous year, as the railhead was rapidly advancing eastward across the Great Basin, a party of special commissioners, appointed by the President of the United States, was directed to examine the facilities of the Central Pacific Railroad and its telegraph line. Their report, filed in January 1869, provides an

During the hustle and bustle of construction, Cisco, boasting a population of 7,000, was, for over a year and one-half, the eastern terminus of the railroad. — ALFRED HART, SOUTHERN PACIFIC COLLECTION

After the terminal moved east, some buildings were torn down and others were left to decay. Eventually, a fire left nothing but a freight house and a platform. (BELOW) By the 1890's, Cisco had taken on a more placid demeanor. Many of the lower spurs survived until the 1940's, being used by outfit cars and the Maintenance of Way Department. — GUY L. DUNSCOMB COLLECTION

In the haste of Central Pacific construction, many mountain ravines were spanned by trestles, then later, as circumstances would permit, were replaced by more substantial structures. Such was the case at the Upper Cascades were 244 feet of a former trestle litters the ground below a recently constructed truss bridge. — R.A. MILLER JR. COLLECTION

early and factual description of the roadway and facilities of the railroad through the Sierra Nevada mountains of California.

The railroad, extending eastward from Sacramento over the summit of the Sierra to the big bend of the Truckee River (Wadsworth) was built to a maximum grade of 116 feet per mile and a minimum radius of 573 feet. The crossties were cut from the adjacent forests which abounded with cedar, sugarpine, red and white fir. Iron rails of 60-pounds to the yard were laid throughout with the exception of the snowbelt where somewhat heavier rail was utilized. The extra rail weight was partly distributed in the web to raise the top of the rail above the ordinary clearance of the car wheel flanges and above the accumulation of ice upon the track (or so they thought). Across the district, there were 15 tunnels in number and their character and location are presented here. Although 16 tunnels had been originally contemplated, it should be noted that one bore at Tunnel Cut was abandoned because the rock was found to be too soft.

No.	MILE-POST	APPROXIMATE LOCATION	LENGTH	FINISH
1	166.4	Orel-Blue Canon	481.4	Approaches timbered
2	173.5	Emigrant Gap-Smart	274.0	Timber
3	181.7	Cisco-Tamarack	269.0	Unlined
4	182.0	Cisco-Tamarack	85.0	Unlined
5	185.5	East of Troy	130.0	Unlined
6	194.7	Summit-Lakeview	1659.0	Unlined
7	195.1	Summit-Lakeview	99.5	Unlined
8	195.3	Summit-Lakeview	375.0	Unlined
9	195.9	Summit-Lakeview	223.0	Unlined
10	196.1	Summit-Lakeview	525.5	Unlined
11	196.4	Summit-Lakeview	570.0	Timbered in part
12	196.7	Summit-Lakeview	342.0	Timbered in part
13	201.1	Eder-Tunnel No. 13	870.0	Timber
14	222.7	Wickes-Floriston	200.0	Unlined
15	228.8	One mile west state line	96.0	Unlined

To this list should be added tunnel No. "0", 711 feet, bored through Wildcat Summit between Clipper Gap and Applegate to eliminate the 90 foot high trestle at Deep Gulch. This was opened to traffic on July 24, 1873.

Despite the persistant encroachment of civilization, the glacial geology at Donner Summit today remains largely unchanged from this view taken in the 1870's. The snowsheds are now concrete and the trail is paved, but the massive granite slopes, scarred by the movement of ice over the ages, have yet to yield to man. Magnificent Donner Lake lies in the background. — DONALD DUKE COLLECTION

Summit tunnel No. 6, shown at the right, before completion, was holed-through on August 30, 1867. It was two months before the first train was able to roll through. — DONALD DUKE COLLECTION

The driving of the Golden Spike at Promontory was not the end of railroad building in the west for the "Big Four," although at times, Huntington and his associates would have been glad to be rid of the enterprise. What had loomed as lucrative traffic at the outset, began to fade as the Nevada mine activity — particularly the Comstock Lode operations — went into a temporary decline. Another blow came when the Suez Canal opened. This began to divert heavy tonnage of the Oriental trade which would have otherwise moved across the continent by rail to Pacific ports. While trains continued to roll across the Sierra, the "Big Four" could ill afford to sit idly by and wait for traffic to come their way. They embarked upon developing a network of lines radiating from the mainline which, in time, would garner the lion's share of the railroad business in California. Indeed, in the 18 years following the driving of the Golden Spike at Promontory, the 690 mile pioneer Central Pacific would expand, in seven western states, to embrace some 5,500 miles of line.

At first the builders of the Central Pacific confined their activities to extending the road east from Sacramento, although authorized by Congress to build west to the Pacific Ocean. In the meantime, the Western Pacific Railroad of California was formed (no relationship to the more recent railroad of the same name). This line was organized December 13, 1862, to build a railroad from San Jose, the projected terminus of the San Francisco & San Jose Railroad, to Sacramento via Niles, Livermore and Stockton. This enterprise was headed by Timothy Dane and Peter Donahue, principal officers of the San Francisco & San Jose Railroad. Construction began in San Jose during January 1865, and reached Niles in 1866. The available money for the enterprise was used up long before the Western Pacific was completed and it was sold to the Contract & Finance Company, a Central Pacific subsidiary, which not only completed the railroad but extended it from Niles to Oakland. At long last, the transcontinental railroad reached tidewater.

As time went on, the "Big Four" began to look at other railroads developing within California, with an eye toward protecting their interests. The Sacramento Valley Railroad, an early rival in the Sacramento region, had fallen on hard times since the days of Judah's involvement. Projected to build to Placerville, the road had only completed 22 miles to Folsom, before a reorganization was necessary. Once revitalized, the little line barely reached Shingle Springs before the "Big Four" acquired an interest in 1865. Under their control, the railroad was ultimately extended to Placerville in 1888.

The Central Pacific, on its push eastward into the mountains, intersected the line of the California Central Railroad at Junction during the early part of 1864. This railroad had been incorporated in 1852 to build north from Folsom, and a junction with the Sacramento Valley Railroad, to Marysville, but by 1861, the line had only reached Lincoln, a distance of 18.5 miles. Encountering financial difficulties, the Yuba Railroad was incorporated to carry on the work. Meanwhile, in June 1863, the California & Oregon Railroad was organized to build north from Marysville into Oregon. The "Big Four" were operating all these companies by October 1867. The 8.2 mile line between Folsom and Junction was torn up during 1868, in lieu of the Central Pacific's shorter route from Sacramento. Following a couple of reorganizations and consolidations, the "Big Four" pushed the railhead north to Redding by 1872. This became the mainline to Oregon and eventually a through route to Portland was achieved in 1887.

Meanwhile, other promoters were at work. The California Pacific Rail Road Company had been incorporated during 1865 to build a line of railroad from the wharves at South Vallejo to Sacramento. This line was in operation to the west side of the Sacramento River by November 1868. The river was spanned and on January 15, 1870, the "Cal-P" was into Sacramento itself, crossing the track of the Central Pacific near the foot of I Street. After April 1871, this organization, through careful acquisition, commanded a large share of the freight and passenger business on the Sacramento and San Joaquin rivers. In May, the road threatened to build a competing line to Ogden via Davis(ville), Oregon and Idaho. A look at the map clearly shows that the "Cal-P" was headed straight for the Feather River Canyon. Such activities were viewed with alarm by the "Big Four" and through a series of maneuvers, the "Cal-P" was solidly in the Central Pacific camp by August 1871. The California Pacific continued to operate as a separate entity until July 1, 1876, when it was then leased to the Central Pacific.

On another front, a rival transcontinental, the Southern Pacific, had been organized in 1865 to construct a line of railroad south from San Francisco, through San Jose to southern California, then east through Arizona territory. The "Big Four" again moved in and were in control of this enterprise as early as 1868. A consolidation of several smaller independently held companies in 1870 resulted in a new Southern Pacific Railroad which was under the direct and exclusive control of Huntington and his associates. With the paperwork out of the way, work continued on the southern route starting from a point on the Central Pacific between Sacramento and Oakland

The isolated, but vital Summit complex at the crest of the Sierra grade as it appeared about 1874. The large structure to the left is Cardwell's Hotel, while the turntable and enginehouse tracks branch off to the right. The mainline curves to the east, center, and ducks into tunnel No. 6. — G.M. BEST COLLECTION

which was later known as Lathrop. Los Angeles was reached during the fall of 1876 and work continued east from that point, ultimately forming the "Sunset Route."

Huntington and his associates on March 17, 1884, created the Southern Pacific Company and long-term leases were tendered to all the properties of the Southern Pacific and Central Pacific Railroad companies. Thus, it was in this way that the pioneer Central Pacific became closely associated with the affairs of the Southern Pacific Railroad and the line up and over the Sierra undeniably linked with the SP. In time, all identity of the former was lost although the two roads did not formally merge on paper until 1959.

The west had its "Pacific Railroad," but to quote one old-timer in a fading page of *Railroadman's Magazine* "The Central Pacific was short of almost everything needed for good railroading — short on engines, short on sidings, just about all out of signals and plenty low on telegraph stations. About all they did have enough of was short curves, steep grades and single track." This is an easy enough criticism to make, in light of later developments, but the infant Central Pacific was light years beyond the rutted and tortuous wagon roads that had preceded it.

First settled in 1839 by John Augustus Sutter, a Swiss military officer in the service of Mexico, Sacramento became the principal operating point for this new railroad across the Sierra, and by 1849 it boasted of a population approaching 4,000. A year later the town had increased to 10,000 inhabitants and continued to grow at a rapid pace. During 1854, Sacramento was chosen as the capital of the state of California. By reason of its central position in the vast and fertile Sacramento Valley, the place became a distributing and wholesale point of great importance.

During 1867, the original Central Pacific yards and support facilities were augmented by a 29-stall roundhouse, car shops and planing mill. These became the nucleus of the Sacramento shops, which at one time, were the largest single employer of labor in the west. New locomotive construction was undertaken, as well as the design and construction of hundreds of freight and passenger cars, marine engines, winding machinery

The first 16-stall wood roundhouse to be built at Truckee lasted less than a year. Consumed in flames during 1869, it was replaced by this structure (LEFT) about 1875. — DONALD DUKE COLLECTION (BELOW) The first through Central Pacific train entered Truckee 119.5 miles east of Sacramento, on June 19, 1868 and from that day forward the place has held prominance in the railroad's operation. Activity crowds the Truckee yards about 1870, with two trains ready to depart west. Helpers, all steamed up, wait patiently in the clear. — STANFORD UNIVERSITY SPECIAL COLLECTIONS

While in passenger service between Truckee and Wadsworth on the Truckee Division, engine No. 1011 poses for the camera at Truckee in the 1890's. — H.K. GAGE, MR. & MRS. ROGER ZWANSINGER COLLECTION

This imposing 22-stall roundhouse, built after the devastating fires that ravaged Truckee from 1868 through 1883, was constructed of Rocklin granite. Completely circular, the structure was one of three similar structures on the combined Southern Pacific System. The other two were located at Houston, Texas, and Algiers, Louisiana. — GUY L. DUNSCOMB COLLECTION

This deck truss bridge originally spanned the Little Truckee River at Boca. — SOUTHERN PACIFIC COLLECTION

Central Pacific tracks followed the course of the Truckee River for nearly 70 miles. This view, taken about 1870 just below Truckee, looks down the track to the west. — C.E. WATKINS, GUY L. DUNSCOMB COLLECTION

for cable railroads and general foundry and machine work on contract. Here too, were the offices of the Sacramento Division which, in its infancy, extended eastward over the Mountain to Truckee, Nevada County, a distance of 119.5 miles. During 1868, and for a number of years after, trains on the district were governed and run by the clock of G.M. Parker, a Sacramento watchmaker, who was located at 34 K Street.

Eastward from Sacramento, the first point of operating significance occurred at Junction, 18.2 miles out, where a day telegraph station was maintained to handle Oregon Division trains leaving or joining the main stem. Rocklin, at 22.1 miles, was the point at which helpers were added for the run to the summit. By August 1869, the facilities here included a woodshed of tremendous size, a station, a roundhouse made of granite which accommodated 28 locomotives, a turntable and a water tank. A 24-hour telegraph office was maintained in the station. It is unclear when train crews began taking assignments here, but the record shows Rocklin originating freight trains as early as 1871.

Fueled by the railroad and local granite quarries, Rocklin grew rapidly. On Front Street facing the tracks, saloons soon dominated a major portion of the business district. Rocklin exhibited the same incendiary tendencies as most frontier towns by burning to the ground in 1869, and once again in 1870. Fire destroyed the roundhouse in 1873 taking ten locomotives with it. The first depot, and John Sweeney's Saloon which also occupied the premises, burned in 1891. In each case, rebuilding was commenced soon after and Rocklin figured greatly in the operation of the road over the Mountain for nearly 45 years.

East of Rocklin, a string of day telegraph offices accompanied by sidings, dotted the railroad. Newcastle was 31 miles out, Colfax 54.2 miles, Gold Run 64.3, Alta 68.7 and Blue Canon 78 miles east of Sacramento. Emigrant Gap, 83.5 miles out and deep in the snowshed district, had a 24-hour telegraph office as did Cisco and Summit. At the latter point, situated at the west portal of tunnel No. 6, 105.2 miles east of Sacramento, the Central Pacific also erected a wooden enginehouse with stalls for twelve locomotives, a turntable, for the convenience of helper engines, and the Summit Hotel.

At the east end of the Sacramento Division, 119.5 miles from Sacramento, the railroad established an engine terminal at Truckee. Truckee Division crews then took over for the 69 mile run to Wadsworth, Nevada. By reason of its location at the foot of the hard climb to the west, Truckee was a point where helpers accumulated. A 16-stall roundhouse was built in town to accommodate these engines as well as the snow equipment that was used to clear the line over the summit.

Truckee flourished as did other railroad towns. A brisk lumbering and ice business added to her fortunes. The town was for many decades the only readily accessible leisure time mecca for lumberjacks, railroaders and miners who patronized the scores of saloons, eating and gaming houses. Perhaps Truckee's greatest attraction was the profusion of bordellos. Originally clustered along the river, they were by the end of 1871, more conveniently located along Jiboom Street, behind the main commercial row. The river front location was abandoned to Truckee's Chinese population. Legend has it that the term "Redlight District" actually originated in Truckee with the railroad men leaving a red lantern lit outside the particular lady's crib to indicate that it was occupied.

Probably Truckee was as rough and tumble a town as any of its contemporaries, with the exception of Bodie. Following a decade of shootings, robberies and other highbindery, a "601" committee was formed. Patterned after a similar group in Virginia City, these vigilantes succeeded to some degree in quieting the town.

Part and parcel of being such a volatile frontier town were the great fires which consumed the place with annoying regularity. The first fire, in 1868, reduced the settlement to ashes, then another the following year claimed the Central Pacific roundhouse. Then a series of fires in 1870, 1871 (three separate blazes), 1874, 1875, 1881, 1882, and 1883 burned everything from the business section to new Chinatown. The blaze of 1883 brought about the erection of a new local landmark since the wooden engine house, the second one to be built in 15 years, was heavily damaged. From the ashes rose an imposing 24-stall roundhouse composed of Rocklin granite. Resembling a Medieval battlement, the Truckee roundhouse became one of three completely circular roundhouses on the Southern Pacific system with the other two located in Houston, Texas, and Algiers, Louisiana.

A handful of telegraph offices, in the 69 miles from Truckee to Wadsworth, handled the movement of trains in the early days. Prosser Creek was six miles from Truckee, followed by Boca, Verdi and Reno. A short distance of 1.5 miles seperated Prosser Creek and Boca, but there were 35 miles between Reno and Wadsworth.

Wadsworth, Nevada, situated on the Truckee River where it makes the big bend north to Pyramid and Winnemucca lakes, had been settled by white men in 1854. The original settlement known as "Drytown" was the place where emigrants, weary from the long trek west across the Great Basin, first encountered green grass and water. As the country grew, the place became a shipping point for the minerals of Churchill County (borax, salt, soda), stock, wool and trout from the Truckee River. In 1868, the Central Pacific established Wadsworth as headquarters for the 201-mile Truckee Division which extended from Truckee, California, to Winnemucca, Nevada. The town held this distinction until May 1, 1895, when the Truckee Division was split at Wadsworth and the lines west were added to the Sacramento Division. That portion east of Winnemucca, formerly the Humboldt Division, was annexed to the Truckee Division on June 15, 1885. Then, in turn, all lines east of Wadsworth were placed under the jurisdiction of the Salt Lake Division superintendent. Temporary car and machine shops and a roundhouse were erected at Wadsworth in the early days but in time they outgrew their surroundings. Therefore, during the

CENTRAL PACIFIC STATION LIST — 1874 SACRAMENTO & TRUCKEE DIVISIONS

140	*Sacramento	215	China Ranch	263	Stonewall
143	American River	218	*Blue Canon	265	Union Mill
148	Arcade	221	Owl Camp	266	Proctor's Mill
155	Antelope	222	Chinn's Siding	266.5	*Prosser Creek
158	*Junction	222.5	Putnam Siding	267	Camp 16
162	*Rocklin	223	*Emigrant Gap	268	*Boca
165	Pino	230	Crystal Lake	270	Camp 18
168	*Penryn	232	*Cisco	271	Camp 19
171	*Newcastle	235	Tamarack	272	Camp 20
176	*Auburn	238	Mountain Mill	273	Bronco
183	Clipper Gap	239	Cascade	278	State Line
189	New England Mill	241	Patterson's	284	*Verdi
194	*Colfax	242	Summit Valley	294	*Reno
199	Cape Horn Mill	245	*Summit	302	Vista
205	*Gold Run	252	Strong's (Canon)	314	Clark's
207	Dutch Flat	254	Stanford	322	Salvia
209	*Alta	256	Millers	329	*Wadsworth
210	C.C. Mill (Alta Shed)	257	Donner Lake		
218	Shady Run	260	*Truckee		*-denotes telegraph office

-Mileage is calculated from San Francisco via San Jose and Niles.

In the remarkably clear view above and on the adjoining page, one has a glimpse of Reno on the rise as a commercial center and freighting point, circa 1884. Facing west from the vantage point of the Virginia & Truckee depot roof, Commercial Row fronts the tracks on the left and Central Pacific's freight station on the right. The Sierra range rises in the distance. — GUY L. DUNSCOMB COLLECTION

summer of 1883, ground was broken across the river where plenty of space was available for new yards and shops and all the necessary appurtenances.

Drytown continued to exist until noon, April 15, 1884, when a fire broke out in the yardmaster's office in the old depot. Within ten minutes, the depot, the post office and the Wadsworth Hotel were in flames. Spreading rapidly, the fire had four-fifths of the town reduced to ashes within three hours. Climaxing the incident, snow commenced falling and continued to fall far into the next day creating quite a scene. After things cooled down, Wadsworth's residents picked up what was left and moved across the river to join the railroad.

The town was rebuilt at its new location and by 1888 could boast of a population approaching 700. Dispensers of liquid refreshment included the "White House," perhaps the most genteel saloon in town, the "Wadsworth," the "Nevada House," the "Only," the "Columbus," and the "Reception" where the popular game Klondike and other fascinations vied for the railroader's dollar. Counteracting the influence of these dens of inequity, the good citizens tried to make the town respectable by setting out hundreds of poplar, cork and elm trees, erecting churches and patronizing the Truckee Division library. The library, the best in the region, was an institution evoking the strongest civic pride. It contained some 2,500 volumes, a reading room with all the principal papers of the west in evidence and an elegant, beautifully bound Bible on a black walnut altar, which was the gift of Central Pacific Master Mechanic A.J. Stevens.

At their peak, the railroad facilities at Wadsworth consisted of a yard nearly two miles long with six tracks at its broadest point and it employed two switch crews each shift. A 20-stall roundhouse employed 40 men. The car shop kept 22 men busy repairing an average of 300 cars per month, and a large machine shop, comprised of six stalls and fitted with all the latest equipment, had three or four engines undergoing heavy maintenance at all times. This facility kept an additional 100 men busy.

The labor force in the shops and roundhouse at Wadsworth was comprised primarily of Chinese.

Facing east, the Central Pacific crossed Lake Street and stretched in an unbroken tangent toward the wasteland of Nevada. The four-stall CP engine house may be seen in the middle distance. The V&T mainline to Carson City and the Comstock swung off to the right. Connecting with the Central Pacific at Reno, V&T fortunes rose during the years 1873-1878 when as many as 35 trains a day fueled the Big Bonanza at Virginia City. — GUY L. DUNSCOMB COLLECTION

Indispensable during the construction of the railroad, many of the race settled in the railroad towns which they had helped to build. In addition to such basic services as launderers and cooks, the Chinese worked on right-of-way gangs, as laborers in the shops and, in some cases, as at Carlin, Nevada, even hostled locomotives. The way points of China Ranch and Chinn's Siding high in the Sierra, attested to their contribution to the construction effort. Closely identified with the Central Pacific Railroad in the early days, the Chinese, in time, came in for a great deal of retribution.

The first party of three Chinese sailed from Hong Kong to California in 1848 aboard the bark *Eagle*. By January 1852, their numbers within the state had increased to 7,512 men and eight women. The first groups flocked to the mines where they worked abandoned claims. Once the supply in California was exhausted, the Central Pacific began importing them on a large scale. This labor was contracted for under Chinese law. Bound to their company until all claims were paid, the wealthy and powerful "Six Companies" contractor had the power of life and death over a Chinese

Locomotive CP No. 96, the *Clipper*, poses at Wadsworth, Nevada, about 1875. Situated at the big bend in the Truckee River, 35 miles east of Reno, Wadsworth predated Sparks as the division point. — GUY L. DUNSCOMB COLLECTION

laborer or "coolie." Offenders faced tribunals composed of their own people, whose processes and decrees were executed swiftly and without regard for local laws.

The Chinese tended to cling to the ways of the Orient, finding it difficult to blend into western culture. This at times manifested itself in outbreaks of violence. Stumbling in the darkness one night, the wife of a veteran Mountain hoghead was horrified to discover, a few yards behind the Blue Cañon depot, the body of a chinaman strung up from a yellow pine — the victim of the mysterious Tong wars. Their weakness for opium was plastered across the pages of *Harpers* and other east coast weeklies with regularity. The Chinese tended to gather in a particular quarter of a city which local authorities frequently viewed with disgust and horror. During 1876-77, a period of general discontent grew among Californians due to little rain and poor crops, and an anti-Chinese movement began to take shape. This was followed by a great falling off in gold production and an economic slump during which the movement intensified. Thus, during May 1882, immigration of Chinese was suspended for ten years. They were burned out of Truckee during 1885-86 and also in other towns along the line during the same period.

Still, the Chinese were a novelty and the Pacific tourist, traveling out west by train, wanted to see but two things, the wonderful mines of Virginia City and the armies of Chinese. The closest many got to the mysterious Celestials was to view their handiwork from the cushions aboard the *Express* as they traveled the upper reaches of the Sierra.

The tourist, a comparatively new element in the far west, was the result of the completion of the Pacific Railroad. Stub passenger service had been provided during the construction from Sacramento out to the terminal behind the advancing front. The first scheduled passenger trains commenced with Central Pacific's timetable No.1, effective June 6, 1864 (four days premature), which covered the 31 miles from Sacramento to Newcastle. There was only one passenger-and-mail, and two freight-and-passenger trains listed in each direction. Train Nos. 1, 2 and 3 operated in both directions. Timetable No. 2, effective May 13, 1865, extended the service to Auburn.

Regular passenger service between Sacramento and Promontory, Utah Territory, was inaugurated on May 15, 1869, five days after driving the Golden Spike. From Promontory, passengers were obliged to transfer to a Union Pacific train bound for Omaha but, after September 6, 1869, this transfer was effected at Ogden. Connecting trains allowed travel from Sacramento to Chicago in five days, seven hours; to New York in seven days. Simply known as the *Express,* No. 1 from Sacramento to Truckee required eight hours 35 minutes to complete the run, circumstances permitting. No. 2, westbound, covered the same territory 25 minutes

CENTRAL PACIFIC RAILROAD.
No. 1, TIME CARD No. 1.
To take effect Monday June 6th, 1864, at 5 A. M.

TRAINS EASTWARD.					STATIONS.	TRAINS WESTWARD.			
Frt and Pass No 3	Frt and Pass No 2	Pass & Mail No 1.				Frt and Pass No 1	Pass & Mail No 2.	Frt and Pass No 3.
5 PM leave	1 PM leave	6.15 A M, L			Sacramento		8.45 A M arr	12 M arr.	6.40 P M ar.
5.50 / 5.55 } mt frt	2.15	6.55	18		Junction	18	3	11.20	5.55 / 5.50 } mt. Ft
6.09	2.38	7.05	22		Rocklin	4	7.40	11.07	5.37
6.22	2.55	7.15 meet F	25		Pino	3	7.15 mt pass	10.56	5.25
6.40	3.30 PM arr	7.30 A M arr	31		Newcastle	6	6.45 A M, L	10.30 A M, L	5 P M, L

Trains No. 2 and 3 east, and 1 and 3 west, daily, except Sunday.
Trains No. 1 east and 2 west, daily.

LELAND STANFORD, President.

faster.

On the morning of the last day on the long journey west aboard No. 2, travelers were treated to the "grand and exciting rush" down the west slope of the Sierra and around Cape Horn. Guide books to rail travel in the far west, like Adams and Bishop's *Pacific Tourist,* glorified this entrance into California as the gateway to a veritable fairyland. "A grander or more exhilarating ride than that from Summit to Colfax on the Central Pacific Railroad you can not find in the world... the rush and vehement impetus of the train and the whirl around the curves past the edges of deep chasms among forests of magnificent trees fills you with wonder and delight."

In addition to train Nos. 1 and 2, there was one mixed or emigrant train run each way on a daily basis as an extra from May 15, 1869, through November 13, 1887. A special *Palace Car Express,* on an 81-hour schedule between Omaha and San Francisco, was tried for a brief period that fall. Commencing October 5, 1869, this special was due to depart San Francisco each Monday at 7:30 A.M. Westbound, the special departed Omaha each Tuesday at 9:15 P.M. The fare was $168.00 for a double berth.

Commencing on January 1, 1873, Nos. 1 and 2 became the *Atlantic & Pacific Express* and then on April 26, 1875, the eastbound schedule became the *Atlantic Express* and the westbound the *Pacific Express*. The Pullman Company took over operation of the Silver Palace cars on July 1, 1883 and introduced through sleeping car service between San Francisco and Chicago. The first diners made their appearance during 1892. A second pair of through trains was assigned to the "Overland Route" on November 13, 1887. The trains, which remained nameless, carried the numbers 3 and 4. The *Golden Gate Special,* an extremely high-class extra-fare train, was operated for only one season, from December 5, 1888, through May 14, 1889. Departing on a weekly schedule from Council Bluffs, Iowa, and San Francisco, California, the trains were operated extra as no schedule number was ever assigned. By August 1889, train Nos. 5 and 6, the *Oriental Mail,* made for a third set of trains in daily operation between San Francisco and Chicago. Train Nos. 5 and 6 were soon dropped, however, and by the mid-nineties, the schedules eastbound were No. 1, the *Atlantic Express,* and No. 3, the *European Mail*. Westbound, the *Pacific Express* ran as No. 2 and the *Oriental Mail* as No. 4. Local passenger train Nos. 11 and 12 served Reno, Truckee and other settlements along the Truckee River canyon. Foothill communities between Colfax and Sacramento were served by locals which carried the Nos. 25 and 26. This service commenced on July 1, 1892.

Freight schedules on the Mountain, as of November 5, 1871, fell into two groups. Train Nos. 5 and 7, originating at Sacramento and destined for Ogden, Utah, were transcontinental in nature, as were Nos. 6 and 8 on the westbound run which terminated at the Oakland wharf. Supplementary schedule Nos. 5½ and 7½ originated at Rocklin and terminated at Truckee. Nos. 6½ and 8½ covered the same territory westbound. Although definite confirmation is not available, it is surmised that similar local schedules extended this service from Truckee to Reno, or Wadsworth.

Transcontinental freight traffic, as of July 1, 1890, had increased enough to warrant placing in the timecard, schedules No. 9 eastbound and No. 10 westbound. By this time the unique fractionated schedules for local trains had been discontinued in favor of more conventional listings. Nos. 19 and 23 eastbound and Nos. 20 and 24 westbound now operated between Rocklin and Truckee while schedule Nos. 11 and 12 handled Truckee-Reno traffic.

Long-haul westbound trains carried the personal belongings of emigrants, manufactured goods, machinery, tools, oils, other fuels and miscellaneous essentials needed in an emerging economy. Eastbound trains handled basic products of the west such as cattle, hides, orchard crops and grains. Eighteen million pounds of wool moved over the Mountain in 1877. Also, tucked in among the expected products were the fabled silk trains and a million pounds of seal skins, shipped east during 1876.

Local trains serviced the quarries at Rocklin and Penryn, the fruit sheds in the foothill district, the many sawmills along the line and the ice harvesters which clustered in the narrow canyon between Truckee and Verdi. Here the Central Pacific passed through a region where conditions were just right for the natural preparation of ice, namely it was very, very cold. In an age where ice was imported to Sacramento and San Francisco at great expense from as far away as Alaska and even Boston, the prospects of local production attracted great interest. All that was needed was to dam a stream, wait for the surface to freeze and then harvest the stuff by sawing it into blocks. Serious ice harvesting began during 1868 in the Summit Valley, but when the railroad reached the Truckee River canyon, the focus of the industry moved to the east side of the mountains where it was cold and the snowfall was not as great. The Boca Mill & Ice Company began operations during 1868, using its own pond for ice harvesting in the winter. This firm was joined by others who located along the railroad at such seasonally bleak points as Artic, Donner, Truckee, Polaris, Prosser Creek, Boca, Iceland (which had formerly and unexplicitly been named Cuba!), Wickes, Floriston, Essex and Verdi. All in all, more than 26 companies worked the Sierra ice business over the years but along the way there were two great amalgamations, one in 1882 forming the Union Ice Company, and another in 1891 forming National Ice which narrowed the field to three producers with Tahoe Ice Company becoming the third successful independent company. In season, two to three ice trains a day departed Wadsworth (and later Sparks), switching the various ice plants. The ice, among the heaviest commodities handled, was shipped in old box cars enveloped in sawdust or straw. The ice was used in San Francisco and other west coast cities and also, to cool the Washoe mines. With the development of the insulated refrigerator car, ice was shipped east to the grand hotels of New York City and New Orleans where it was widely regarded for its purity.

The same water used to make such pure ice, was also a principal ingredient in Boca Beer, a product of the same region. Established in 1875, the brewery at Boca was an enormous shipper of brew, bottling some 30,000 barrels a year. Its fame spread to Paris where it became popular at the 1883 World's Fair. The waters found at Blue Cañon were widely regarded as the purest of any found along the Central Pacific and thus, were shipped in tank cars to Rocklin and Sacramento for railroad and domestic use. Much of this water was used to replenish the tanks of thirsty locomotives which congregated at these points.

These locomotives had increased in size and number since the day in 1863 when C.P. No. 1, the *Governor Stanford,* first arrived at the docks in Sacramento. This 4-4-0, or American type, manufactured in the east by R. Norris & Sons in 1862, was followed by many others of similar wheel arrangement, and then by the 4-6-0 Ten-Wheelers. In the 1860's, three, four or five 4-4-0's were required to haul a train of 20 cars over the Mountain. The early 4-6-0's were not much good in this service and were primarily used in the desert. In the 1870's, heavier 4-4-0's were delivered but it was not until the spring of 1882 that a significant advance was made in mountain locomotive design. CP No. 229, outshopped in April, was of a 4-8-0, or Mastodon type, and powerful enough to haul 20 loads — or 422 tons — at ten miles-per-hour on the Donner grade. Twenty of these were built by Cooke and operated a number of years on the Mountain. They were followed by Schenectady cross-compound 4-8-0's and SP-built cross-compound 2-8-0's and Vauclain compounds, six of which could take a train of 60 or 70 cars over the Sierra.

Freight helpers were based at Rocklin and Truckee for Sierra mountain service and at Wadsworth for service east over the Hot Springs grade. Passenger helpers double-headed east from Rocklin to Truckee then double-headed back after a layover, although, with the light trains of the period, the additional power was not essential on the westbound run from Truckee to Summit.

In the early days, wood was the only locomotive fuel available but with direct rail connections to the east, coal was brought into those areas where wood was scarce. East of Wadsworth, coal was the principal fuel, but as late as 1893, virtually all locomotives working west between that point and Rocklin were wood burners. In the special instructions to Sacramento Division employees, a long-standing rule cautioned enginemen not to create a hazard by throwing odd-sized wood over the side of the tender of a locomotive that was in motion.

The possibility of being struck by a flying chunk of cord wood was not the only uncertainty to railway operations in the high Sierra during the latter half of the 19th century. On a district where level track was at a premium, dragging a train uphill was one thing but the ability to hold it back on the descent down the other side was of far greater importance to those directly involved. In an age innocent of the automatic air brake, brakemen controlled the train by means of applying and releasing staff hand brakes. Westinghouse introduced the straight air brake on passenger equipment during 1871 and the automatic air brake on freight cars during 1882. Even though most home road equipment had been converted over by the early nineties, this primitive and dangerous means of braking was still frequently required. About half the midwestern road's cars received in interchange still had no air brakes even though a trainline pipe was provided so they could be cut into air brake-equipped trains.

Passenger trains were not permitted to exceed 25 miles-per-hour over any part of the road except on special order. Freight trains were held to 10 miles-per-hour east of Junction and 12 miles-per-hour west of that point. Despite these precautions, runaways did occur, often with spectacular results. The story is told of the *Yuba,* a McKay & Aldus Ten-Wheeler, CP No. 25, which came down the grade too fast and went over Cape Horn, and on down into the American River canyon where scavengers eventually stripped her bare. The late D.L. Joslyn, the dean of Southern Pacific locomotive historians, reported that in 1905, as a young sprout, he made an investigation of the river's bottom but it revealed no trace of the locomotive save some oil cups.

Another threat to life and limb was the primitive link and pin coupling system used in the early days. Many brakemen were killed or maimed while attempting to insert the pin or hold the link in position. Even as late as 1892, virtually all SP couplers were of one link and pin variety or another, but Janney automatic couplers (which were compatible with link and pin) were beginning to make an appearance. By the turn of the century, these safer devices were in general use. For many years, however, one or more missing fingers were the mark of high seniority and experience among trainmen.

Another problem was the confusion generated by conflicting locomotive numbers. The Central Pacific, although being operated by the Southern Pacific, was a separate entity as far as rolling stock was concerned. In other respects, the two roads were operated, for all practical purposes, as one road. The intermingling of power created a dangerous situation. Sacramento Division veteran engineer Christ Rasmussen, through the pages of an old *Railroad Man's Magazine,* recounted just such an incident. On the night of February 6, 1889, Rasmussen was firing CP No. 225 on the westbound passenger run between Truckee and Sacramento. Double-heading on the point was CP No. 70. Their train, No. 4, departed Truckee one hour and 15 minutes off the advertised with a "run late" order. At Blue Cañon, they picked up an order which read "MEET ENGINE 23 AT GOLD RUN." At Shady Run they found engine No. 23 in the hole with no reasonable explanation as to how it got there. At Gold Run yet another No. 23, the one mentioned in the order, appeared in the siding. With the order fulfilled, and the meet with No. 23 safely behind them, train No. 4 highballed out of Gold Run only to have a cornfield meet with yet another No. 23 about a mile outside of town. At the investigation of the incident, it was brought out that the train at Shady Run was headed up by CP No. 23, the train at Gold Run was powered by SP No. 23 and the collision involved Virginia & Truckee No. 23 which had been borrowed for snowplow service!

Problems of this nature were soon averted. During 1891, all locomotives under the Southern Pacific system, including those of the Central Pacific, were renumbered under a logical plan which avoided duplication.

Not all the hazards of railway operation in the early days were generated by primitive equipment and practices. From time to time, outside events would hamper the flow of traffic. Crime was one of them. Eighteen months after the Central Pacific started running a through train, the first train hold-up in the west occurred. No. 1, the *Atlantic Express,* which had departed November 4, 1870, was the victim. The train consisted of a locomotive, coach, sleeper and baggage/express car containing over $60,000. As No. 1 picked its way over the Sierra, Big Jack Davis and a band of cutthroats, loitering around an abandoned mine in Nevada's Peavine Mountains, laid plans to relieve the train of its valuables. Their chance came at Verdi, Nevada, as the train slowed to negotiate a tight curve. Men in masks jumped aboard, climbed over the woodpile into the cab of the locomotive and compelled the engineer to yank the whistle cord which sent the brakemen leaping for the hand brakes. Conductor Mitchell walked up and was confronted by seven masked men who forced him to unhook the baggage car from the rest of the train. Then off sped the engine and baggage car with all the loot. At conductor Mitchell's insistance, the brakes were released on the remaining cars of the train which then rolled off in hot persuit. A mile down the canyon the head end of the train was reached. The crew and messenger had been herded into the express compartment and the thieves had made off with $40,000 in gold and notes. The gang was soon rounded up, but it is interesting to note that within 24 hours, at Independence, Nevada, the same train was robbed by a different group.

Labor unrest severely disrupted service during 1894. Following the panic of 1893, a national railroad union movement was organized by Eugene V. Debs. His American Railway Union succeeded in attracting many CP and SP employees although road engineers and conductors held out. With unemployment at high levels, unrest was the order of the day. Various groups of unemployed workers called "armies," who rallied around General Coxey's national movement, arrived in Sacramento on April 6, 1894, led by General Kelley. At the capitol they were joined by another 5,200 men and, on May 10, 1864, they seized a train at Arcade station in Sacramento and headed for Rocklin. The local constable arrested the engineer and, when trouble developed, shot one of the invading army and escaped with his prisoner. Fearing lynchings by the so-called "army," the people of Rocklin released the prisoner. Meanwhile, alerted to the disturbance, the militia was dispatched to Rocklin and the strikers disbursed. The period of unrest continued and soldiers were placed at other railroad points like Truckee and Reno. Late in June, A.R.U. employees of the Southern Pacific were ordered to refuse to handle Pullman equipment because of an A.R.U. strike against the Pullman Company. At 11:00 P.M. June 28, 1894, a general strike was called against the SP. Much violence and disruption ensued and it was August 26th before the strike was called off. The men went back to work, but much ill will came of the affair and blacklists of men who had been implicated in the strike held hostile offenders out of work for several more years.

Perhaps the most significant and certainly the most enduring obstacle for the railroad to overcome in operating over the high Sierra was (and still is) the weather. From the very beginning railway operations have been complicated by snow. Fully 50 miles of the line are above 5,000 feet and, by reason of its strategic location north and east of the Golden Gate, the pass experiences the brunt of most Pacific storms. Annual snowfall averages from about two feet at Colfax to 35 feet at Summit. At the latter point, 86 percent of the total precipitation falls as snow.

Judah underestimated the snow problem. In measuring a total accumulation of 13 feet at the summit, Judah in his report to the directors dated October 1, 1861, theorized that...

> "It is only necessary then to start an engine with snow plows from the summit each way after the commencement of a storm clearing the snow as it falls. A similar course of procedure at each successive storm will keep the track open during the entire winter...a crust forms upon the snow which prevents its drifting badly...the only point where we shall encounter a level surface of snow is in Summit Valley for about two miles. By elevating the tracks at this point, no trouble will be anticipated."

Judah's successor, S.S. Montague, tended to minimize the problem as well. In his report of December 1865, however, he indicated that some form of protection might be needed...

> "The heavy snowfall in the immediate vicinity of Summit, amounting in the aggregate to 10 or even 12 feet in depth and a much heavier accumulation at some points due to drifting will render it necessary to provide a substantial protection, either by timber or masonry, to ensure the successful and uninterrupted operation of the road during the winter months. The principal points requiring such protection occur upon the eastern slope and within two miles of Summit...at the only points where any real danger of obstruction from this cause (slides) existed, the line has been thrown so far into the hill that the entire roadbed will be cut in the solid granite and so protected by masonry and timberwork that any slides that may occur will pass harmlessly over the track without interfering in the least with the passage of trains...that portion of the line requiring this rather unusual protection does not exceed 100 yards. Properly constructed I do not entertain the slightest apprehension of any stoppage or disturbance of trains due to the causes alluded to. As we approach the summit and for the greater portion of the distance through the snow belt the roadbed will be formed by light side cutting or embankments, thus facilitating the removal of snow from the tracks..."

Montague and the directors of the Central Pacific were shocked into reality by the winter of 1866-67. Total snowfall was nearly 40 feet and snow averaged 18 feet on the level at Summit. The snow came early and stayed late. By March 1867, there was 15 feet in the Summit Valley. As it began to melt, slides created tremendous problems with track and right-of-way being swept away. Slides above Alta carried away a number of buildings and completely destroyed a large trestle near Cisco.

Although every known appliance was used to keep the road clear that winter, including the largest and best snowplows then available, it was found impossible to keep the road open half the time and then only by employing an army of men with shovels. It was decided that the best positive means of protecting the railroad from the elements would be to construct snowsheds and galleries throughout the heavy snow district.

Some experimental sheds were built in the summer of 1867. Montague's report for that year anticipated but nine miles in the upper reaches of the line would require sheds, covering the track in cuts only. Snowplows would be depended upon for clearing embankments but experience soon proved that it would be best to make the shed covering continuous through the deep snow belt. By the spring of 1868 snowshed constuction began in earnest. Men were gathered from all quarters — some 2,500 — and, with six trains to distrubute material, a great deal was accomplished. Work continued until fall, but after two months of shoveling snow to clear for foundation work, the snow overwhelmed the shovelers and put a stop to the operation. By this time, 23 miles of shed and galleries were in place — 13 miles of them continuous — and, with this protection reinforced by 2,500 shovelers, the line was kept open through the winter of 1868-69, except for about ten days in February.

The *Sacramento Union* reported that on February 9th, a heavy snowslide occurred in the morning about a mile above Emigrant Gap carrying away about 300 feet of snowshed and 100 feet of track. Connections were maintained only by the more rugged of the passengers footing it from Cisco to Emigrant Gap, around the blockade, a distance of seven miles. Trouble with the big bridge at Butte Cañon kept the line closed to through trains until the 19th. This same section of line, which parallels the formation known as Smart Ridge, is as troublesome today as it was more than a century ago.

The first sheds were constucted very much after the manner of a house with a peaked roof, similar to today's "A" frame construction. The logs comprising the posts and braces were felled in the adjacent forests of pine, fir and cedar and primarily hand hewn. Neighboring sawmills provided the planks for roofs and sides. The design was not entirely successful as buried posts and braces soon began to rot and, with subsequent forcing out of line followed its melting. The boards covering the roof were largely of sugar pine laid longitudinally without battens. With melting snows, water came down on the roadbed in torrents.

Most of the new shed constuction in 1869 was of a flat roof design. This type of shed, at first built without rafters, sagged under the heavy snow load. Heavier timber later allowed for a 25 foot depth of snow on the roof. This design proved resistant to changes in alignment and with the substitution of ponderosa or yellow pine for the sugarpine and stone footing for wood blocks, the rot problem was overcome as well.

By 1873, shed construction was essentially complete. Chief Engineer Montague was able to report that year, that "more than 30 miles of these galleries were built, consuming 44,639,552 board feet of sawed timber, and 1,316,312 lineal feet of round timber, equivalent in the aggregate to 52,537,424 board feet measure of sawed timber and 721 tons of iron and spikes." The cost of the original snowshed construction is not clearly recorded but historian Erle Heath estimated in 1925 that it amounted to at least $2 million.

The sheds contributed materially to the successful operation of the railroad over the high Sierra but the public tended to ignore the benefits when passing through the long, dark and smokey passage. Indeed, while reporting on the blockade of 1869, in which the sheds first proved their worth, the *Sacramento Union* found time to remark that "the sheds are frequent and provoking as they shut out many of the most magnificent mountain views." Early efforts to overcome these objections were made in the form of windows placed in portions of the sheds to allow a cleared view of the more interesting vistas. But breakage by snow and other causes compelled their abandonment. Then a plan was adopted, wherein, every other vertical slat was removed to allow as maximum a view as was possible. These were replaced in advance of each winter season.

Summer tracks were adopted in a number of places in the snowshed district. These were laid outside and adjacent to the sheds, affording tourists the best possible view of the surrounding

The first experimental snowsheds were erected in the summer of 1867. Work was underway at the east approach to tunnel No. 10, 1.5 miles east of Summit where Alfred Hart took this photograph. — SOUTHERN PACIFIC COLLECTION

The early sheds were fashioned in the manner of today's "A" frame construction but proved unsatisfactory when under heavy snow loads. Later designs incorporated a heavily reinforced flat roof. — R.A. MILLER JR. COLLECTION

territory. Useless in winter, the frogs to these tracks were taken out in advance of each season so as not to accumulate ice and present an unnecessary hazard to operation. Still, the sheds remained unpopular and often when annual inspection parties toured the district, the suggestion was made to abandon most of them.

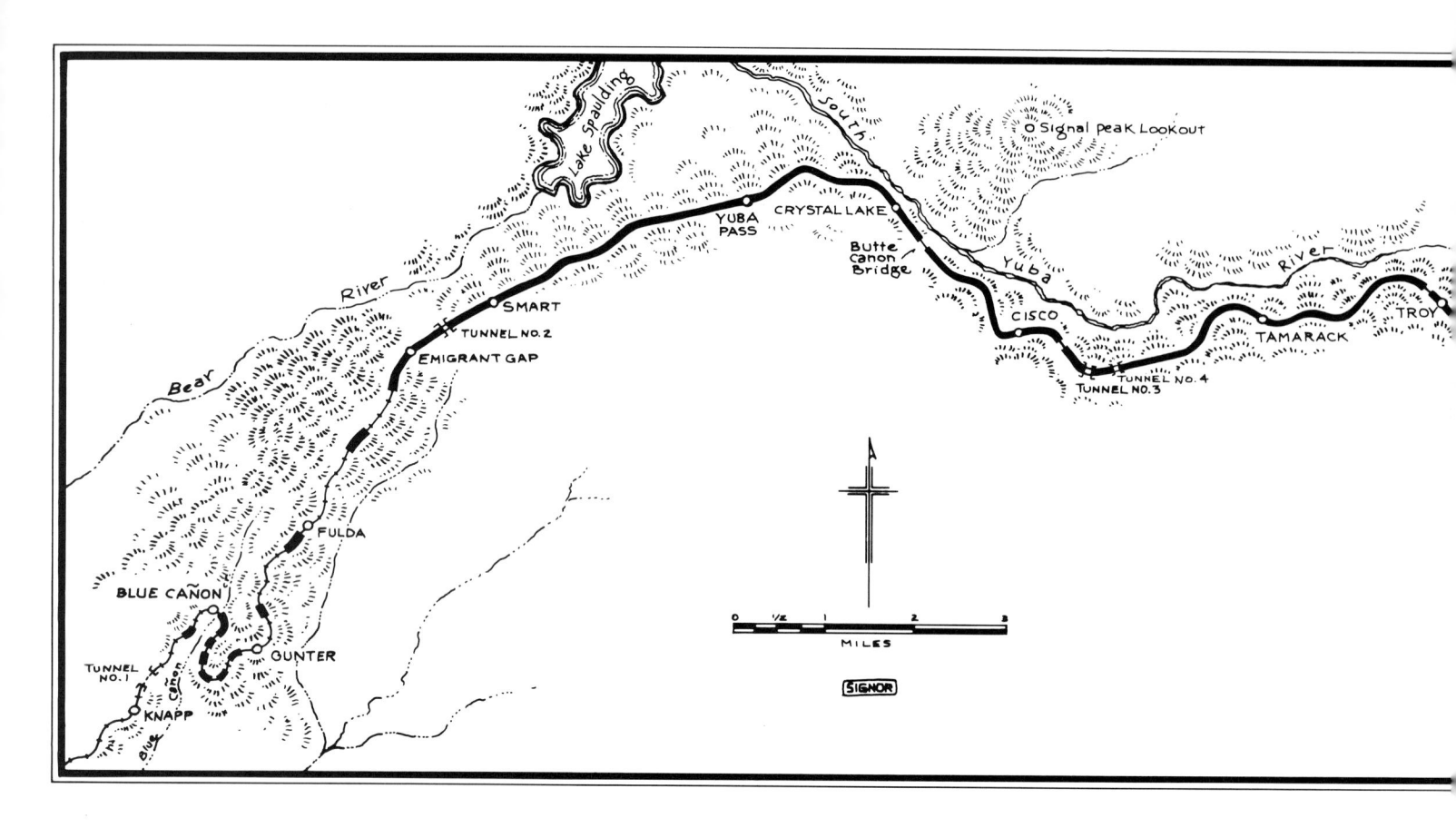

During the season, the sheds were not the only line of defense against storm. Huge pilot plows were also affixed to engines that were regularly assigned to the district. Bucker plows had been developed after the blockade of 1865-66. The first of these, the CP No. 1, left Sacramento shops on October 24, 1866. Resembling a huge wooden wedge, it was mounted on freight car trucks and weighed in at twelve tons, although, after its first runs, weight was increased to 19 tons by the addition of pig iron. By the time of the Golden Spike ceremony at Promontory, four such plows were in service. All in all, ten bucker plows were turned out of the Sacramento shops between 1866 and 1884.

With the bucker plow and six to twelve engines, a run was made at a snowdrift from some distance away with every engine "down in the corner." Snow literally would spurt aside once the drift was hit and would continue to be forced alongside until the outfit was stopped by a build up of pressure at which point the plow and engines backed up for another run — that is unless the plow or a locomotive was derailed which was a frequent occurrence. Bucking snow was a term that carried much meaning in those days and to say it was thrilling work was to put it mildly. As the banks of snow were built up on each side of the track, they would become too high for the plow to remove the accumulation. Therefore, after each pass, it was necessary to excavate chambers in the side of the snow banks into which the snow on the next trip of the plow could be deposited. This necessitated an army of shovelers. At Shady Run a huge camp was set up and ten monster ranges were utilized in cooking meals for the crews. During blockades, the same camp provisioned stranded trains.

Flangers were developed during 1876 to clean out snow and ice packed between the rails which otherwise would fill the flangeways and result in derailments. Riding a flanger was anything but pleasant as the operator had to ride on an open flat car raising and lowering, by hand, the plows which were arranged beneath. The flanger had to be operated at a high rate of speed in order to throw snow and ice aside, therefore, the operator had to be constantly on the alert.

The future of the bucker plow was limited largely due to the development in Canada of the "Rotary Steam Shovel" during 1884. In 1885, the first rotary was built in the United States, under patent, by the Cooke Locomotive Works. Successful tests, during the winter of 1885-86 on Union

SNOW SHEDS & TUNNELS
June 28, 1921

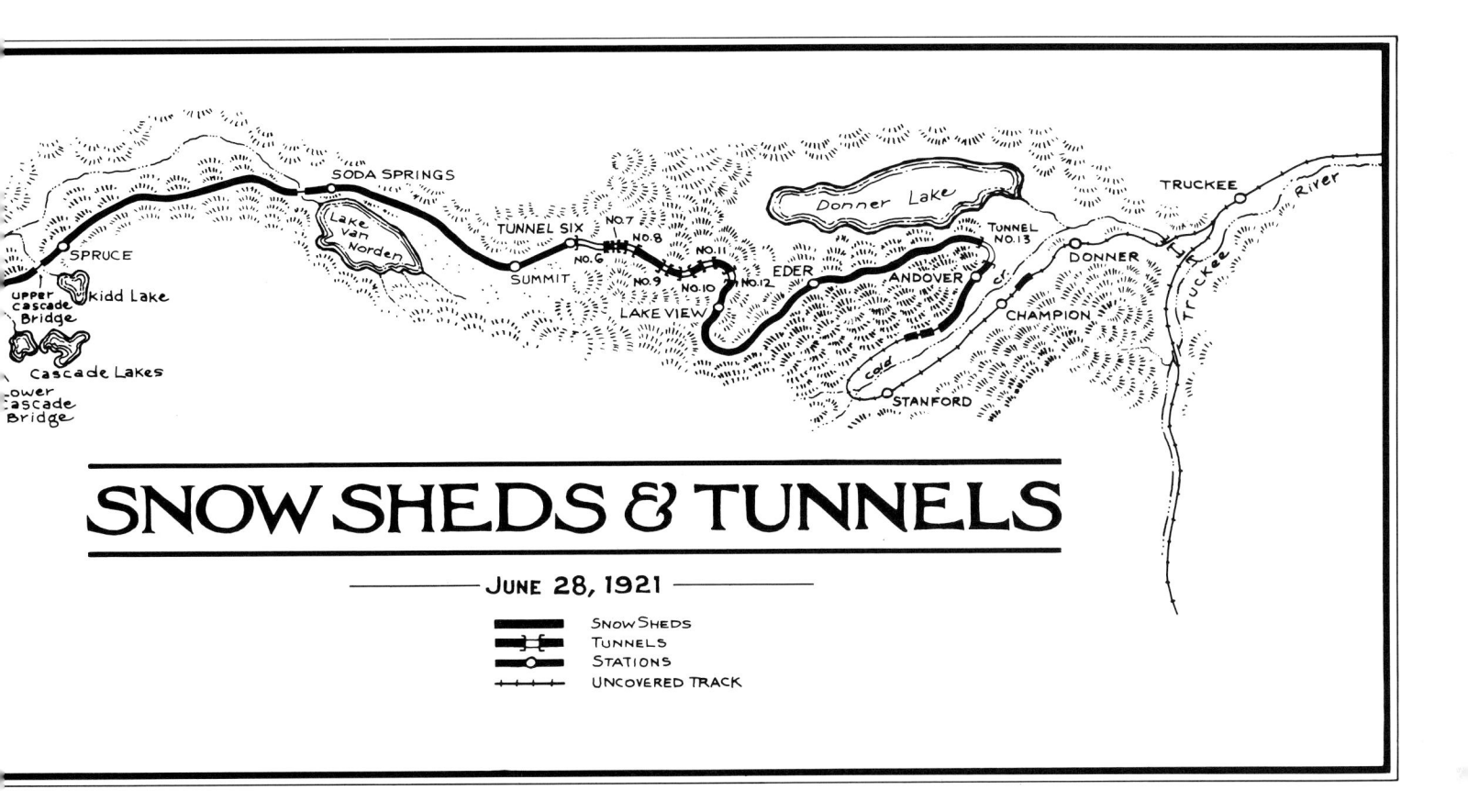

- Snow Sheds
- Tunnels
- Stations
- Uncovered Track

Pacific's Oregon Railway & Navigation Company, led Southern Pacific to order one for its subsidiary Central Pacific and the Donner grade. This was Leslie rotary, No. 5, built by Cooke in December 1887. Unfortunately, the machine arrived too late for the winter of 1887-88 and spent its first two years in comparative idleness. It was used to clear summer sidings and to plow out the Truckee yards each spring, handling these tasks easily considering the difficulties encountered with other methods, but otherwise, the new rotary spent most of its time in the Truckee roundhouse.

All of this equipment and the sheds themselves, were put to the test as the terrible winter of 1889-90 descended upon the high Sierra and indeed, the entire west coast. Charles Fredrick Crocker described the worsening conditions in a dispatch to the *Railway Gazette*...

"The first storms of the season commenced about the middle of October and for that season were very severe in intensity. In the latter part of October and early November about a week or ten days of cessation was followed by the inauguration of a storm, the distinctive storm conditions of which have not abated up to the present (January 27, 1890). The storm has remitted in its fury for the space of one or two days occasionally in the period, but we have experienced a storm condition... without abatement for a period of 70 days, during which time we have had at least 60 days of actual precipitation of rains in the valleys extending a very considerable distance up the flanks of the mountains, with snow on the higher altitudes and summits of all the mountains in the state... uniformly accompanied by tempests of wind which filled the air with fallen as well as falling snow which drifted in the cuts made by snowplows... alternating Arctic and Equatorial currents, as are usual in these storms, have varied the temperature within 24 hours many degrees. Five or six inches of rain has at times fallen on twelve feet of snow threatening the inundation of valleys below. A following Arctic current suddenly changed the temperature freezing this melted mass into ice making the use of snowplows impossible... in many of the cuts and narrow ravines through which the road passes in the mountain region. Drifts reach the enormous depth of 30 to 50 feet and make the use of snowplows wholly out of the question covering trains out of sight... in places on the line of the Central Pacific the snow is from 150 to 200 feet deep on top of the snowsheds and a special force of carpenters is employed to strengthen them to prevent their being crushed. Other forces are attempting to relieve them by removing snow...

It began snowing along the entire line from Ogden to Colfax December 20th and has continued uninterupted since... from Reno to the summit the thermometer descended to 30 degrees below zero. As the new year dawned, 600 men were at work fighting to keep the line open over Donner Pass.

The bucker plows were proving woefully inadequate in coping with the mounting drifts. On the 2nd of January, one of these primitive devices along with the six engines being used to propel it, became hopelessly mired in blowing snow two miles above Blue Cañon. The line was closed until the 5th when the plow and locomotives were freed with the aid of a new rotary and 200 shovelers.

For the next few days the line remained open but with considerable difficulty as heavy snows descended again and the last through train passed over the division on January 14th. By this time the accumulation of snow was astounding. Fully 24 feet of snow lay on the level at Summit, twelve to 18 feet at Emigrant Gap, Cisco and Cascade, twelve feet at Blue Cañon, eight feet at Alta, Dutch Flat and Gold Run, seven feet at Colfax and four feet at New England Mills. Cuts along the entire line from Blue Cañon to Gold Run were drifted full. The rotary was doing excellent work but the job was too great for only one machine. General Superintendent Fillmore later speculated in the *Railway Gazette* that if they would have had three or four rotaries instead of one, it would have been possible to keep the road open without serious delay.

Meanwhile, another bucker plow had become snowbound about two miles west of Blue Cañon and along with it five locomotives derailed, so an urgent order was wired to the east for two more Leslies. Another model of steam plow, the Cyclone, was brought out on a demonstration run to clear the line from Ogden west which in places had drifts ten to 15 feet deep. It was very successful in going, across the Great Basin, throwing the snow with great force. Officials eagerly awaited its arrival in the mountains.

On January 18th the *Sacramento Union* reported that...

Eastbound trains that had left Wednesday the 15th were not yet as far as Blue Cañon. The foremost is about two miles this side of Blue Cañon with one of the bucker plows ahead of it. This evening the plow was working hard to clear the road through to the station and had about accomplished the task when a huge snow drift slid down and literally buried the whole concern. The bucker plows which started on Thursday January 16th to clear the track at Tunnel 13, between Summit and Truckee which got corralled in the snow, is still there. Another plow started to help extricate the blockaded snow thrower but had not got more than a few yards out of Truckee when it too floundered in the snow and was unable to proceed... it took another bucker plow and five engines 36 hours to get to Tunnel 13, five miles west of Truckee.

Another plow and three locomotives derailed and plunged down an embankment near Cape Horn Mills killing a brakeman and injuring three others. General Manager A.N. Towne, in a dispatch to the *Railroad Gazette* reported that...

The last passenger train that went up the mountain required 19 of our most powerful locomotives and a push plow to get it over and even with this power it got stalled near Emigrant Gap. This was the last trip possible to make with the push plows. After that they had to depend entirely upon power plows to throw the snow out of the deep cuts... when I left the office tonite there were 1,245 shovelers between Colfax and Truckee and more on the way.

This was in spite of a strike among the shovelers for a raise from $2.00 to $3.50 per day on account of the extremely harsh conditions.

At last, the great storm subsided enough to allow crews to make some headway and on January 31st, after 16 days, the blockade was finally raised. This released from Truckee eight westbound trains containing 59 cars of passengers and mail, as well as those trains held on the west slopes. A brief respite was at hand but by February 17th snow was falling again and by the 22nd 55 inches had accumulated and it was still falling.

The winter of 1889-90 was one for the record — not to be approximated again for nearly a half century and because of it the bucker plows were, for the most part, retired soon after and the more efficient rotaries took their place. Another rotary arrived in time for the mid-February storms and performed as was now expected, but the Cyclone plow failed miserably. Upon reaching the Mountain District, the Cyclone was put to use at Strong's Cañon, on the summer track which had remained untouched all winter. Four engines were used to push the plow into the drift where it immediately choked up so solidly that it was necessary to melt snow from the auger with steam. Then a single engine pushed a rotary onto the siding and opened it up with no difficulty. The Cyclone later failed in tests at Cascade siding and in the Truckee yards and was never used on the Mountain again. Clearly the rotaries had proved their ability to cope with the high Sierra snow and

By the spring of 1868, the construction of snowsheds and galleries in the high Sierra was in full swing. In the above scene, work was underway that summer at Cascade on a project which ultimately protected over 30 miles of railroad at a cost of $2 million. — ALFRED HART, SOUTHERN PACIFIC COLLECTION

A few years later, a westbound train emerges from the sheds at the same location as shown above. A change of season clearly illustrates the necessity of the sheds. — R.A. MILLER JR. COLLECTION

Central Pacific bucker snowplow No. 1, weighing in at 19 tons, was constructed in the Sacramento shops. — G.M. BEST COLLECTION

Besides the sheds, bucker plows constituted the railroad's primary defense against snow. A bucker plow poses for the camera, at the left, at Cisco in the 1880's. The idea was to ram the plow into the drifts with enough speed and power to force the snow to the side. When it stalled, the plow would draw back, as shown below, for another run at it. — BOTH GUY L. DUNSCOMB COLLECTION

"Bucking snow" was a term that held much meaning in the early days and to say it was thrilling work was putting it mildly. Roaring into a snow bank at speed, with such unseen dangers as fallen trees, rock and ice, was a contributing factor to the frequent derailments and even death. (RIGHT) Photographer L.E. Graham was on hand in Cold Stream Canyon to record this bucker incident. The plow is completely buried in the drifts to the right of the second engine. (BELOW) At least seven wood burners shove a bucker plow through the drifts in Cold Stream Canyon. Anywhere from six to twelve engines were employed simultaneously in this demanding service. — ALL R.A. MILLER JR. COLLECTION

45

The heavy snow in the high Sierra so overwhelmed the bucker plows, that Central Pacific was an early and enthusiastic supporter of the Leslie "rotary steam shovel." Developed in Canada during 1884, Leslie licensed its manufacture to the Cooke Locomotive Works and the fifth Leslie rotary to be built in this country was delivered to the Central Pacific early in 1888. (ABOVE) CP rotary No. 2 and crew pose at Cascade soon after its delivery. — R.A. MILLER JR. COLLECTION (LEFT) The rotaries proved their worth during the terrible storms of 1889-1890. — GUY L. DUNSCOMB COLLECTION (BELOW) The only "Cyclone" snowplow acquired by the road is shown in the Truckee yards in mid-February 1890. The screw-like snowplow failed to measure up to the standards set by the rotaries. — R.A. MILLER JR. COLLECTION

46

Continuous storm conditions prevailed in the high Sierra for nearly 70 days, from mid-November 1889 through February 1890, creating the kind of weather that legends are made of. At one point, 24 feet of snow lay on the level at Summit with drifts twice that. Snow piled up in such record proportions that the railroad was blockaded for 16 days. In the two photos at the right taken at Blue Cañon, twelve feet of snow had accumulated on the level, making it the point of farthest penetration on the west slope. — BOTH STANFORD UNIVERSITY SPECIAL COLLECTIONS (BELOW) Truckee was digging out from under as much as 18 feet of snow in February 1890 when H.K. Gage took the photograph shown below. — COURTESY MR. AND MRS. ROGER ZWANSIGER

they have been close at hand ever since, ready to leap into the fray.

The sheds also proved to be invaluable in the battle with King Snow. Not a foot of shed was lost during the entire storm and where they were in place, the line was kept reasonably free of snow. The extreme difficulties encountered in maintaining operations over a strip 1.5 miles long near Cascade, where the sheds had burned the previous summer, underscored their importance. In the past, abandonment of the costly and ungainly structures had been discussed and so it was decided that this portion would not be rebuilt and the rest gradually abandoned. The directors appeared to place undue confidence on their other defenses to keep the line open. But, as in the past, it was this strip which repeatedly was blockaded with drifts ranging from 20 to 25 feet in depth and all efforts were centered on this section the last four days before the January blockade was lifted. Following this episode, the burned strip was rebuilt and snowsheds became a permanent item of the maintenance of the road over the Sierra.

The fire that destroyed the stretch of shed at Cascade in the summer of 1889 was not the first, nor was it the last to create problems for the railroad. The fire hazard of such an extensive frame structure was substantial. Exposed from without to forest and brush fires and from within to incendiary hazards of railway operation — sparks from the locomotives, hot brake shoes, lantern illumination and the like — sheds resembled a giant tinder box waiting to ignite. This condition was augmented by the strong contrasts between the winter and summer conditions on the Donner grade. Traditionally, more than half the total precipitation falls in January, February and March while a barely perceptible three percent falls during the five to six month long dry summer.

During the Central Pacific's first full year of operation, (1869-70), and well before the snowsheds had reached their greatest extent, a fire destroyed nearly 4,000 feet of shed in one instance and 1,200 feet in another. A shed fire was an awesome thing and the destruction of property and loss of life was often great. Stories are told of one Sacramento Division Superintendent whose heart was stilled forever as he emerged from his office car in the sheds to view the scene of one such holocaust, and of another who was driven mad by similar circumstance. The necessity of providing proper fire protection for the sheds was a major priority and in time an elaborate system for fire prevention and control was established.

During the summer of 1870, three fire trains were set up and deployed in the shed district at Blue Cañon, Summit and Truckee. Later, following disastrous fires near Summit during September 1892 in which a fire train was trapped, a fourth train was assigned to Cisco. The first engines, so assigned, were the *Governor Stanford, Grey Eagle, Unicorn* and *Merced*. Along about 1890, standard Ten-Wheelers began to be assigned to the service. They were equipped with a Duplex fire pump designed to deliver 300 gallons of water a minute through a 1,000 foot 2.5-inch hose. Each train was set up with two water cars, hose, and a full complement of ladders, axes, buckets and similar apparatus. During the season, the trains were under steam at all times and crews were on duty day and night. Responding to an alarm, the trains would observe no speed limit other than what caution might dictate and they would blow a high-pitched steam siren continuously en route to the fire.

The fire trains were only as good as the detection system which would sound the alarm. During 1876, it was recognized that from a prominent mountain peak on the west slope of the Sierra Nevada known as Signal Peak or Red Mountain, it was possible to observe, with only minor interruption, the entire line of railroad from Blue Cañon to Summit. That year a telephone line was run from Cisco to the summit of Red Mountain and a lookout was erected at an elevation of 7,860 feet for the express purpose of detecting and reporting fires. This is understood to be the first practical use of a telephone on the Southern Pacific lines. During the summer months, two watchmen were located in this lookout on 12-hour shifts. To aid them in their observations, an ordinary engineer's transit was installed. A wire needle attached to this would travel over a copper plate of sufficient size to accommodate a range of about 180 degrees. Etched on the plate was a true line of the snowsheds together with mileposts, alarm boxes and other well established points. Thus, the exact position of the transit in relation to the sheds was available at all times. Etched on the glass bay window was an exact line of the sheds as seen through the transit so as to determine their location at night. All in all, 26.4 miles of sheds were visible from the lookout. The watchmen would scan the district with field glasses and upon noticing smoke or fire, the transit was trained on the spot to determine its exact location. The watchman then telephoned the agent at Cisco, who called out the fire train. Furthermore, the watchman reported to the agent at Cisco every half hour.

There were two points, within Red Mountain's range of vision, obstructed from view by spurs of the mountain range. (These obstructions were utilized in placing the casings composing the bay windows of the lookout.) During the fire season, observation stations for the sheds from Summit were maintained on the top of tunnel No. 6 east to tunnel No. 13 and on top of tunnel No. 3 for those portions obscured from view at Red Mountain. No apparatus was maintained at either station except for the telephone which was linked to the central fire office at Summit.

Augmenting this arrangement was a series of telegraph boxes, 48 in number, spaced less than one mile apart, which extended throughout the snowshed district. Watchmen, patrolling equally given portions of the sheds, reported every hour via these boxes or sounded the alarm if there was trouble. Their report was registered automatically on a tape device, called the "Gerry Machine," located in the central fire office at Summit and, as a matter of record, in the district roadmaster's office at Truckee. This tape was continually monitored during the fire season and upon the appearance of an alarm, the nearest fire train was summoned. Additionally, alarms were located in several of the more important parts of the sheds, which, when operated by track walkers or other personnel, set off bells at Summit and other points.

Certain precautions were taken in the sheds themselves, to limit the spread of fire. Early on, 150 feet of galvanized iron was substituted for the wood at every half mile point but in a fire situation, this proved ineffective in checking the spread of flames. A shed fire would race beyond the metal section in a "chimney effect." It was determined that in order to break this draft, it would be necessary to create openings. The solution was the telescoping shed, a 96 foot section of shed on wheels which, during the summer months, was hitched to a locomotive and hauled into an adjoining shed. These were set up where necessary to create a break in the sheds every 5,000 feet. At their greatest extent, there were 17 telescoping sheds in place.

The sheds were the principal feature of the Donner grade, a trademark if you will, and although not unique to the Central Pacific, they had the most extensive deployment of the structures in North America and as such, were easily recognized and cursed by tourists. They proved to be a vital and enduring tool for the maintenance of the railway over the Sierra Nevada mountains and dominated and influenced operations on the district well into the 20th century.

An early fire train is ready for service somewhere below the sheds in the 1890's. Note the two homemade tank cars behind the engine. — G.M. BEST COLLECTION

Mallet No. 4029 hisses quietly in the long shed at Truckee on February 21, 1922. — SOUTHERN PACIFIC COLLECTION

2

The Harriman Influence 1900-1929

The Central Pacific Railroad was, beginning in 1884, leased to the Southern Pacific Company. At this time, all money for its operation and physical improvements were advanced by the Southern Pacific who was actively engaged in railroad construction throughout the west. The SP could only offer the Central Pacific just enough money to essentially maintain the property in operating condition. Concern was expressed over the CP's ability to meet its obligations on the government debt it had incurred during its construction days. A solution to this dilemma was reached by Huntington during 1899 but, in so doing, it was necessary to reorganize the Central Pacific. A new company, the Central Pacific Railway, fully controlled by the Southern Pacific Company, began business on August 1, 1899.

Essentially unchanged since the original construction, difficulties were encountered in operating larger and more modern equipment over the old roadbed and raising speeds commensurate with the times was out of the question. Central Pacific's physical plant was ripe for upgrading and, with the reorganization of the railroad, engineers were dispatched into the field with instructions to make surveys that would reduce grades and curvature.

At this point in time, the long shadow of Edward Henry Harriman was cast over the destiny of the Central Pacific and the Donner grade. During 1897, Harriman, a skillful financier and railway executive who had made his mark in the reconstruction and re-equipping of the Union Pacific, had obtained control of the property through auction. In the succeeding five years, nearly $45 million was expended to bring the insolvent, dismembered and decrepit Union Pacific to the forefront as the most modern and efficient railway in the hemisphere. Harriman's plans were global in aspect and, seeing the Central Pacific as a logical extension of his system, he sought to buy it but Huntington would not sell. His only recourse then was to acquire the entire Southern Pacific system and, following Huntington's death in August 1900, he gained that opportunity. Through a series of skillful financial negotiations Harriman had, by March 1901, enabled the Union Pacific to acquire from Huntington's estate and others, enough outstanding stock to control the company. He was elected chairman of the SP executive committee in April and assumed the presidency on September 26, 1901.

Almost at once, the same visionary program that had been applied to the Union Pacific was directed towards the Southern Pacific. During the eight years of Harriman's direct administration, more than $240 million was expended on new equipment, reconstruction, and the development of new lines either by purchase or new construction. Attributed to Harriman is the remark "Spend it in a week if you can," a directive given to SP's General Manager Julius Kruttschnitt who had just been handed $18 million for improvements. Although Harriman died in September 1909, with much still to be done, his vigorous philosophies on management continued to dominate the policies of the Southern Pacific for two more decades.

This policy stressed the importance of the central "Overland Route" of which the Donner Pass line formed a vital link. Envisioned by Harriman and executed by William Hood, Southern Pacific's chief engineer, was the 84-mile Wadsworth line change, the first in a series of improvements to the Donner grade, which in the next three decades, would take this winding single-track mountain bottleneck and transform it into a modern transportation corridor.

The old terminal at Wadsworth, Nevada, was bypassed due to a line change which extended from a point near Reno to Brown's via Clark's and Hazen. Although longer, the new alignment avoided the 1.5 percent grade encountered in the crossing of the Hot Springs Mountains. The new alignment extended due east from Reno across the Truckee Meadows and it was in this area that a new terminal was planned to replace Wadsworth. This great work, undertaken in the spring of 1902, was perhaps the first major piece of engineering on the Donner Pass line attributed to Hood, a most capable man, who had succeeded Samuel Montague as chief engineer during 1883.

The site of the new terminal was essentially a swamp, and it took six months to fill it with 360 cars of rock a day. During the fall of 1903, the roundhouse foundation was laid and, in February 1904, the transfer of shop equipment commenced. The town of Wadsworth, comprised for the most part of railroad employees and their families, was obliged to move lock, stock and barrel to the new terminal. The move was essentially completed late in June 1904, and the division headquarters, including the station building itself, was relocated to the new terminal of Sparks on June 19th.

Line changes to reduce grade and curvature would speed up operations but, in the Harriman modernization program, signaling, to promote safe operation, received equal attention. Miles of automatic block signals were being set up across the "Overland Route" and elsewhere on the Harriman Lines, to which, operating officials expressed great satisfaction. Along the line from Sacramento over the Sierra, automatic signals were set up between Sacramento and Elvas during August 1904, and between Elvas and Rocklin in the period from December 1906 through January 1907. On the east end between Truckee and Sparks, automatic signals were authorized in January 1905. In filling the gap between Rocklin and Truckee, however, the decision was made to adopt an unusual system of controlled manual blocks, utilizing the Union Switch & Signal Highspeed Electric Train Staff model No. 2.

The staff system, without the necessity of elaborate track circuitry, could be set up more cheaply and quickly than automatic block signals. Nevertheless, at the time the staff was placed in operation on the Donner grade, the necessity of having agents on duty at regular intervals, for the purpose of supervising the work of the fire patrols in the snowsheds, was an important, if not the overriding element in its adoption. Another advantage of the staff system became apparent soon after it was placed in operation. A train, finding any part of the sheds on fire, could immediately back up to the preceeding station in the rear without the danger and delay caused by having to whistle out a flagman to protect against a following train.

The train staff itself was, in its original form, a stick of wood or metal about 20 inches long. When given to the engineman of a train, it signified that he had the right-of-track between two stations, the names of which were painted or engraved directly

— DONALD DUKE COLLECTION

Edward Henry Harriman

on the staff. This right was absolute, regardless of time, rules or conditions, thus making timetables unnecessary as far as safety was concerned. A train running from A to B would have a certain staff and then from B to C another staff of different shape or color and so on. To work around the inconvenience which was caused under this arrangement, whenever the staff happened to be at the wrong end of the section, an electric train staff apparatus was devised. Under this system, each station had a pillar containing a magazine of staffs, say from ten to 25, and with a system of electric locks properly connected from station to station, it was then possible to secure the right-of-track from either end of the section yet, never from but one end of the section at the same time.

The principal was first employed on the London & Northwestern during 1889 and in time it was put to use throughout Great Britain, Russia, Australia and Japan. Its use in North America however, was limited. A number of lines had small installations, with the more notable in place on the Chesapeake & Ohio, the Philadelphia & Reading, the Chicago, Milwaukee & St. Paul and the Santa Fe's line over Raton Pass, in northern New Mexico and southern Colorado. The Donner Pass staff system, extending from Rocklin to Truckee over 98 miles of rough country, was the most extensive installation of this apparatus in North America.

To acquaint the train crews and operators with this new system, Sacramento Division Bulletin No. 23 was issued during January 1905 covering "Instructions and rules governing use of the train staff system." The system itself was placed on line that August. The original staff stations, 38 in number, were spread out across the district, with an average of about 2.5 miles between them. Within the sheds, the staff station was built directly into the side of the structure, with the shed being somewhat widened for a short distance on either side, providing a platform in front of the office. Each station had a bay window, and adjacent to it hung illuminated station signs for identification.

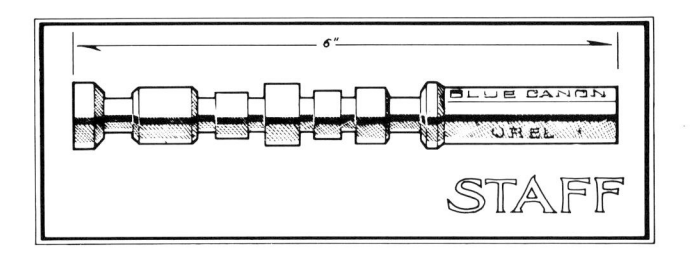

Five additional staff offices were placed in service during World War I to ease traffic conditions. These were set up at Blue Cañon Junction (later Knapp), Keene (later Gunter), Stanford, Donner and tunnel No. 6. The latter was established to facilitate more rapid and flexible movement of helpers between tunnel No. 6 and Summit.

The staff was augmented by a system of fixed signals, deployed throughout the railroad during the summer of 1906, at a cost of $350,000. In open country, these signals took the form of disk or semaphore types, but clearance problems, within the sheds, as well as alternating irregular patterns of darkness and light, prevented the use of conventional signals. What was needed was a compact signal, as yet undeveloped, that would be capable of displaying simultaneous warning both day or night.

A team of SP men, headed up by E.M. Cutting, Sacramento Division Foreman of Signals, tackled the problem. Through numerous trials, they developed a signal so unique that a patent regarding the device was issued April 1903. While experimenting with colored strips of celluloid, Cutting discovered that a fairly good night indication

STAFF SYSTEM ROCKLIN TO TRUCKEE
LIST OF STAFF STATIONS AUGUST 1905

STATIONS	DISTANCE BETWEEN STATIONS	FROM TRUCKEE	STATIONS	DISTANCE BETWEEN STATIONS	FROM TRUCKEE	STATIONS	DISTANCE BETWEEN STATIONS	FROM TRUCKEE
DN Truckee	0.0	0.0	DN Yuba Pass	2.02	31.87	DN Colfax	2.25	65.36
T Champion	3.56	3.56	T Smart	2.76	34.63	T Lander	3.08	68.44
DN Tunnel 13	4.08	7.64	DN Emigrant Gap	1.50	36.13	DN N.Eng.Mills	1.97	70.41
T Eder	2.19	9.83	T Fulda	2.05	38.18	T Applegate	3.31	73.72
DN Lakeview	1.80	11.63	DN Blue Canon	3.15	41.33	DN Clipper Gap	2.97	76.69
DN Summit	2.70	14.33	T Orel	2.64	43.97	T Bowman	3.41	80.10
T Soda Springs	2.96	17.29	DN Midas	2.08	46.05	DN Auburn	3.30	83.40
DN Spruce	2.81	20.10	T Gorge	2.29	48.34	T Zeta	2.98	86.38
T Troy	2.02	22.12	DN Towle	1.80	50.14	DN Newcastle	1.91	88.29
T Tamarack	2.00	24.12	DN Dutch Flat	2.63	52.77	DN Penryn	3.18	91.47
DN Cisco	3.51	27.63	DN Gold Run	2.12	54.89	DN Loomis	2.89	94.35
T Crystal Lake	2.16	29.79	T Magra	3.35	58.24	DN Rocklin	3.91	98.26
			DN Caporn	2.61	60.85			
			T Wirt	2.26	63.11			

DN — Day and night telegraph office. T — day and night telephone office.

could be given with one-half the ordinary round colored lens and, at distances of up to a mile, it was indistinguishable from that of a full lens. Working on this principal, he devised a lightweight, compact, illuminated signal with a single 12-inch bull's-eye. This unit was attached directly to the timbers in the shed. The signal was made to give either of two color indications. This was accomplished by dividing it horizontally into different colored halves and by providing shutters of which the halves could be alternately blinded. The bull's-eye was painted for the day indication and a 6.5-inch color light, in the center, provided the night indication. The shutters were moved by a solenoid.

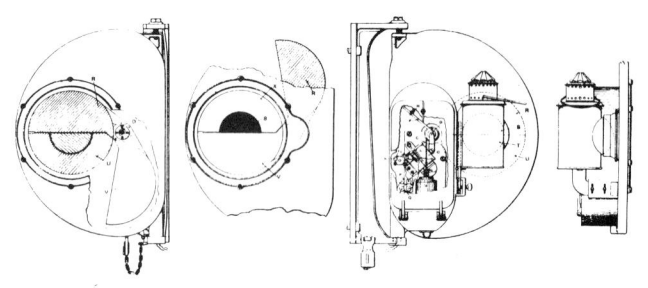

The Cutting Disk Signal — RAILWAY AGE

At the approach to a station that had a side track, there were two such signals affixed one above the other. These were controlled by the operator and were capable of three indications; red over yellow — take siding, green over yellow — proceed cautiously along mainline prepared to stop at staff crane, and green over green — proceed along mainline expecting to secure staff and right-of-track through the next block.

There were drawbacks to the staff system. Without a continuous track circuit, it was not possible to protect against the danger of a train accidentlly becoming detached unless the staff was carried in the rear car which, in SP's case, it was not. Without a track circuit extending throughout the block, it could not provide protection against broken rails. In operation, the staff was delivered to trains by cranes and it was returned by placing it into a pouch and dropping it to the ground at the foot of the staff crane. In order that this transfer could be effected without unnecessary loss of time or personal injury, as had been the case with the original cranes used, a special deliverer and catcher, known as the Keefe Time Saving Device, was substituted for the old cranes after the system had been in operation for several years.

If a staff, when thrown, should accidentally drop down a gorge, as was possible at some locations, traffic would be out of gear on that block until the signal maintainer could be summoned to take out another staff and restore equilibrium to the machines. As an interim measure, in the event a staff was lost, the Superintendent issued train orders to advance a train through the block. Later, a special "balance staff," not to be issued to trains, was devised. The operator, authorized by train order, inserted this special staff into the machine to restore balance.

The first summer, following the establishment of the staff system, the signals used in conjunction with it were made semiautomatic. The upper signals, by means of a track circuit between the fouling points of the side track switches, were set up so they would not clear unless that section of track was unoccupied. Each home signal was also provided with a distant signal of the same type situated approximately 1,000 feet to the rear for upgrade trains and 1,500 feet in advance for downgrade movements. These distant signals were interlocked with the outside switch so they would show yellow whenever the switch was out of position or, whenever the home signal was red. In the vicinity of such signals, the sheds were provided with chimneys to permit the rapid venting of smoke and steam. Each station was also provided with an indicator, fixed above the operator's table, which would show track occupancy or when the switch was set for the siding. At first, all such switches had to be thrown by hand, but in time some came to be remote controlled from the staff office. All switches within the sheds were equipped with lights which burned continuously.

The staff system on the Donner grade remained in place and serviceable for over two decades. But, as time passed, its limits were trimmed in the wake of a vigorous double-tracking program pursued by the Harriman administration. As the double-track encroached upon the staff system limits, the railroad was set up for automatic block signals and the staff stations retired. The first project of this nature, in staff territory, occurred on the west slope commencing at Elvas, near Sacramento. It was completed in two stages with the second track authorized between there and Roseville during February 1907, and from Roseville to Loomis the following July. Thus, at this time, the staff system was retired between Rocklin and Loomis.

Establishing Roseville as a major terminal was coincidental to this work. Judah had favored this location as a natural division point. Indeed, he had enough confidence in the "junction" to secure most of the lots available in the vicinity, with the intent of turning a profit. But his successor, Montague, for reasons not fully understood, decided to locate the terminal three miles further east at Rocklin, from which point helper engines would be required to the summit. Title to Judah's land passed to his heirs and remained in the family until his wife died in 1895, but little profit was ever realized from it. The town of Roseville had originally been laid out during August 1864,

The staff office at Crystal Lake which, due to its isolation, was frequently referred to as Siberia, had quarters for the operators located in the second story. — TED WURM COLLECTION

At the right, the staff office at Champion, located just west of Truckee, was named for F. Champion, an SP agent in the early days. This office was closed August 15, 1924. — SOUTHERN PACIFIC COLLECTION

An eastbound passenger train is about to pass the station at Wirt three miles east of Colfax. — A.C. PHELPS COLLECTION

and growth had been slow but steady, but in the meantime Rocklin had prospered.

In 1905, Rocklin's 26-stall roundhouse was doing a booming business, servicing about 1,200 locomotives a month. Approximately 140 employees worked in the local shops and car department, with another 150 in train service. Twenty-one freight crews, based at Rocklin, were in Mountain service. Rocklin's monthly railroad payroll was between 25,000 and 30,000 dollars. However, traffic increases after the turn of the century placed a difficult burden on Rocklin. During 1903, an expansion program, aimed at doubling the capacity of Rocklin's yards, still left them inadequate for the business. Rocklin was rapidly becoming a bottleneck.

In February 1905, a team of railroad officials arrived in town to look over the facilities as a possible site for a new roundhouse of greatly increased capacity, with a yard 7,000 feet long and 800 feet wide, and a total anticipated expenditure of $200,000. Other locations were also under consideration including Roseville, Ben-Ali (near Sacramento), Loomis and the open ground between Rocklin and Loomis. Roseville was eventually selected because of the favorable grade conditions, a quantity of available open ground and, most importantly, because of its strategic location, something Judah, in his wisdom, had anticipated 40 years earlier. Here, within the confines of one yard, it would be possible to reclassify incoming freight for its destination to the north, east, south or west. The same facilities could also make over incoming trains from the Sierra for the lighter grades of the valley districts, as well as break the valley trains into sections for the heavy Mountain District east of town.

Work began on the yards at Roseville early in 1906, and the move from Rocklin was completed two years later. During the summer of 1907, the yards at Roseville were completed enough to allow for making up trains. With an engine and caboose, crews for the Mountain would be called out of Rocklin with an engine and caboose to run down to Roseville to pick up an eastbound train. With a tonnage train, the run was made to Rocklin, and there, the helpers would be added. This operation proved rather unsatisfactory, as a "hogback" on the mainline just west of Rocklin would cause these trains to stall. In this event, the customary procedure was to whistle for a yard engine to help drag the train in, but many times an engine was unavailable and doubling was necessary.

The facilities in the new yards were largely in

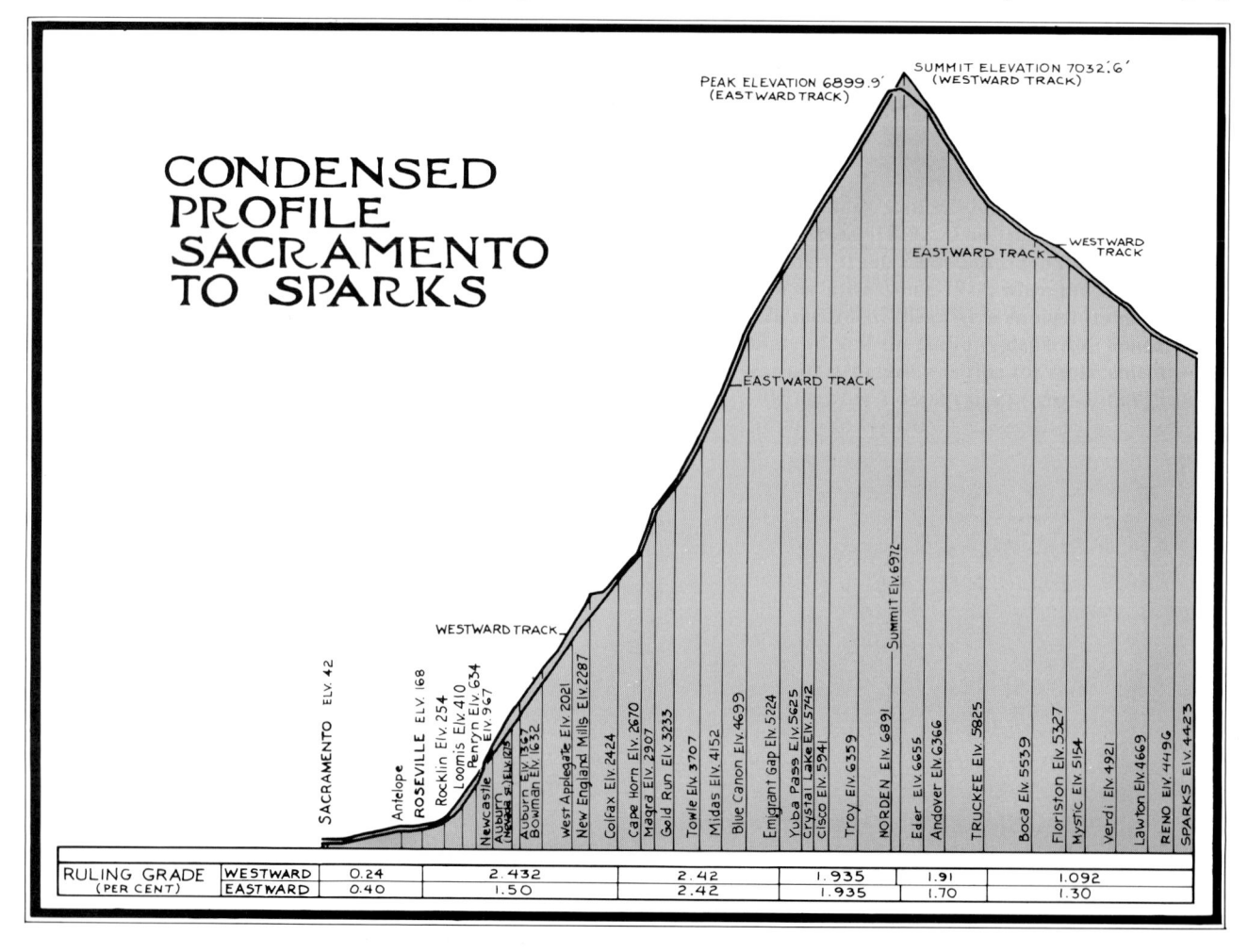

place and the crews organized and called out of Roseville commencing on November 4, 1907. Two yards were built on descending grades on either side of the double-track mainline, which ran through the center of the yards. All classification tracks were laid on a 0.4 percent grade at the western end of the yard. Classification was done westerly and the cars were drawn back by way of runaround tracks. Other facilities in the new yards at Roseville included a 32-stall roundhouse with provisions for doubling the capacity, a 350,000 gallon water tank, a machine shop, 56,000 barrel oil tank and the necessary scales, car repair tracks, storage tracks and buildings.

Rocklin's usefulness ended March 1, 1908, and the last moves from the former terminal were completed April 25th. After that the town faded from the operating scheme of things. In recognition of the fact, a "funeral" was held April 18th at Porter's Hall in Rocklin. Attending the event, hosted by the roundhouse crew, were friends and acquaintances wishing to pay their respects. Refreshments were served.

Farther up the grade and out of deference to the stiff grade in the immediate vicinity, a second-track was authorized in January 1908 between Gold Run and Alta, a distance of four miles. When completed, the staff station at Dutch Flat was discontinued.

During the early Harriman years, a serious study was undertaken of all available alternatives for providing a second-track over Donner grade. Harriman advocated an entirely new line with reduced grade and curvature. Similar projects had recently been completed in Nevada, across the Union Pacific and in California, such as the monumental Bayshore Cutoff near San Francisco, which clearly demonstrated that cost was an object of little consequence in order to achieve the desired result.

The limitations of the Donner Pass line were well defined. Eastward tonnage had to contend with a 2.2 percent maximum compensated grade between Rocklin and Colfax and a 2.4 percent grade between Colfax and Summit, although, the rise slackened somewhat above Emigrant Gap. Trains encountered a comparatively light maximum grade of 1.0 percent westbound between Sparks and Truckee, but a stiff 2.0 percent from that point to Summit. To complicate matters even more, 50 miles of line was in deep snow country.

A number of options were proposed by Hood and his staff. An entirely new single-track line was surveyed between Rocklin and Truckee, with a maximum compensated grade of 1.5 percent. A similar line change had been proposed between Roseville and Rocklin but, with helpers now being added at Roseville, there was no need for this costly work and it was dropped. In order to gain distance, it was necessary for the proposed track to deviate widely from the existing alignment. A notable feature of this proposal was the plan to bore a 27,480-foot tunnel (a little over 5.2 miles) from a point in the vicinity of Spruce to a point in the vicinity of Lakeview, at an elevation of 6,306 feet. The line would then skirt north of Donner Lake before rejoining the existing alignment just west of Truckee. Two more short tunnels would be necessary along the north bank of Donner Lake.

This same 5.2-mile tunnel was incorporated in another less ambitious scheme of simply creating a new 16.57-mile line between a point near Troy and Truckee. The estimated cost of this undertaking, at the time, hovered near ten million for single-track line and 14.7 million if it was to be double-tracked.

It was during this period of speculation that the daring scheme of a long tunnel under the mountains was considered. The concept was not a new one, having captured popular fancy as far back as the 1870's when former California Governor John Bigler had proposed a water/rail tunnel through the summit of the Sierra. Incorporated in a 28.5-mile line change from Fulda to Truckee was a double-track tunnel, 18.5 miles in length, whose total estimated cost would be close to 31.4 million. Electrification of the railroad through a tunnel of such magnitude would be essential for a successful operation. In calculating the costs involved in this great tunnel, Hood had figured that the construction of feeders and overhead, substations and the purchase of six electric locomotives would increase the overall cost of the project to 34.6 million.

The figures and method of operation, for the proposal, were based upon a recently electrified portion of the Great Northern line over the Cascade Mountains about 100 miles east of Seattle, Washington. About three miles of railroad extending from Wellington to Cascade through the 13,873-foot Cascade tunnel were involved. Here, the first three-phase electrification of a trunk railway in the United States was placed in operation during July 1909. Formerly this had been a coal-fired operation and as such, many difficulties were encountered going eastbound against the 1.7 percent grade, due to smoke, gases and condensation from steam accumulating within the tunnel. Hydro-electric generated power was fed into a 6,000-volt overhead and transformed to 500 volts on board the locomotives. The system was designed for potentially being used over the entire mountain division of the Great Northern, over which electrification was ultimately extended. But at the time of the Hood study, the electric locomotives merely dragged each train, steam locomotives and all, through the long tunnel.

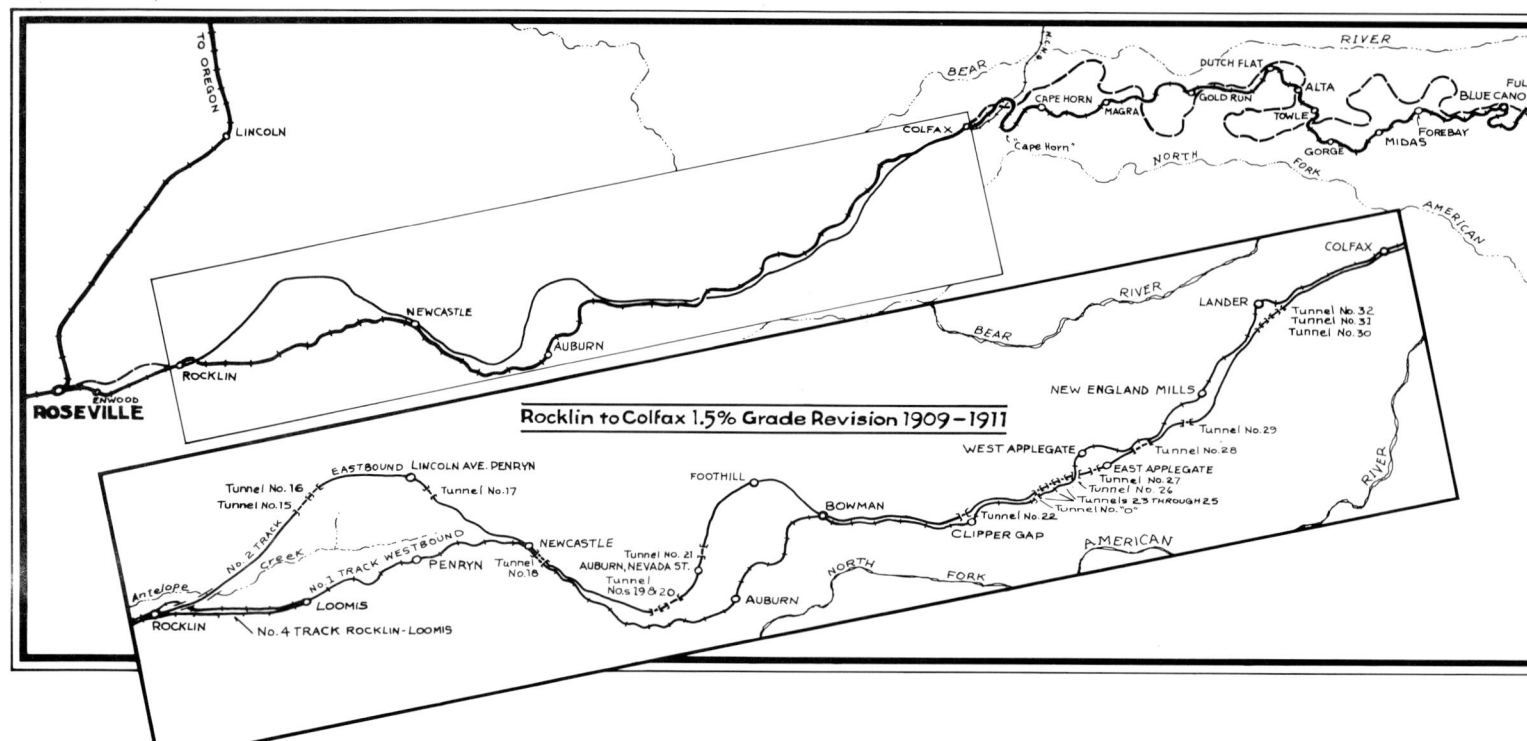

Although electrification of the lengthy Sierra Tunnel was limited in scope, the idea of electrifying the Donner grade in its entirety had not escaped the consideration of Harriman and his planners. During the fall of 1907, Julius Kruttschnitt, Director of Maintenance and Operations for the Harriman Lines, directed Alan H. Babcock, Southern Pacific's electrical engineer, along with Frank J. Sprague, who had been retained as consulting engineer, to study the possibilities of electrification between Roseville and Sparks, a distance of approximately 139 miles. For nearly three years, Babcock had been studying the possibilities of a change in motive power from steam to electricity, and had collected much of the necessary data on which a report could be based.

Aside from the problems of economics and suitability, certain difficulties would have to be addressed before such an undertaking could commence. The heavy snows and violent storms, indigenous to the region would have to be considered in the erecting and maintaining of transmission lines so they would work without interruption. Interference from snow in the operation of a 3rd-rail, if used, could cause problems. In the spring, precautions would be needed due to short circuiting caused by the melting snow, leaving the possibility of fire in the sheds due to such shorts. Commenting on the problem of electrification of the line over the Sierra, Julius Kruttschnitt remarked in the *Wall Street Journal* in January 1910 that:

Eastern critics may be inclined to the opinion that we are dallying in this matter. We have found that it pays well to make haste slowly with regard to innovations. Electrification for mountain traffic does not carry the same appeal that it did two years ago. Oil burning locomotives are solving the problem very satisfactorily. Each Mallet-compound locomotive, having horsepower in excess of 3,000, hauls as great a load as two of former types, burning 10 percent less fuel and consuming 50 percent less water.

Although the question of how to surmount the rocky summit of the Sierra was still not finalized, the desirability of a new easy grade line in the lower elevations was never seriously debated. During the spring of 1909, funding was secured and work commenced on the 1.5 percent grade between Rocklin and Colfax, with the expectation that this low grade line would eventually be continued all the way over the mountains.

Erickson & Petterson of San Francisco had the contract for the first 20 miles of new line from Rocklin to Clipper Gap, while the Utah Construction Company of Ogden handled the remaining eleven miles into Colfax. William Hood oversaw the work as Chief Engineer, while A.J. Barclay acted as engineer in charge.

The original alignment between these points was 31.6 miles long with a maximum 2.2 percent grade opposing eastbound traffic and a maximum curvature of 10 degrees. The new line was to be 30.8 miles long with a maximum 1.5 percent grade and a maximum curve of four degrees. To achieve these savings in grade and curvature in a shorter distance, much heavy work was necessary, including 17 tunnels and two major bridges.

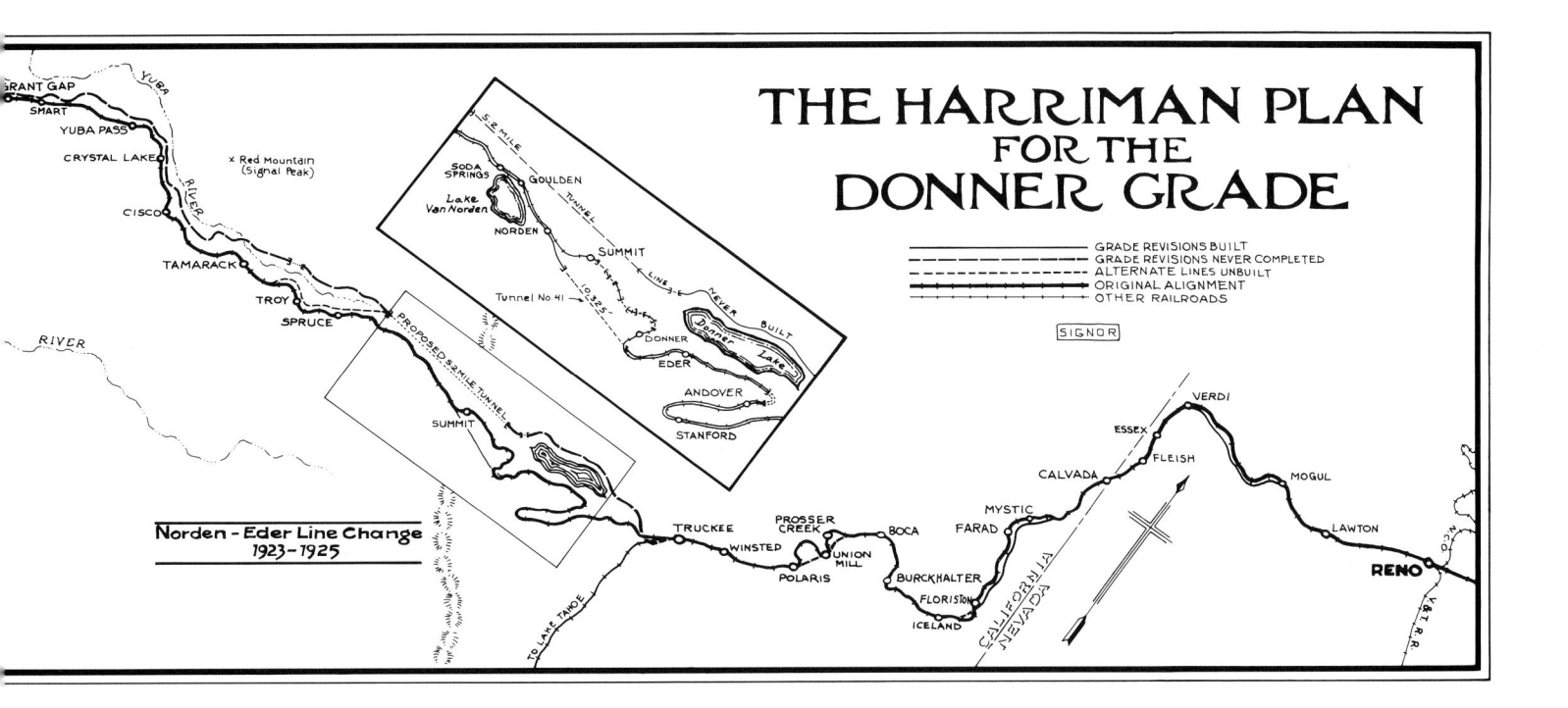

There was considerable difficulty in getting the necessary right-of-way at reasonable prices. People, who would ordinarily be willing to give it away for the construction of a new railroad, seemed to take the opposite course where the improvement of an existing line was concerned. At length, the right-of-way was secured, although construction was delayed in starting to bore tunnel No. 21. The reason for the delay was that at one point it became necessary to acquire the corner of a churchyard in order to continue work.

During the length of the construction project, no work trains were run on the original line due to the fact that there would have been too many delays, as train service was so frequent. With the electric train staff system in use, work trains could not be operated on the mainline by flagging. Thus, a great deal of construction track was built which crossed the mainline at various points under the protection of simple electric interlockings. From the original line, many temporary spurs were built for the delivery of materials and supplies to construction camps, tunnels and heavy cuts. There were a number of places, however, some distance from the original line, to which no spurs were built. To reach these places all equipment had to be hauled overland, sometimes as much as 2.5 miles. At Auburn, for example, locomotives, cars and steam shovels were hauled for a mile and one-half through the streets of town. Track was laid ahead of them and the shovels, under their own power, hoisted themselves uphill with cables.

Eastward from Rocklin the original line was relocated some 6,000 feet in order to allow the new grade to pass over it. Between this separation and Newcastle, the low-grade line diverged widely to the north, piercing three tunnels — No. 15, 1,896 feet, No. 16, 769 feet and No. 17, 1,639 feet. Tunnel numbering took up where the original tunnels left off. Original tunnel No. 15, between Mystic and the state line, had been daylighted just prior to the commencement of the project.

About two miles of the original line were relocated in the vicinity of Newcastle in order to keep it south of the new second track, thus eliminating some curvature in the process. The two tracks then passed through tunnel No. 18 before diverging, as the original line continued at a higher level. At 991 feet, tunnel No. 18 was the only double-tracked tunnel required between Rocklin and Colfax.

Auburn Ravine was bridged by a 540-foot trestle, 90 feet above the stream bed on a three degree curve. Three more tunnels were drilled in this vicinity. These were tunnels No. 19, 368 feet, No. 20, 1,239 feet and No. 21, 1,200 feet.

The most troublesome work was encountered in building the new line between Bowman and Applegate. The old grade constantly interfered with the new location, but the lines were at different levels so that simple double-tracking was not feasible. In this section, four more tunnels were required — No. 22, 1,024 feet, No. 23, 843 feet, No. 24, 292 feet and No. 25. This tunnel, 763 feet in length, required a cut so close to the original line that it could not be excavated without spilling material on the old line. Therefore, a shoofly was built around the south side of the work to temporarily carry the original mainline. There were other places in this

The date was May 14, 1909 and the camera was trained (LEFT) on the 698-foot long tunnel No. "0." (BELOW) By November, work was underway on adjacent tunnel No. 23 in conjunction with the Rocklin-Colfax double-tracking project. A temporary material spur was in place. — BOTH SOUTHERN PACIFIC COLLECTION

By April 18, 1911 the new tunnel and second track are in operation. The Bowman-Applegate section created many problems because the old line constantly interfered with the new line at different elevations. — SOUTHERN PACIFIC COLLECTION

section, while not so cramped as in this case, that could not be excavated with steam shovels. At these points the work was done by hand.

At Applegate, the new line was carried 30 feet under the original right-of-way in a skewed concrete subway, designated tunnel No. 26, and between this point and Colfax six more tunnels were required, the longest of which was No. 28, 3200 feet. Beyond tunnel No. 32, near Lander, and on to Colfax, a distance of two miles, the original line, which frequently crossed the second track, was abandoned and a new simple double-track line was built. Included in this great project, which was completed and placed in operation during the spring of 1912, was an extensive revision of the Colfax yards in which the yard trackage was straightened, extended, a wye built and plans laid for the erection of a substantial concrete engine house. As with other sections of double-track, the staff system was dismantled, eliminating ten staff offices, and automatic block signals were set up using, for the most part, Union Switch & Signal style "B" lower quadrant semaphores.

The first through freight train movement over the length of the new line occurred March 31, 1912, and effective April 7th all eastbound through passenger trains took to the new line. The original mainline was reserved for westbound trains and was designated the No. 1 track. The new low-grade line became the No. 2 track and was used exclusively by eastbound trains. With the two flyovers, a good portion of the double-track between Rocklin and Colfax was now left hand running.

The new cutoff, with its increased capacity and constant grade, was a success in all respects. The only negative aspect of the work came from shippers at Loomis who complained about the loss of express shipment of perishables on train No. 24, a condition soon rectified. The short stretch of double-track between Rocklin and Loomis, laid prior to the grade revision, was designated the No. 4 track. Certain eastbound passenger trains, like the *Sierra,* the *Pacific Limited* and the Colfax Locals, handling mail and express for Penryn and Loomis, would use this track as would local freights working the fruit sheds. Trains, having timetable or train order authority, would use No. 4 track from Rocklin to Loomis and then proceed up No. 1 track against the current of traffic to Newcastle where a crossover to No. 2 track was made.

Coincident with the second tracking between Rocklin and Colfax, the section from Reno to the first siding west, Lawton, was double-tracked, as was the section from Truckee to Winstead, the first siding east. Both of these stretches were completed during the early summer of 1910. In the fall of 1912, with the Colfax project behind them, a force of men went to work extending the double-track down the Truckee River canyon from Winstead to Lawton. The second-track was laid adjacent to the existing track where it was feasible, but to even out grades and reduce curvature, about 19 miles of line between Lawton and a point west of Floriston were laid at a different level than the original track. The new line in this section was completed and placed in operation in May 1915. The westbound track from Sparks to Truckee was held to a one-percent ruling grade. Although a number of stretches exceeded this figure, they were so short they were considered "momentum grades."

In the same period, double-tracking was extended on the west slope from Colfax to Blue Canon. Even though the steepest grades to be encountered on the hill were in this section, there was no slackening of the grade. The second track was laid, for the most part, adjacent to the original line. In this work, extending from Colfax to Gold Run and from Alta to Blue Cañon, a great steel viaduct was erected at Long Ravine and two double-track tunnels — No. 33, 1,331 feet and No. 34, 410 feet, were driven at Cape Horn. The former, cutting out the perilous trip around the "Cape" was dubbed the "Panama Canal" by some witty conductor. The only other major work required was to widen tunnel No. 1 near Orel in order to accept the second track. Lost in the project were the staff offices at Colfax, Wirt, Caporn, Magra, Gold Run, Towle, Gorge, Midas and Orel.

This work failed to conform to the grade revision contemplated by Harriman and engineered by Hood. In order to hold to the 1.5 percent maximum grade, it took a costly and widely divergent course of 36 miles to span the distance that the existing grade covered in 25. But the climate for financing such great works was changing. The United States Government, in accordance with the Sherman Anti-Trust Act of 1890, had filed suit in Federal Court on February 1, 1908, seeking to break up Harriman's "Associated Lines." Harriman died the following year, leaving the future of the summit tunnel clouded. Julius Krutschnitt wired Hood, in January 1911, seeking more conservative estimates to present to the "Committee." Building the summit tunnel line from Cisco to Truckee had been figured at $6 million. Hood now offered an estimate of $2.3 million for simply double-tracking the present line between the two points. Even this proposal was not acted upon.

The government complaint led to a 1913 Supreme Court decision, obliging the Union Pacific to divest itself of all its Southern Pacific stock. Then, in February 1914, another blow came when the government attempted to separate the Southern Pacific and the Central Pacific. The subsequent battles over who should control the Central

Pacific — either the SP or the UP — of whether it should remain a separate entity, dragged on for nearly a decade. In the interim, all innovation and improvement to the Donner grade was shelved.

Unfortunately, while improvements were curtailed, traffic swelled and the 41-mile stretch of single-track from Blue Canon to Truckee, through the sheds, became a bottleneck of serious proportion. Indeed, it was during 1913 that an all time record of 18 passenger trains were regularly scheduled on the Mountain between Sacramento and Sparks. During the first three decades of the 20th century, through passenger trains, regularly scheduled over the Mountain, virtually doubled. Sections of these trains and local passenger service to the western foothill communities and towns along the Truckee River added to the congestion.

A general realignment of passenger schedules had been implemented system wide on October 15, 1899, making odd numbers westbound (toward San Francisco) and even numbers eastbound, where formerly the reverse had held sway. With the inauguration of Nos. 1 and 2, the *Overland Limited,* transcontinental schedules on the "Overland Route" increased to six a day. *Sunset Magazine,* the official house organ of the Southern Pacific's passenger department, described the new all-vestibuled train as one composed of the finest equipment — a veritable "Aladdin's Carpet" — possessing all the comforts that a comfortable mind could suggest. Fully twelve hours were shaved off the, then best, eastbound schedule and four hours off the westbound, the strictly deluxe, extra-fare limited, composed entirely of Pullman Palace cars.

At this time, train Nos. 3, 4, 5 and 6 rounded out the long distance schedules on the Mountain. Westbound, Nos. 3 and 5 were both known as the *Pacific Express;* Nos. 4 and 6, the *Atlantic Express.* This confusing situation existed until May 14, 1904, when No. 5 was renamed the *Western Express* and No. 6 the *Eastern Express,* the first in a series of name changes for these trains. Sacramento-Colfax local service had been established July 1, 1892 as No. 25 (east) and No. 26 (west). On April 9, 1899, these locals had been renumbered Nos. 33 and 34. As of October 15th the numbers were reversed. Service was extended to Towle for most of 1900 due to this town's increased importance as a lumbering center.

The *Reno Passenger,* train Nos. 13 and 14, came on line on April 5, 1903. Train Nos. 9 and 10, the *Fast Mail,* were inaugurated December 31, 1905. Train No. 9, handling mail and express exclusively was, prior to the coming of the streamliner *City of San Francisco* in the 1930's, the fastest scheduled train to operate over the Mountain.

Train No. 10, while basically a mail and express train, handled more passengers than No. 9 did and over the years carried more names than any other train on the Southern Pacific system. The first change came during 1908 when No. 10 became the *China & Japan Fast Mail.* Later the train carried the names *California Mail, San Francisco Limited, Atlantic Express, Salt Lake, Gold Coast* and *Pacific Limited.*

Train Nos. 37 and 38, Sacramento-Colfax locals, were added May 29, 1908, and later became train Nos. 109 and 110 in 1911. These were extended to Sparks during 1913 as the *Mountain Special* and the *Newsboy,* respectively. On September 12, 1909, train Nos. 98, 99, 100 and 101, all Truckee-Sparks motors, were placed in service, marking the beginning of McKeen Motorcar service on the Mountain. Eighteen passenger trains were now plying the Donner grade's sinuous rails on one stretch or another.

Prior to Depression, a series of reschedulings, discontinuances and reinstatements occurred with few new trains introduced. The exceptions were the inauguration of the *St. Louis Express,* Nos. 21 and 22 on November 14, 1920, the *Gold Coast Limited,* Nos. 27 and 28 on November 14, 1926, and the *Tahoe* which assumed schedule Nos. 21 and 22 on September 25, 1927, reflecting the broad gauge service recently extended to the scenic mountain lake.*

Although passenger trains were running over the district with increasing frequency, the movement of freight with all the attendant problems encountered in boosting it over the Sierra divide, was the primary cause of congestion, As part of the Harriman System, the "Overland Route" to the Pacific was the most direct outlet for goods gathered in the east and funneled onto the Union Pacific. The same held true in reverse. Manufactured goods, livestock, petroleum, lumber, tea, silk and other miscellaneous items were handled on long-haul trains. But, by far, the most significant commodity involved in this transcontinental trade was the movement of fresh fruit and vegetables from the farms and orchards of the west coast to consumers in the mid-west and east.

The Overland perishable business had had its humble beginnings back in 1884 when the first acceptable carload of California oranges reached Washington D.C. The business had increased yearly but, as no organized system for handling perishable shipments on a national scale was available, growth of this traffic was modest. How-

---

* For those readers seeking more detailed information on Mountain passenger trains over the years, the Appendices of this volume contains an exhaustive compilation of such trivia assembled by devotee Albert C. Phelps of Auburn, California.

PACIFIC FRUIT EXPRESS

ever, technology was advancing and seizing the opportunity, the managements of the Union Pacific and Southern Pacific railroads joined together in organizing the Pacific Fruit Express Company. They were soon joined by the Western Pacific Railroad. The PFE Company, incorporated in the state of Utah on December 7, 1906, was charged with the responsibility of purchasing and maintaining a fleet of refrigerator cars and with the construction and operation of bunker icing plants throughout the west.

The PFE Company accommodated the grower by expanding his market and, as his business grew, so did PFE. An initial fleet of 6,600 40-foot wood-sheathed refrigerator cars, with a capacity of 30,000 lbs. of fresh fruit or vegetables, were ordered. By August 1920, 15,394 of these distinctive orange and brown cars were in service with another 4,000 on order.

A necessary part of the refrigerator car operation was the manufacturing of ice, as each reefer had bunkers which held large quantities of ice and salt and since periodic replenishing of the bunkers was essential to maintaining the desired temperatures within the car on their long haul east. At one time, PFE maintained seven natural and 18 artificial ice manufacturing plants at strategic points along the Harriman Lines. On October 9, 1909, the PFE Company placed into operation, at Roseville, a giant precooling plant. Erected of brick and reinforced concrete, it was the most significant structure in the new yard in terms of size and traffic development. The new plant, by employing a new intermittent vacuum process, was able to precool a cut of 24 cars of fruit registering at 70 or 80 degrees down to 40 degrees in two hours, and had a daily ice making capacity of 250 tons. In time, the perishable business would come to be the single most important commodity handled at Roseville. By the fall of 1925, Roseville was icing between 700 and 800 reefers a day and this plant had been expanded many times over.

In general, perishables gathered from as far south as Bakersfield and Santa Margarita in the San Joaquin and Salinas valleys and from as far north as Klamath Basin and the Rogue River Valley in Oregon, as well as everything in between, was routed through Ogden Gateway by way of Roseville. Long strings of reefers packed with vegetables from the Salinas Valley, grapes from Napa, pears from Oregon, melons and oranges from the San Joaquin, peaches, plums, apples, cherries or what-have-you, would accumulate at Roseville. Arranged in "blocks," the cars were re iced and forwarded east over the Mountain.

On the long haul east, the perishable blocks received high priority in train make up, motive power assignments and dispatching. The schedule time for the perishable blocks was, by the mid-teens, trimmed down to 60 hours and 15 minutes between Roseville and Ogden with 18 hours of that time allotted for the trip over the Mountain from Roseville to Sparks. Allowing for wartime congestion, the schedules were increased by one hour across the Sacramento Division on December 23, 1917. To illustrate the scope of traffic in the year 1919, for example, 567 Roseville fruit blocks moved over the Mountain, 237 Los Angeles-Ogden orange blocks, 44 Turlock cantaloupe blocks and 33 Exeter orange blocks. As a war measure, the United States Railway Administration diverted 52 additional fruit trains, all Western Pacific blocks, east over the Mountain. The practice was to assign each block a number if it consisted of more than ten cars of fruit. Although it was a year-round business, the perishable movement assumed epic proportions at the peak of the harvest season. A slow trickle of the colorful cars during January and February would give way to a flood of them during late summer and early fall. The

FRUIT BLOCKS OPERATED EAST OUT OF ROSEVILLE OCTOBER 27, 1919

Roseville Fruit Block Number	Green Fruit Block Number	No. of Fruit & Vegetable Cars	Left Roseville	Arrived Sparks	Time Lost
407	597	25	2:50 A.M.	10:30 P.M.	40 minutes
408	598	40	3:00 A.M.	5:15 A.M.	7 hours 15 minutes
409	599	44	4:45 A.M.	5:00 A.M.	5 hours 15 minutes
410	600	45	11:45 A.M.	6:55 A.M.	10 minutes
—	601	26	2:05 P.M.	8:35 A.M.	30 minutes gain
411	602	33	3:05 P.M.	2:00 P.M.	3 hours 55 minutes
412	603	39	4:45 P.M.	3:55 P.M.	3 hours 50 minutes
413	604	39	11:59 P.M.	8:50 P.M.	1 hour 50 minutes

following table lists the perishable movement, out of Roseville, for a busy day during October 1919.

All of the delays, to the 19 hours allotted on the district, were attributed to dense traffic in the sheds. Although a shed fire seriously delayed block No. 408 and No. 409, the loss was compounded even more because of the wait for relief crews on account of the federal hours of service law.

Of equal importance to the shipper was the availability of empty precooled cars and, as a result, it was the practice to run special trains of empty refrigerator cars, returning from the east in blocks of 50, at speeds approximating passenger train schedules.

In the lower foothills of the Mountain itself, a fair amount of perishable activity was generated. During the Alberta and Bartlett pear season, three switch crews were kept busy on summer nights pulling as many as 25 refrigerator cars out of Loomis; 40 out of Newcastle. They were then taken down to Rocklin and set out. A double-headed Mallet cab hop out of Roseville would assemble a train at Rocklin (with the "soft bellies" or wooden underframe cars behind the helper) and by the time it reached Colfax, the cab hop was a full grown fruit block. During the spring of 1926, in order to speed up the handling of this traffic, an ice deck of modest capacity was erected at Colfax just west of the roundhouse. The Pacific Fruit Express Company harvested ice on Donner Lake and re iced the reefers at a 21-car capacity facility in the Truckee yards. This arrangement proved inadequate for the business, however, and in 1920, a new 110-car ice deck and manufacturing plant was built at Sparks and the Truckee facility was closed. Predating the Truckee operation, Boca at one time, was the scene of a bunker icing operation, utilizing the natural harvest from adjoining ponds.

Other Mountain District local traffic included the production of the granite quarries at Rocklin, and following the San Francisco fire and earthquake of 1906, they experienced a modest boom in production. At Flint, just west of Auburn on the westbound track, the Mountain Quarries Company (later Pacific Portland Cement) serviced a limestone deposit, with an eight-mile standard gauge line, across the American River Canyon. The tributary Nevada County Narrow-Gauge had been feeding the mines of the rich Nevada City-Grass Valley district since 1876 from a connection with the SP at Colfax. A long shed was provided at Colfax, at which freight was transferred between narrow and standard gauge cars. West slope logging railroad operations were centered in the Towle-Blue Cañon-Emigrant Gap section with the Towle Brothers having far flung operations in both Placer and Nevada counties. During 1902, they sold their equipment to the Read Timber & Lumber Company. The latter outfit worked the country south and east of Fulda through World War I. The firm, Birce & Smart, worked the Bear River drainage from Southern Pacific connections at Smart and Yuba Pass. During 1912-1914, the Pacific Gas & Electric Company, in order to aid in the construction of the Lake Spaulding hydroelectric project, assumed portions of both the Birce & Smart logging railroad at Smart and the former Towle Brothers right-of-way between Orel (renamed Forebay) and the Bear River.

The east slope was the scene of large scale lumbering operations and during the construction of the Central Pacific, a number of mills were active along the line — at least a dozen in the eight miles from Truckee to Boca alone — all feeding the railroad and the mines of the Washoe. As the local timber was depleted, lumbering operations became centralized at Truckee, Boca and Verdi along the SP mainline, and logging railroads were extended out into the surrounding mountains. Some of these railroads gained "shortline" status such as, the far flung Boca & Loyalton Railroad, the Hobart Southern and the Lake Tahoe Railway & Navigation Company. The latter operation, catering primarily to the tourist trade, was leased to the Southern Pacific during 1925, broad gauged, and operated for nearly two decades as that road's Lake Tahoe Branch.*

One element of the forest products industry was the production of paper. During 1900, Crown Willamette Paper Company built a pulp and paper mill along the Truckee River at Floriston. The Southern Pacific was engaged to transport four foot lengths of cordwood to the mill, on conventional flatcars. As many as 100 cords a day were brought down from Hobart Mills to Truckee and the SP interchange. During October 1918, Crown Willamette constructed a short spur at Stanford and a tramway was set up there to bring cordwood from the headwaters of Cold Creek. The principal production of the Floriston pulp mill was tissue wrap for the California fruit industry.

The size and capacity of the motive power, charged with moving all this traffic over the mountains, was in a perpetual state of evolution. Shortly after the turn of the century, Harriman Standard Consolidations were assigned in Mountain freight service and Standard Ten-Wheelers assumed passenger schedules. While these locomotives performed yeoman service on the grade

---

*Those readers seeking full particulars of these and other east slope operations are kindly referred to the detailed accounts of historian David F. Myrick contained in *Railroads of Nevada & Eastern California,* Volume One, (see bibliography).

and were used successfully system wide, the usual complaints, regarding gas, smoke and visibility within the sheds and tunnels of the Donner grade, were voiced. The larger the engines became, the greater the outcry. Electrification was considered as a solution to many of the problems encountered in operating a mountain railway and, as previously outlined, was seriously considered in the Sierra Nevada Mountains. During May 1909, as Alan H. Babcock and the electrification committee pored over cost estimates and proposals, a revolutionary form of steam locomotive arrived at the Sacramento Shops that, ultimately, was to lead to the scrubbing of the idea of electrification entirely. Mallet compound locomotive No. 4000, a 2-8-8-2 type, with 26 & 40x30-inch cylinders, 56-inch drivers and a total weight on drivers of 394,150 pounds, was the state of the art in mountain locomotive design. Other locomotives with similar specifications were already logging impressive records for the Great Northern Railway in the Cascade Mountains of Washington State. The Southern Pacific had ordered two of these 2-8-8-2 locomotives and, during the summer and fall of 1909, carefully tested them against the regular freight power then in use on the Mountain.

Consolidation No. 2564 was the first to be evaluated in tests conducted between Roseville and Summit on June 9, 1909. Nine loads and six empties were behind the tender for a total weight of 478 tons. On June 11th, another test was conducted with 483 tons behind the drawbar — close to the engines tonnage limit. After allowing sufficient time to assimilate the data collected, on November 6th and again on November 9, 1909, the Mallet No. 4001 was tested over the same territory. On the first trip, the engine handled 19 loads and nine empties for a total of 1,006 tons. The No. 4001 handled 1,105 tons on the second trip. The fuel used by each locomotive was Kern River oil. During the trips, a great deal of data was compiled and the consumption of water and fuel carefully monitored. The Company was quite pleased with the Mallet's performance. Statistics indicated that the engine could handle more tonnage than two of the Consolidations combined, while achieving considerable savings in water and fuel consumption per ton mile. Additional economies were achieved as the Mallet used only one crew.

On paper the Mallet was just the thing for the Donner grade, but the smoke and gas accumulation in the sheds was worse than ever and created a situation so intolerable that the men refused to work on them. The lengthy boiler compounded the problem by restricting visibility within the sheds. Something would have to be done to minimize these problems before the Mallets could operate routinely on the Mountain.

Locating the cab at the front of the engine could go a long way in solving the dilemma. Since oil was now generally in use as fuel, locating the crew at the tender end of the unit was no longer essential. Thus, a Southern Pacific trademark, the cab-ahead Mallet, was born. The remainder of this first batch of Mallets was changed at the factory to operate cab first, with the vanguard of the new design arriving during February and March 1910.

Crews, apprehensive to the idea at first, soon appreciated the comfort and safety afforded by the cab's forward location. Two versions of the engines were developed. The Mallet Consolidation, in the configuration 2-8-8-2, was designed for freight service. This series, Nos. 4002-4048, constructed during 1909, 1911 and 1912, had 26 & 40x30 cylinders, 57-inch drivers, weighed 435,000 pounds on drivers and developed 85,040 pounds of tractive effort. This series worked so well that a Mallet Mogul in the configuration 2-6-6-2, was designed for passenger service. This series, Nos. 4200-4211, constructed in 1911, had 25 & 38x28-inch cylinders, 63-inch drivers, weighed 396,000 pounds on drivers and developed 65,920 pounds of tractive effort. This design was not as successful as the freight version. In the snowsheds, the cab end swung so far out on the curves that on occasion, corner posts were torn out. The engines tracked poorly and had a tendency to derail. On February 5, 1912, one mile east of Applegate, No. 4208, on its maiden run, went down an embankment with the prestigious *Overland Limited,* and soon after that, the whole series was fitted with four-wheel lead trucks which seemed to rectify the

COMPARATIVE TONNAGE RATINGS — MOUNTAIN *

Type	Class	Numbers	Roseville-Colfax Eastward Track	Colfax-Sparks Roseville-Colfax Westward Track	Truckee to Summit
4-6-0	T	2235-2378	1,030-1,660	560-920	1,060-1,080
2-8-0	C	2500-2751	1,600-1,890	880-1,060	1,020-1,230
2-10-2	F1	3600-3652	2,730	1,520	1,760
2-10-2	F3	3653-3667	3,110	1,730	2,010
2-8-8-2	MC2-6	4000-4048	3,815	2,170	2,500
4-6-6-2	MM2	4200-4211	3,185	1,795	2,070

*Ratings in "Ms" — units of 1,000 pounds.

The wreck of the *Overland Limited* near Applegate, in the early morning hours of Monday, February 15, 1912, was directly attributed to the unstable lead truck of engine No. 4208. The Mallet was on its maiden run. — GUY L. DUNSCOMB COLLECTION

problem. In either case, the crews referred to the Mallets as "Wamps" or "Wampusses." In time, other engines were experimented with in Mountain service; the super-heated 3200 series Mikados, the 3600 series 2-10-2's and three-cylinder 5000 series 4-12-2's, all with little success. Nothing seemed to suit the particular operating characteristics of the Donner grade like the "Back-Up Mallets." Used at various times throughout the Pacific Lines, the cab-forwards were developed especially for the Sierra sheds and remained a fixture on the district as long as steam lasted.

Engines assigned to the Roseville-Sparks district had certain identifying features. To reduce the force of the exhaust against the roof of the sheds, exhaust splitters — a V-shaped casting — were applied to the stack of each locomotive in order to deflect the exhaust to the sides. The top boards, at the junction of the roof and walls of the sheds, were removed to vent the deflected exhaust. The benefits were twofold. The sheds were kept relatively clear of smoke and steam, and the roof boards, which had previously tended to rattle loose with the passing of trains, now remained secure. Another feature, below the cab window of regularly assigned Mountain engines, was the staff catcher apparatus.

During the spring of 1912, as soon as a sufficient number of Mallets were in service, all engineers began and ended their runs at Roseville instead of Sacramento. With the Mallets in routine service east out of Roseville, operations became more or less standardized. A Mallet would be utilized as the road engine while one or two additional engines might be cut in 13 cars ahead of the caboose. A Consolidation was added to the point at Colfax for the stiff climb through Gold Run and then cut at Emigrant Gap. The Mallet helper near the rear of the train would continue on to Summit where it would then cut out. Consolidations were used as helpers out of Colfax due to the limitations of the 65-foot turntable at Emigrant Gap. The turntable at Summit was extended to 105 feet in order to accommodate the Mallets. At Roseville, roundhouse No. 2, which had remained unfinished for several seasons following the initial construction effort there, became the Mallet house. Sixteen of the 32 stalls were extended 20 feet and the turntable pit was blasted out and extended to accept a 105-foot span. A balloon track, installed at Truckee, accommodated Mallet helpers added there for the westbound climb up to Summit. All of this work was accomplished during 1910-1911.

Trains were normally filled out to the tonnage limit of the power. However, the Green Fruit trains were handled somewhat differently. Limited to 56 cars straight out of the ice deck at Roseville, these expedited trains operated with a Mallet road engine and one Mallet swing helper 13 cars ahead of the caboose to Summit, with the Emigrant Gap helper added on the point at Colfax. These trains frequently exceeded their 18 hour schedule time over the district, if all conditions were favorable. Runs of 16 hours and 30 minutes, between Roseville and Sparks, were known to have occurred.

The fruit block's rapid pace over the Mountain was something of an achievement, for the time. Passenger trains usually fared even better, but general freight operations over the Sierra Nevada, during the first few decades of the 20th century, were characterized by long hours and harsh conditions. So much so, that excess miles were allowed in order to attract men to work the district, a policy still in effect today. In freight service, this amounted to as much as 32 miles between Sacramento and Truckee. Even helpers between Roseville and Summit were allowed 17 extra miles. Since the men were paid by the mile, this amounted to an increase in the size of the paycheck.

Relief crews or "Dog Catchers" were the order of the day. In fact, the Federal 16-hour law created so many difficulties that regular Dog Catching crews were assigned at Truckee with hours-of-service relief their only assignment. Fruit blocks or stock extras seemed to be the only freight trains with a chance of making it over the road. One "old timer" recalled making a 16-hour relief for an eastbound train at Emigrant Gap and 16 hours later the train had only moved 1,000 yards, into the siding at Smart! Still, this was an improvement over the days before the 16-hour law. "Dutch" Nagel was fired for falling asleep, staff in hand, after 72 hours of continuous duty. The Brotherhood got him back to work after a spell, but when the Federal law was imposed, "Dutch" was in the forefront of those cryin' that a living couldn't be made with the reduced hours.

In trying to operate the railroad over the Sierra, the imposition of the Federal hours of Service law created many difficulties for the Southern Pacific. For years train crews had worked two districts, Rocklin (later Roseville) to Truckee and Truckee to Wadsworth, but line relocations in 1904 and the new yard at Sparks changed the latter terminal to Sparks. This, plus the signalling of the Mountain and the move to Roseville in 1907, led the SP to attempt running crews through from Roseville to Sparks the following March, which eliminated the Truckee crew change. Almost immediately, problems were encountered with crews crowding the 16-hour law. The Mallets, with their increased efficiency stalled off the inevitable for a time, but during late 1911, a decision was made to break the run into two districts once again. Blue Cañon, at the west end of the snowshed belt and the approximate midway point, was selected. From this point, the "West End" extended to Roseville some 60 miles, while the "East End" extended on to Sparks, a distance of 79 miles.

Blue Cañon, previously nothing more than a wayside point of minor nature, experienced a modest boom in population and, nestled in the narrow canyon as it was, housing was suddenly at a premium. The crews rented rooms in people's homes, erected cabins of cast off shed timbers, or stayed in the old Woodbury Hotel which was widely regarded as a fire trap.

The addition of more Mallets, the completion of the Rocklin-Colfax Cutoff and double-track between Truckee and Sparks, about 1913, led the SP to eliminate the Blue Cañon crew change. But the crush of wartime traffic, commencing late in 1916, strained the capacity of the Donner grade, and the resulting slowdown forced the reestablishment of the Blue Cañon crew change that fall, this time to continue until the completion of double-tracking nearly 10 years later.

The men with seniority would often bid in the Blue Cañon-Sparks run "as an outing" during the summer months but, as a rule, they preferred the "West End," "Sunset Jobs" or the valley runs of the Sacramento Division. The "East End" had the grades, the sheds, the weather and the long mileage. The problems with snow have already been mentioned, but the biting cold was another factor to be reckoned with. Although less of a snow problem, the temperature in the Truckee River canyon could become so frigid that thermometers didn't even register. Under these conditions, train air brake systems could freeze up without warning, rendering the brakes ineffective. Temperatures of 20 and 30-degrees below zero have been repeatedly recorded in such locations as Boca and Floriston.

To the miserable brakeman, forced to ride out on top of the cars between Andover and Sparks, whether it was 20 or 30-degrees below zero was a moot point. "Why I had on all the God damned clothes I owned" recalled one veteran, "and I was so padded I could barely walk. One minute you were sweating next to the cookstove in the caboose, and the next you were frozen solid to the running board. The young extra man usually was assigned the rugged job of fourth brakeman. If one had any seniority at all, the job was entirely avoided. Still, someone had to do the job, and a trick often used, in order to escape the biting cold, was to tie a lantern to the brake staff and then hide out on the "monkey deck" which, on a Mallet, was between the engine and the tender.

Then, there were the interminably long sheds and tunnels on the district with their attendant peculiarities of operation. Even with cab-forwards in regular use, hazards existed. Smoke and gas, driven by prevailing winds, would often overtake the crew in the cab. This condition occurred when working upgrade westbound at tunnel No. 13, a particularly notorious area in this regard. For such situations, respirators were provided on all locomotives.

Between Blue Cañon and Truckee and between Rocklin and Colfax, night signals on trains, switch lamps and wayside signals were required to be displayed at all hours of the day and night. Flagmen were required to hang two Dietz lanterns under the rear platform of the caboose so a constant vigil could be maintained in order to look for freshly splintered ties, indicating a derailment or dragging equipment. If discovered, the train would be stopped by setting the conductor's valve in the caboose.

To get the elemental tasks of railroading accomplished, in an age innocent of radio communications, an elaborate system of whistle and lantern signals were developed. This system was all for naught within the sheds, since visibility was often restricted to less than a car length and whistles could scarcely he heard over the roar of the engines and the rumble of the trains. The only effective means of communication within the sheds was the brake pipe. When a train pulled into a siding, the lead engineer would release the brakes and let the slack run back on the helpers, who would then set their independent brakes as soon as the train stopped. When the lead engineer was ready to go, he would make a heavy application of the brakes, then release them — as a signal to proceed — and to warn the helpers to release their brakes and to work steam. At the summit, brake and signal lines were tested and all retaining valves turned up. After the helper was cut from the train, the air brakes were set on all cars by opening the angle cock at the rear of the caboose in what is known as a "plug test." When the engineer had restored the air, if authorized, the train could then depart.

Marks on the posts within the shed, indicating the distance in car lengths from the switches at each siding served as the only means for letting the lead engineer know if his train was in the clear, or that the rear end crew was about to line the switch. Other marks indicated where to spot for water or fuel.

As a precaution against fire, in the showshed district, enginemen were requested not to dump carbide from gas generators. Similarly, fusees were not allowed. All flagging in the sheds was done by placing torpedoes on the rail. So great was the roar in the sheds, that torpedoes could not always be heard, but a well-trained nose could smell them. Hot boxes could be detected in the same manner, as could sticking or extremely hot brakes, which were frequent occurrences on the district due to the severity of the grades.

The slope of the Sierra grade was steep enough to warrant special precautions in order to prevent the uncontrolled movement of trains. West from Summit to Roseville, trains faced a total descent of 6,855 feet in 87 miles. A train working from Truckee upgrade at full steam towards Summit had to stop in a little more than a train length, after emerging from tunnel No. 6. This was done in order to stop short of a mainline switch left lined to an escape track, leading out of the sheds and onto the ground — a precaution against runaways. Helpers were then cut, brakes tested and retainers turned up. The escape track switch was then lined for the mainline and, when the train had passed

Dietz lights, seen here in their brackets at the rear of the caboose, were lit day and night in the sheds.
— SOUTHERN PACIFIC COLLECTION

over it, relined for the derail track. On the long descent to Roseville, stops to cool wheels and inspect freight trains were required at Spruce, Crystal Lake, Blue Cañon, Gold Run, Colfax and Auburn. Retainers were only required on westbound runs down to the Long Ravine Bridge. Eastward trains used retainers from Summit to Truckee and were required to make inspections at Stanford and Verdi. The number of tons per operative brake in the train were also restricted; 50 tons on the west slope from Summit to Loomis and 55 tons on the east slope from Summit to Truckee.

Most of this also applied to passenger service but, as an added precaution on these trains, the air and signal lines were tested at Truckee, Blue Cañon and Colfax as well. In the matter of braking trains on the district, there was little margin for error. The men had a profound respect for the Mountain and its grades. Around potbelly stoves in roundhouses and "cryin rooms" across the division, sobering stories were related. Stories like the night No. 210, while cutting her helpers at Summit, slipped backwards down the grade, silently gathering momentum in the sheds only to crash through the station at Cascade and over the edge into the canyon. One had to be on his toes at all times.

The Donner grade served as a proving ground for the development, testing and improvement of brake systems. During April 1908, for example, when Westinghouse was developing an improved triple valve, official tests were conducted on the district. In these tests, conducted between Zeta and Rocklin, high-wheeled Atlantic No. 3026, a dynamometer car and eight passenger cars were given every trial that might come up in ordinary usage. Another train, of 90 empty oil tank cars, was also rigged with the equipment and tested under the same conditions, in each case with favorable results.

The rapidly increasing density of trains was complicating an already difficult and time consuming operation, as the Harriman lines funneled traffic over the district to fuel a rapidly developing west coast. New records were continually being set. The first twelve days of November 1913 saw 474 trains operated over the Sierra Nevada mountains with 44 trains handling 496 cars on the peak day. These figures did not include the light engines, the Newcastle switcher, construction trains working between Sparks and Truckee on the double-track, snowshed work trains or the Truckee-Sparks motor, but these figures would double by the end of the decade.

A major contributing factor to this increase was the United States' involvement in World War I. The crush of wartime traffic led the government to assume control of the railroads on December 28, 1917. The Donner Pass line came under the direction of SP President William M. Sproule, who was designated District Director of the Central Western Region of the United States Railway Administration. Sentries were placed at tunnels and bridges across the district as a precaution against saboteurs. Perishable schedules were lengthened due to the congestion. Of the 627 extra troop trains operated over the Pacific Lines during 1918, only 106 were operated over the Sierra, but regular transcontinental schedules were frequently run in many sections to accommodate the military.

After laboring under the supervision of the U.S.R.A. for several years, the railroads were handed back to their owners on March 1, 1920, much the worse for wear. Coming as it did at the advent of another perishable season, perhaps the most pressing crisis for the Southern Pacific was the availability of Pacific Fruit Express refrigerator cars. The fleet was scattered all over the United States, and many had gotten into service on roads and territories where it was never intended that they should go. As of April 1, 1920, only 1,500 PFE refrigerator cars, out of a fleet of nearly 15,000, were on the Pacific Lines. An order for 4,000 new cars was immediately placed and the long process of rounding up the strays began.

Rebuilding war weary track and equipment was a big problem. In the case of the Central Pacific/Southern Pacific, money for this important task was not readily available due to government interference. Not satisfied with having successfully broken up the Union Pacific and the Southern Pacific systems, the Federal Government, on February 11, 1914, had again brought suit, this time to separate the Central Pacific and Southern Pacific. The subsequent battles over who should control the Central Pacific — either the SP or UP, or whether it should remain a separate entity —

dragged on for nearly a decade. Finally, on February 10, 1923, the Interstate Commerce Commission decided that common ownership with the Southern Pacific was in the public's interest and on June 11, 1923, the Justice Department approved the order.

This court order was the signal to unleash major improvement projects around the system. On the Donner grade, this meant the completion of double-track over the 40-mile gap between Blue Cañon and Truckee. Gone now were the daring schemes of low grade lines, great tunnels and electrification. Instead, the new second track was laid, for the most part, adjacent to the existing track. The project took two and one-half years to complete and, although, less ambitious than those plans on the drawing board a few decades earlier, considerable difficulties were encountered in bringing it to a successful completion.

The first phase of construction involved second tracking from Blue Cañon to Emigrant Gap. Construction commenced March 6, 1923 and the 5.3 miles were completed August 15th of the same year. Included in this section at Blue Cañon and Emigrant Gap were 65-car center sidings and a new 80-foot covered turntable at the latter point. One unusual feature of this work was the commandeering of the Emigrant Gap fire train to furnish water to the contractor's steam shovels and donkey engines.

Commencing on April 10, 1923, 6.5 miles of second track was laid on the east slope between Truckee and Andover. Included in this section, which was completed August 5, 1923, was a new center passing track at Stanford and an extension of 733 feet to the siding at Andover.

Authorization for the remaining 28.4 miles from Emigrant Gap to Andover came November 9, 1923, and it was by far the most difficult portion of double-track to be built in the Sierra. Complicating an already challenging side-hill location, which left little space for storage of materials and the erection of camps, was the fact that nearly all the right-of-way outside tunnels were protected by snowsheds. Before any grading could be done, these had to be removed and then replaced before the heavy snow season arrived. As many as 20 steam shovels were employed simultaneously. Material, removed from cuts, was moved in narrow-gauge cars, hauled by donkey engines, on tracks which frequently crossed over the mainline, in order to widen fills on the outside. Extreme care was taken, by electric interlockings, to protect through trains which ran with a frequency approaching every 23 minutes during the summer and early fall. Twenty gangs of 25 men each busied themselves at shed work, while two work trains distributed materials.

Notable features of this final section included the erection of four steel viaducts over Butte Cañon, Upper and Lower Cascade creeks and the Yuba River, each approximately 400 feet in length. There was also a 4,000-foot westbound siding installed at Yuba Pass and Troy, center sidings at Crystal Lake and Troy, an 80-foot turntable at Cisco, in addition to, seven new tunnels.

But the most significant features were to be found in a 5.36-mile line, independent of the original grade, which reduced the summit elevation by 132.7 feet and shortened the line by 1.29 miles. Incorporated in this section was a summit tunnel, nearly two miles in length, which was holed through at 8:15 P.M. on August 25, 1925. By September 19th, the track was laid and the first train, 55 cars of green fruit, passed through. This was not the 5.2-mile tunnel proposed in the early years of the Harriman administration, but at 10,322 feet, this tunnel, designated No. 41, was the third longest in the continental United States at the time. It was only exceeded by the 23,176-foot Hoosac Tunnel of the Boston & Maine and the 14,413-foot Cascade Tunnel on the Great Northern. At its west approach, a 6,000 foot siding was laid, as was a similar one adjacent to the original mainline, which was now considered the westbound track. Additional support trackage and a 100-foot turntable was set up at the junction of the two lines. This new installation, entirely covered by snowsheds and equipped with a modern concrete station, became Norden. On March 10, 1926, Norden assumed all the functions that had previously been carried out at Summit in regard to the cutting of helpers, communications and maintenance. The facilities at Summit were soon abandoned.

The final gap in the second-track was completed October 15, 1925. Once in operation, these new facilities opened up a tremendous bottleneck on the Mountain and made for a near continuous run of double-track, extending 242 miles from Oakland Pier to Sparks, Nevada. Along with the new track came a number of fundamental changes to the physical plant and to the methods of operation over the Sierra Nevada Mountains.

When an automatic block system was set up, utilizing Union Swtch & Signal style R 3-color light signals, the staff system was soon retired and the apparatus and many of the stations employed in the system were dismantled. The following summer, an interlocking plant was set up at Norden in order to speed up the handling of helper engines and reduce congestion even further at this strategic point. The 48-lever electric interlocking plant at Norden was placed in operation on September 23, 1926.

The completion of double-track precipitated the

decline in shed mileage. Prior to 1922, the entire 29.3-mile length of snowshed remained intact, but during the construction of the second track, 9.4 miles of these sheds were abandoned and never rebuilt. However, new snowsheds, over the new tracks built in connection with the second tracking, were constructed, which brought the total length up to 22.9 miles. The sheds were expensive to erect, maintain and protect. Officials were placing renewed confidence on the snow fighting machines assigned to the district. This, in 1926, included six rotary snow plows, of which, four were the largest and the most modern design, seven flangers and three spreaders. In the ensuing years, mile after mile of sheds would be retired. So much so, that by 1950 only a little over four miles would remain in place. The lookout station at Red Mountain was abandoned in 1934, following the retirement of the last sheds within its preview. In a freak accident, the last watchman to be assigned to the outpost was electrocuted. While standing on a steel plate, lightening struck the telephone line he was using to place a call to Cisco. His job was not filled and the incident closed the last chapter on the 58-year history of the lookout.

The fire trains, which had once been deployed at Truckee, Summit, Cisco and Blue Canon, were relocated when the retreating snowsheds were reduced in number. The Truckee fire train was reassigned to Andover in 1923 and the Blue Cañon train went to Emigrant Gap that same year. By 1940, fire trains still remained at Emigrant Gap and Norden but only in season.

Another operating aspect affected by the completion of double-track was the crew districts. It was now considered possible to run crews all the way between Roseville and Sparks with reasonable certainty that they could make it under the 16 hour law. Thus, on November 3, 1925, crews began running through between these two terminals and Blue Canon quietly faded into the legend and lore of the Mountain.

The completion of double-track ushered in what might be termed the modern steam era on the Donner grade. The old days of railroading in a barn were rapidly drawing to a close.

Recently completed double-track near Truckee. — SOUTHERN PACIFIC COLLECTION

The Arcade Station, long a Sacramento landmark, dated from 1879. Over the years, a multitude of passenger trains passed through the venerable structure. Even as late as June 1924, when the photos on this page were recorded, there were enough trains in evidence to amply fill out the station's departure board. But the 45-year old structure was ripe for replacement. — (ABOVE) GUY L. DUNSCOMB COLLECTION, (LEFT) SOUTHERN PACIFIC COLLECTION

No.	TRAINS LEAVE DAILY	LEAVE
10	Roseville Colfax Truckee Reno Ogden D.&R.G. Connections	1.15 A.M.
16	Roseville Marysville Chico Redding Portland	1.40 A.M.
13	Oakland San Francisco	3.55 A.M.
5	Benicia Oakland San Francisco	4.20 A.M.
19	Oakland San Francisco "PACIFIC LIMITED"	5.00 A.M.
21	Benicia Oakland San Francisco	6.55 A.M.
65	Galt Lodi Stockton Lathrop Modesto Merced Fresno	7.10 A.M.
45	Davis Dixon Elmira Suisun Oakland San Francisco	7.20 A.M.
210	Roseville Newcastle Auburn Colfax	7.30 A.M.
47	Davis Dixon Suisun Benicia Oakland Truckee	8.10 A.M.
532	Freeport Hood Walnut Grove "MIXED"	8.30 A.M.
31	Galt Lodi Stockton Fresno San Francisco Los Angeles	9.00 A.M.
59	Puget Sound Express Woodland Willows Redding Portland	10.00 A.M.
59	Connects For College City Grimes Colusa Hamilton	10.00 A.M.
56	Roseville Marysville Chico Gerber Redding Dunsmuir	10.30 A.M.
1	SAN FRANCISCO OVERLAND LIMITED	10.45 A.M.
24	Roseville Auburn Colfax Truckee Reno Tonopah And Goldfield	11.15 A.M.
29	Davis Suisun Benicia Oakland San Francisco	12.30 P.M.
23	Oakland San Francisco	2.15 P.M.
2	SAN FRANCISCO OVERLAND LIMITED Ogden And East	2.35 P.M.
152	Folsom Latrobe Placerville	3.00 P.M.
17	Davis Benicia Oakland San Francisco "SACRAMENTO SPECIAL"	3.10 P.M.
34	Roseville Newcastle Auburn Colfax	3.40 P.M.
63	Southern Cal Express. Stockton Fresno Los Angeles	4.10 P.M.
22	Roseville Colfax Truckee Reno Ogden	4.40 P.M.
58	Roseville Marysville Chico Gerber	4.50 P.M.
209	Davis Dixon Elmira Suisun Benicia San Francisco	5.20 P.M.
27	Davis Dixon Suisun Benicia Oakland San Francisco	7.05 P.M.
65	Davis Woodland Williams Willows Orland Corning Gerber	7.20 P.M.
67	Marysville Knights Landing Woodland Davis	7.25 P.M.
20	Ogden And Eastern Points "PACIFIC LIMITED"	7.35 P.M.
6	Roseville Auburn Colfax Truckee Reno Westwood Susanville	10.15 P.M.

X DENOTES TRAIN HAS DEPARTED

Architects Bliss & Fairweather of San Francisco were called upon to design a new Sacramento terminal. Looking east early in 1925, in the above aerial view of Sacramento, ground is already being cleared for the new station. — GUY L. DUNSCOMB COLLECTION Sacramento Shop pet No. 1276 graced the butterfly train sheds of the new depot for many years. (RIGHT) The locomotive fairly glistened with nickel-plated fittings and burnished copper piping. Aluminum paint highlighted running boards, smoke box and stack. — A.S. MENKE COLLECTION (BELOW) The new station was opened to the public February 27, 1925 at a cost of $2,317,000. — SOUTHERN PACIFIC COLLECTION

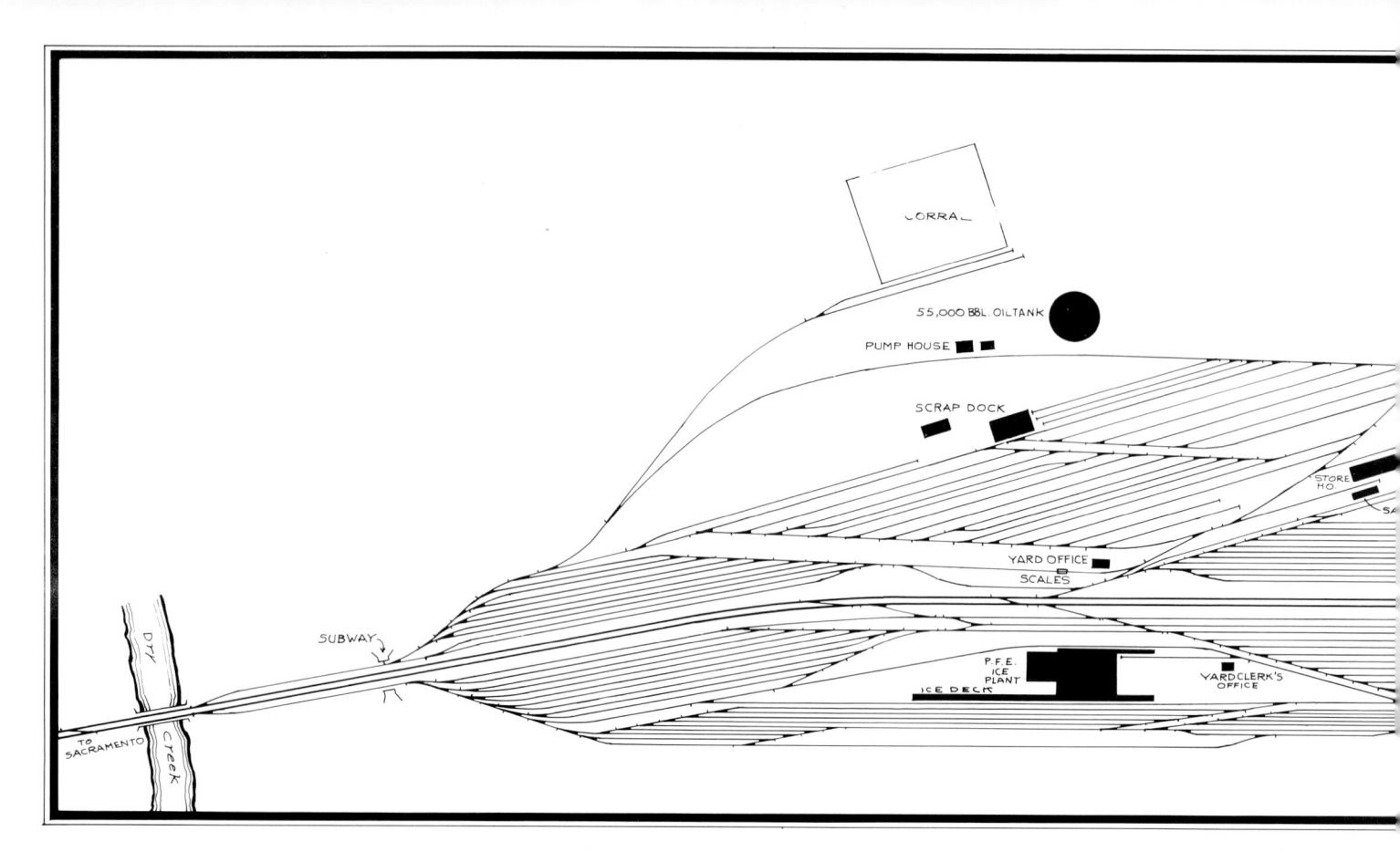

Little in this view of Antelope, looking east in 1923, gives a hint of the vast receiving yard which now occupies the site. A culvert marker lends the only clue. — SOUTHERN PACIFIC COLLECTION

(OPPOSITE PAGE) Even though favored by Judah as a natural division point, Roseville was, in the early days, little more than the junction between the Ogden and Portland mainlines. Meanwhile, Rocklin, four miles to the east, bustled with activity. But Rocklin was cramped and poorly laid out so it could not handle the tremendous traffic increases which occurred after the turn of the century. After some deliberation, Roseville was chosen in the spring of 1906 as the site for a vast new terminal and by the fall of 1907 the new yards were essentially complete. Two years later, when the view at the right was taken from a balloon, Roseville was well on its way to becoming a major terminal, a position it holds to this day. — ALAN ASKE COLLECTION

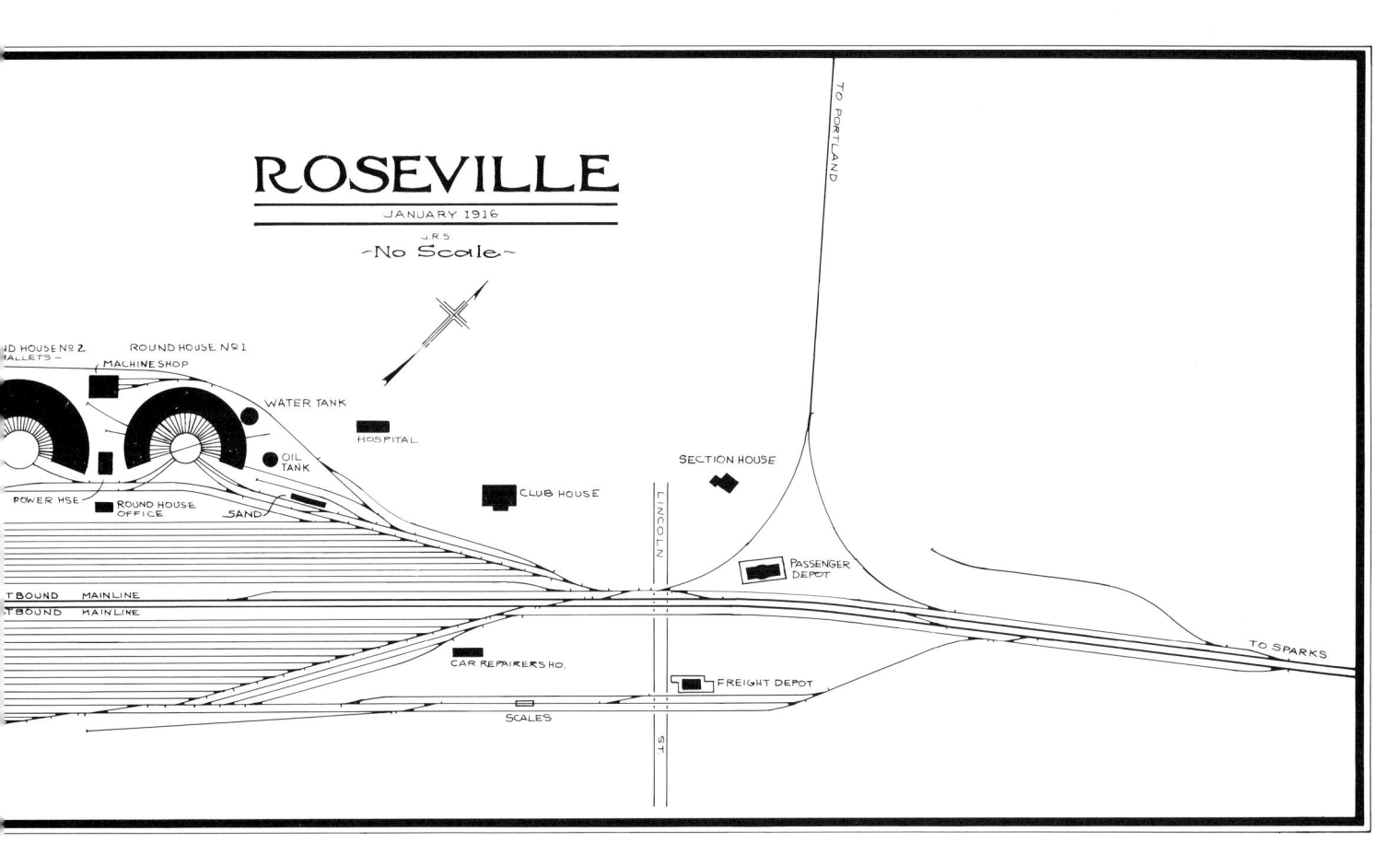

ROSEVILLE
JANUARY 1916
J.R.S.
~No Scale~

Birdseye View R.R. yards Roseville
Copyright 1910 by C.L. Huntington 10102

More important and certainly the most imposing structure at Roseville was the bunker icing and precool plant erected by the Pacific Fruit Express Company in 1909. A joint SP-UP venture, PFE owned and operated a fleet of refrigerator cars and icing stations throughout the west. Much of this traffic, primarily western green fruit, gathered at Roseville and then moved east via the Ogden gateway. Perishables were easily the single most important commodity handled at Roseville during 1928 when the pictures on this and the adjoining page were taken. Looking west from the roof of the ice plant, in the above view, the 200 acre PFE car shop can be seen beyond the creek. Stored sugar beet racks litter the area to the right beyond the mainline. — (ABOVE) SOUTHERN PACIFIC COLLECTION, (RIGHT) LEONARD M. DAVIS HISTORICAL COLLECTION

By 1924, the construction of a second ice plant increased the ice storage capacity at Roseville to 16,000 tons. During the season, some 700 to 800 cars a day passed through the 110-car ice decks in preparation for the rush to the waiting markets in the east. — BOTH LEONARD M. DAVIS HISTORICAL COLLECTION

A variety of interesting cars line the rip tracks (ABOVE) in this panorama taken at Roseville on December 28, 1920. The engine terminal is at the extreme right while the cattle pens appear in the center distance. Here, livestock gathered from points as far away as Ogden, the Imperial Valley and Oregon were fed and rested, then reloaded for final shipment. — SOUTHERN PACIFIC COLLECTION (LEFT) Roseville passenger station from a postcard dated 1909. McKeen Motor Car No. 29 is destined for Colfax. — ALAN ASKE COLLECTION (BELOW) For many years the mainlines ran down through the center of the Roseville yard. A passenger train disappears down the westbound main on a wet day in 1920. — SOUTHERN PACIFIC COLLECTION

The east or "uptown" end of the Roseville yards could be busy indeed. In addition to the parade of mainline trains, considerable flat switching was done here much to the consternation of motorists and pedestrians alike. As business expanded, delays became intolerable and an underpass was eventually constructed during 1948-49.
— A.C. PHELPS COLLECTION

79

Roseville, strategically located at the junction of intersecting lines, one of which was on a substantial grade, attracted motive power on a grand scale. A 32-stall roundhouse, called No. 1, served Roseville at its inception and soon after work commenced on doubling its capacity. But progress on roundhouse No. 2 moved slowly. The introduction of Mallets to the district east of town, during the summer of 1909, escalated the work. By 1922, when the above photograph was taken, 49 freight and 12 passenger Mallets called Roseville home. — JAMES H. HARRISON COLLECTION (BELOW) Roundhouse No. 1 handled smaller valley service locomotives, while roundhouse No. 2 (OPPOSITE) housed the Mallets and other large engines. These two shots date from 1928, while the official portrait (RIGHT) of the "Wampus Stable" dates from the 1930's. With the locomotives in constant use, photographer Dave Joslyn reportedly spent several days setting up this shot. — ALL SOUTHERN PACIFIC COLLECTION

81

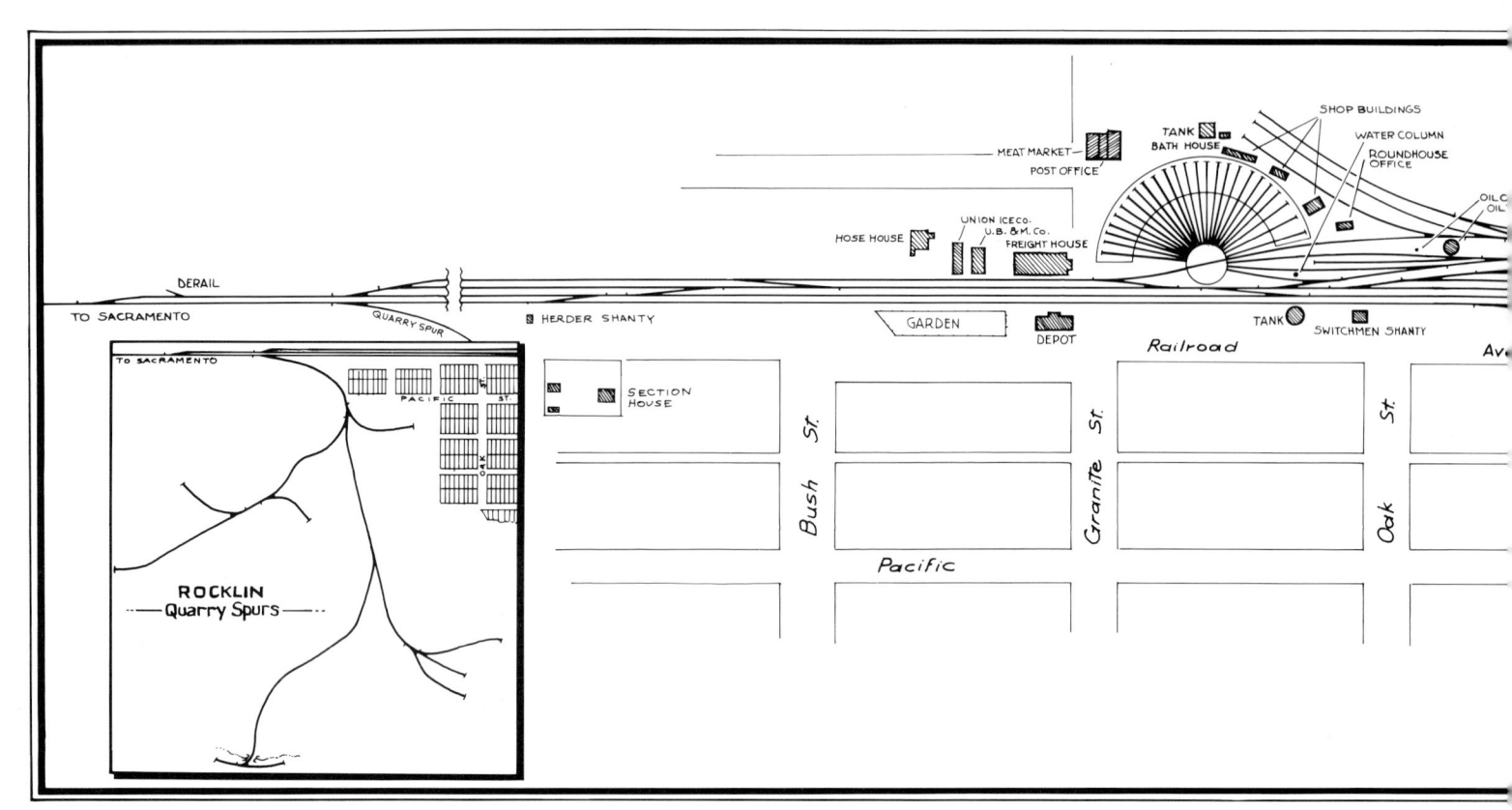

An eastbound passenger train makes a station stop at Rocklin, in the above view, after the turn of the century. A terminal for nearly 45 years, Rocklin was once the home to over 300 railroad men whose monthly payroll in 1905 totaled $25,000. Alas, the local yards were inadequate for modern operation and on March 25, 1908 the last of the functions handled here were transferred to Roseville. — A.C. PHELPS COLLECTION (LEFT) A slight miscalculation led to this predicament at a Rocklin quarry during June 1919. Having helped rebuild San Francisco after the fire, Rocklin's quarries were by this time in decline. — ALAN ASKE COLLECTION

ROCKLIN
OCTOBER 1, 1903

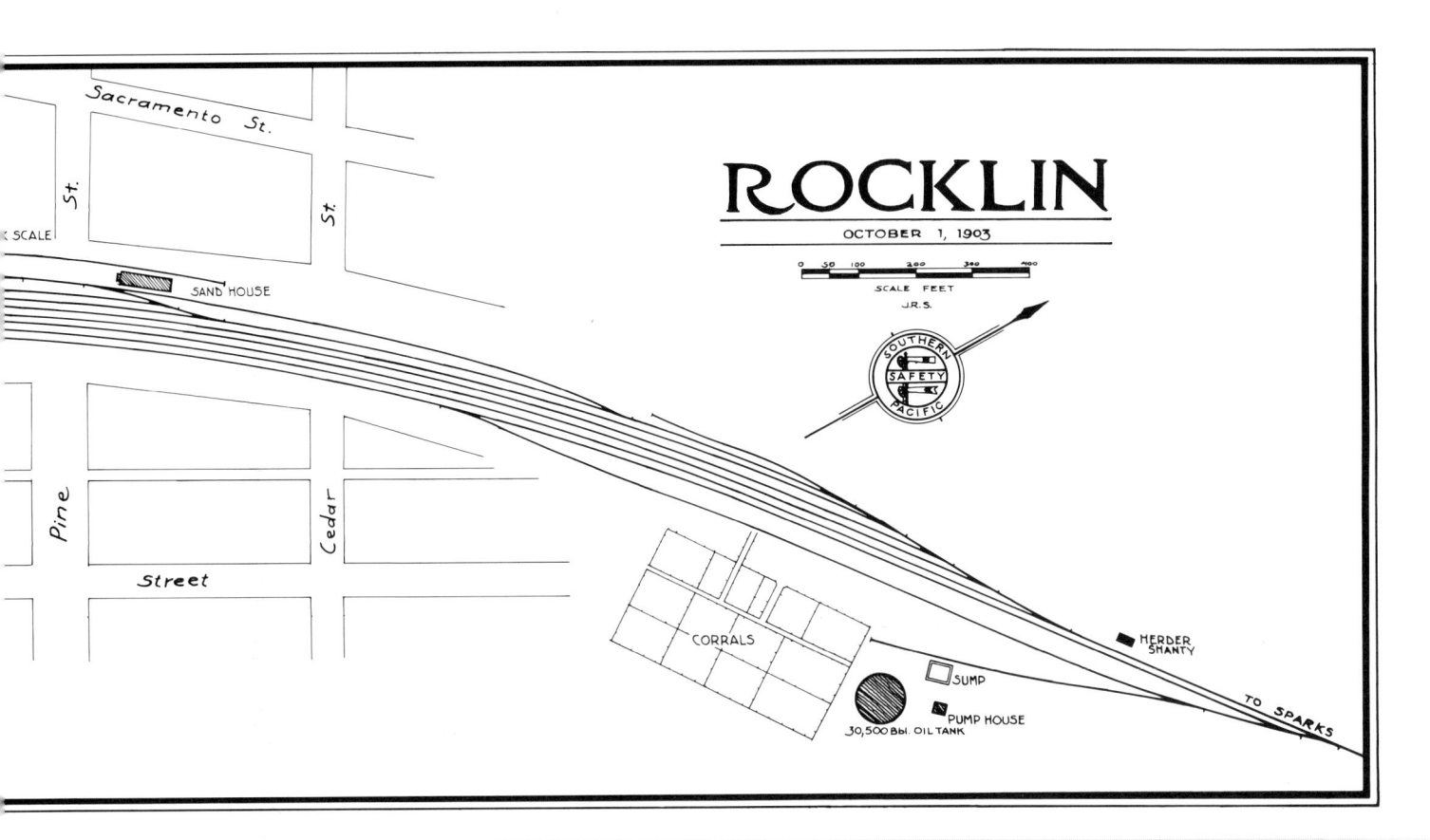

In its heyday, Rocklin's 26-stall roundhouse and shops serviced 1,200 engines a month. Soon after the move to Roseville, the turntable was moved to Placerville. The roundhouse itself was dismantled during 1910 and little by little track and structures were removed. Today nothing remains to remind one of the activity that once was, save an unusually wide right-of-way through town and a crumbling foundation or two. — BOTH ALAN ASKE COLLECTION

During the spring of 1909, work commenced on the Rocklin-Colfax 1.5 percent grade revision. This ambitious project, envisioned by Harriman and executed by his chief engineer William Hood, was the first step in a contemplated plan to double-track and revise the grades all the way over the Hill. Shortly after the first through-train movement over what became the new eastbound track occurred in March 1912, Extra 4003 East (LEFT) was photographed east of Rocklin framed in the steel bridge which carried the new track over the westbound main. — SOUTHERN PACIFIC COLLECTION

Diverging widely to the north, the new line bypassed the great foothill fruit growing district. During the Alberta and Bartlett pear season, as many as 100 cars a night were gathered at points like Newcastle, Loomis and Penryn, then taken down to Rocklin and assembled as solid perishable blocks for movement east. (BELOW) At Penryn, looking west during 1922, hand brakes played an important part in spotting the Penryn Fruit Growers shed on the right. An error in judgement, a brake not properly applied, might drop refrigerator cars into the depot at the end of the spur. — SOUTHERN PACIFIC COLLECTION

Newcastle, shown above, is the scene of great activity in 1909 as work progressed on the new eastbound track. The fill leading to double-track tunnel No. 18 can be seen in the distance while the contractors dinky track appears in the foreground. (BELOW) Further upgrade, a great viaduct 540 feet in length carried the new line, and in this case, the *Pacific Limited,* 90 feet above Auburn Ravine. — BOTH TED WURM COLLECTION (RIGHT) Bypassed to the north, Auburn is served by a second station located on the eastbound track. Train No. 224, the *Sierra,* pauses at Auburn Nevada St. in 1933. — A.C. PHELPS

A Colfax Local drops down the westbound track below Applegate where the new eastbound line is crossed on a skewed concrete subway (Tunnel No. 26). The train, running as an extra, dates the picture as the summer of 1923 or 1924. — JAMES H. HARRISON COLLECTION

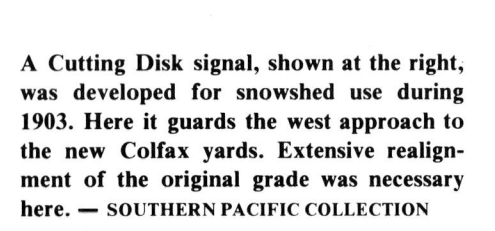

A Cutting Disk signal, shown at the right, was developed for snowshed use during 1903. Here it guards the west approach to the new Colfax yards. Extensive realignment of the original grade was necessary here. — SOUTHERN PACIFIC COLLECTION

As an important town on the west slope of the Donner grade, Colfax was the scene of much activity. (ABOVE) Colfax-Sacramento local No. 34 waits at the 1892-vintage depot about 1911. McKeen Motor Cars were introduced in this service after March 1, 1909 and closed out in the early 1930's. — DONALD DUKE COLLECTION (RIGHT) Train No. 4, the *Express,* pauses at Colfax shortly before its discontinuance in 1914. — GUY L. DUNSCOMB COLLECTION (BELOW) Train No. 2, the *Overland Limited,* makes an appearance in town on April 2, 1926 behind beefy 4-10-2 No. 5000. — T.T. TABER, A.S. MENKE COLLECTION

Foreman Bat Riordan reportedly kept the new Colfax enginehouse "as clean as a lobby in the capitol." The curve in the foreground and the turntable, holdovers from the original alignment, were in the process of abandonment. The wye was yet to be built. — ALAN ASKE COLLECTION

Nevada County Narrow-Gauge tracks pass to the left of the SP depot in the view of Colfax on a quiet afternoon in 1924. — SOUTHERN PACIFIC COLLECTION

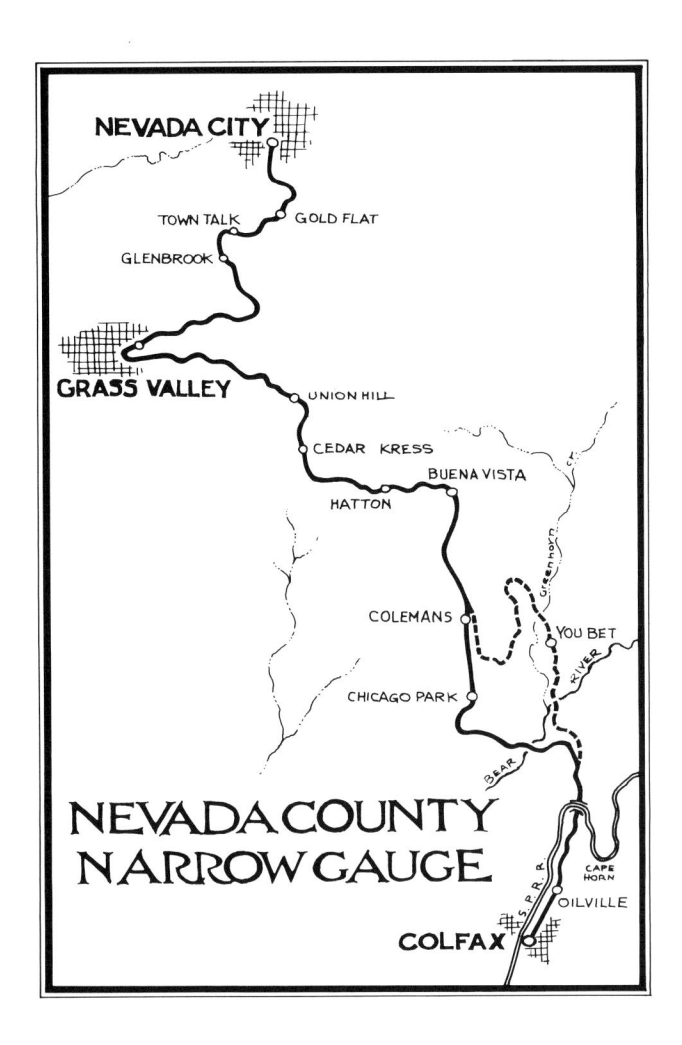

The Nevada County Narrow-Gauge sprang into being in 1875, linking the main "Overland Route" with the rich Nevada City-Dutch Flat gold mining district. (ABOVE) For 63 years the little train was there to meet standard gauge trains as they rolled into Colfax. — ROGER L. TITUS COLLECTION (BELOW) Freight was transferred from broad to narrow-gauge cars along platforms in the Colfax yards. — A.C. PHELPS The last revenue train was operated in July 1942 and the slim rails removed from Colfax in April of the following year.

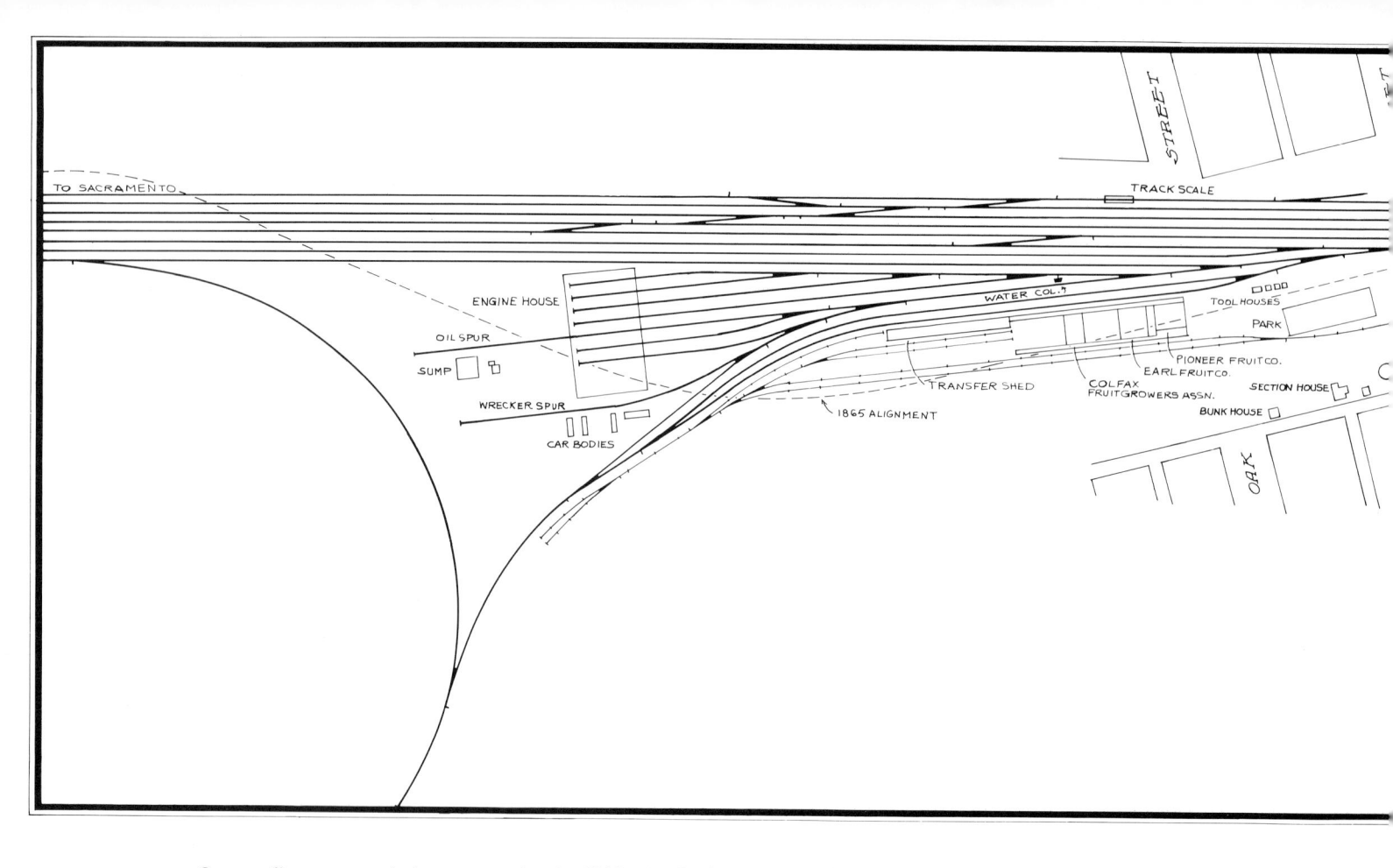

Over a five year period, commencing in 1909, the Colfax yards underwent a major expansion. The original alignment through the area, in the form of a lazy "s," was straightened in stages. (BELOW) Notice the cut beyond the depot in this view. (OPPOSITE PAGE) A new concrete enginehouse, erected during 1911-12, formed a part of this work. Helpers were assigned here after April 17, 1912. The photos were taken May 5, 1915 from the bluffs to the southwest. — BOTH SOUTHERN PACIFIC COLLECTION

COLFAX
MAY 1915

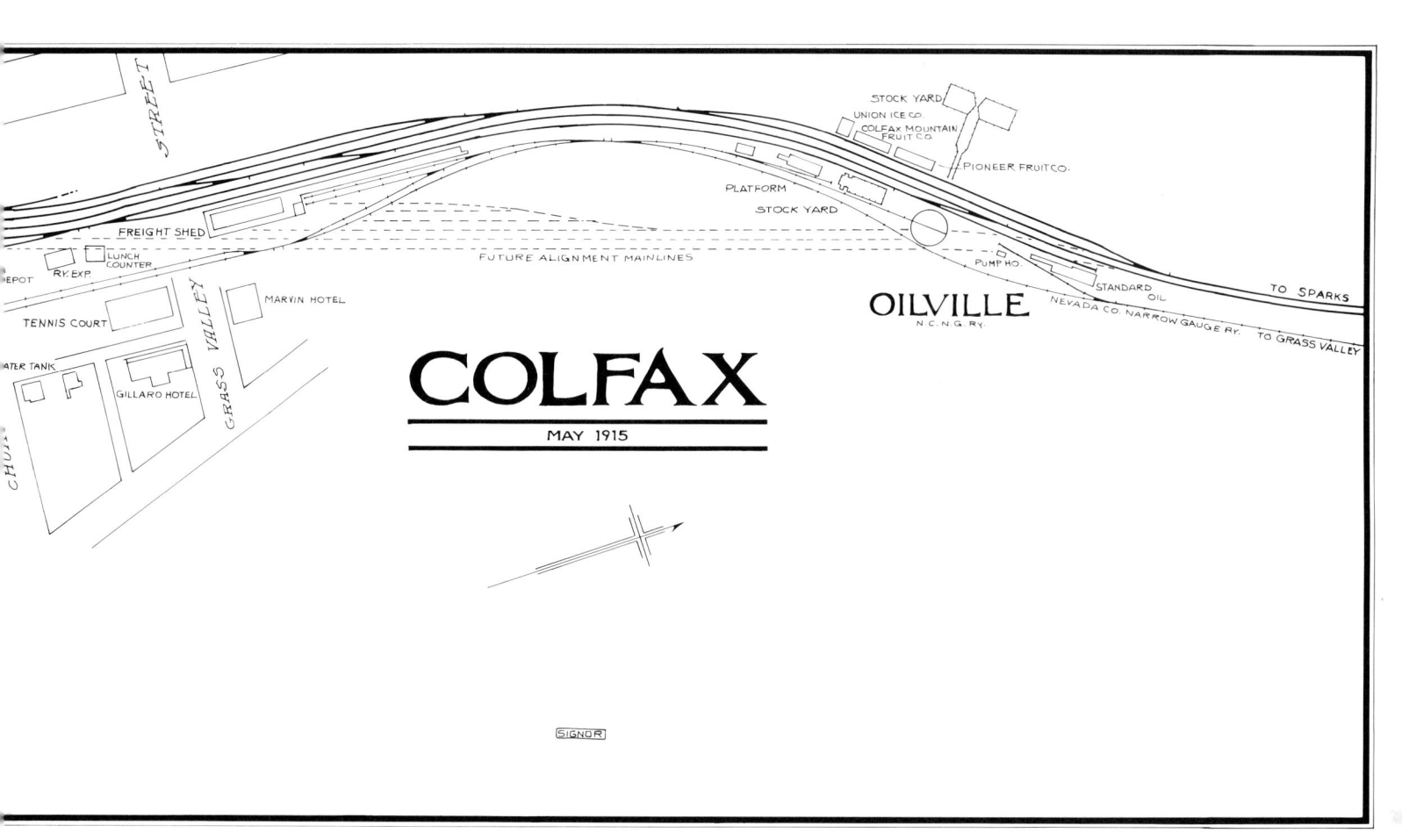

OILVILLE
N.C.N.G. RY.

Train No. 5, the *Pacific Express,* rounds the big curve near Long Ravine just minutes away from a 2:30 P.M. station stop at Colfax. In 1913 double-tracking in this section had not yet begun. — GUY L. DUNSCOMB COLLECTION

A work train places girders on the second viaduct at Long Ravine, February 26, 1914. — SOUTHERN PACIFIC COLLECTION

Coincidental with double-tracking above Colfax, a line change eliminated the spectacular route out and around Cape Horn. Dubbed the "Panama Canal" by the men, the new route cut closer to the ridge, using two double-track tunnels. (LEFT) Work progressed at tunnel No. 33 in February 1914 with the old line towards Cape Horn still in place. (BELOW) Tunnel No. 34 was in daily use the following May. Clearances in the tunnels created problems for passing Mallets, as did gas accumulation on eastbound trains, and it wasn't long before the eastbound line was moved back out on the edge of the precipice. Today, the westbound track is centered in the two tunnels. — BOTH SOUTHERN PACIFIC COLLECTION

A westbound excursion train rolls past Gold Run, 45 miles east of Roseville. — W.C. WHITTAKER

For many years fuel was available at Gold Run. (ABOVE) The road engine on Extra 2715 East takes on oil about 1910. (RIGHT) A wye passed behind the oil pumping plant. — BOTH BILL FISHER

The roadbed in the vicinity of Gold Run stood on tertiary gold bearing gravel. For years, the company employed special agents to protect the right-of-way from attack by miners who were busy sluicing away the surrounding territory. The value of right-of-way as late as 1915, was placed at $9 a cubic yard. Today, this 1918 scene is barely recognizable due to continued hydraulic mining. (RIGHT) The office at Alta stood until the early 1950's. — BOTH SOUTHERN PACIFIC COLLECTION

MOUNTAIN QUARRIES RAILROAD

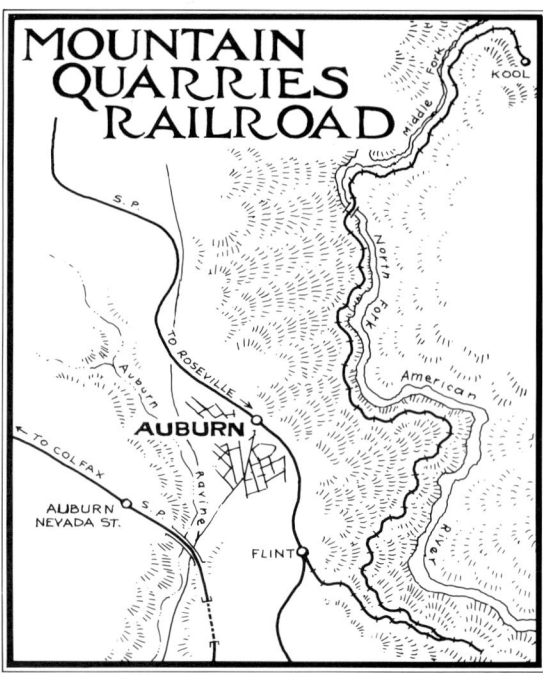

Beginning in 1912, limestone was brought up from the American River Canyon to the SP at Flint, about a mile below Auburn on the westbound track, over a winding eight mile standard gauge railroad. The Mountain Quarries Railroad required a switchback, 18 trestles and a spectacular concrete viaduct over the American River to reach a 700 foot glory hole near Cool station in El Dorado County. Pacific Portland Cement Company Consolidated operated the property. (ABOVE-LEFT) Locomotive No. 102 is seen negotiating the switchback and later photographed in the yard at Flint (LEFT). — BOTH A.C. PHELPS The engine could handle only three loads upgrade and routinely doubled the hill. (BELOW) Abandoned in 1942, the American River bridge, now used by highway 49, serves as the principal reminder of this interesting foothill mineral hauler. — KEN YEO COLLECTION

George Towle, a native of Vermont, along with brothers Allen and Edwin, were all active in Sierra lumbering operations for about 34 years. Beginning in 1868, with a small steam sawmill on Donner Lake, the brothers furnished a large part of the lumber used in the snowsheds and trestles of the Central Pacific. Eventually settling on the west slope at Towle, the brothers' business grew to encompass lumber yards, the manufacture of box shook and the first pulp mill on the Pacific coast. (ABOVE) By the turn of the century, Towle was a bustling community requiring daily local service to Sacramento. Little in this view remains today. The SP mainline east curves off to the left in the foreground. — DOUG RICHTER COLLECTION (RIGHT) As an adjunct to their lumbering operation, the Towle brothers were operating over 35 miles of narrow-gauge logging railroad in Nevada and El Dorado counties before selling out to the Reed Lumber Company in 1902. — D.T. McDERMOTT COLLECTION (LOWER-RIGHT) While the SP was busy during the summer of 1920, Towle was no longer the scene of great activity. — SOUTHERN PACIFIC COLLECTION

One of the more spectacular vistas on the SP in the Sierra, and indeed the entire west, was that of the American River Gorge above Colfax. Long touted in tourist guide books and Company literature, the railroad established a formal viewing platform in 1916 at a strategic overlook a thousand feet above the stream bed near milepost 161 between Midas and Gorge. The location, called American, saw train Nos. 5, 20, and 24 make a scheduled five minute stop here to afford passengers a closer look at this scenic wonder. As a wartime measure, this luxury stop was eliminated in June 1918. The stop was restored on June 27, 1920 and train Nos. 1, 2 and 19, and each made a brief stop. On February 26, 1933, during the Depression, the stop was eliminated and American drifted into obscurity. It became an "additional station" in 1937 and was eliminated from the timetable entirely in 1949. Today, no trace remains of the platform, although the gorge is as spectacular as ever. — R.E. BUIKE COLLECTION (LEFT) The *Sierra* pauses at American in the 1920's. — SOUTHERN PACIFIC COLLECTION

The engineer of an eastbound freight train peers out into the gorge near Knapp during 1916.
— SOUTHERN PACIFIC COLLECTION

Appropriately named, the staff office at Gorge was perched on the edge of an abyss. Gorge was eliminated when double-track was extended through this section during 1913. — SOUTHERN PACIFIC COLLECTION

Tunnel No. 1, a 481-foot bore at milepost 166.4, near Orel (later Knapp) was widened to accept another rail as the double-tracking approached Blue Cañon from the west in the summer of 1913. — SOUTHERN PACIFIC COLLECTION

With traffic increases following the turn of the century, Blue Cañon was established as a turn around point for crews operating out of Roseville and Sparks. Located in a remote and picturesque setting nearly 60 miles east of Roseville on the Sierra grade, the place quickly became a favorite with crews in the summer months. Blue Cañon was a haven for bootleggers and therefore, with the help of the Greek section hands, the crews, working on the double-track in the early 1920's, were kept well supplied. The Blue Cañon depot was surrounded by trains in this summer scene taken about 1910. — GUY L. DUNSCOMB COLLECTION

The Blue Cañon fire train shows off for the camera in the 1920's. For years a fire train was assigned here. (BELOW) A quiet summer afternoon at Blue Cañon could be pleasant indeed. — SOUTHERN PACIFIC COLLECTION

In single track days, a westbound passenger extra prepares to depart Blue Cañon. Effective November 3, 1925, with the completion of double-track, Blue Cañon was abolished as a crew change. — SOUTHERN PACIFIC COLLECTION (RIGHT) Four light helpers pause on the main at Blue Cañon for orders about 1911. The Consolidations are, left to right, Nos. 2655, 2566, 2736, and 2635. — D.T. McDERMOTT COLLECTION

101

At 4,692 feet, Blue Cañon was on the edge of the deep snow belt. The sheds began here, and life in this quaint little community took on an entirely different aspect during the inclement months. (ABOVE) Looking east about 1915, a fresh mantle of snow covers the town. The covered turntable, in the middle distance, is obscured by a grove of trees. — ALAN ASKE COLLECTION (OPPOSITE PAGE) A rotary works through Blue Cañon on February 13, 1922. With a snowfall of 514 inches, the winter of 1921-22 was about average. The photo was taken from above the mouth of the snowsheds looking west. — SOUTHERN PACIFIC COLLECTION

A triple-headed No. 5, the *Pacific Express,* wades through the drifts at Blue Cañon about 1913. — DENNIS M. BEEGHLY COLLECTION

BLUE CANON
SEPTEMBER 1919

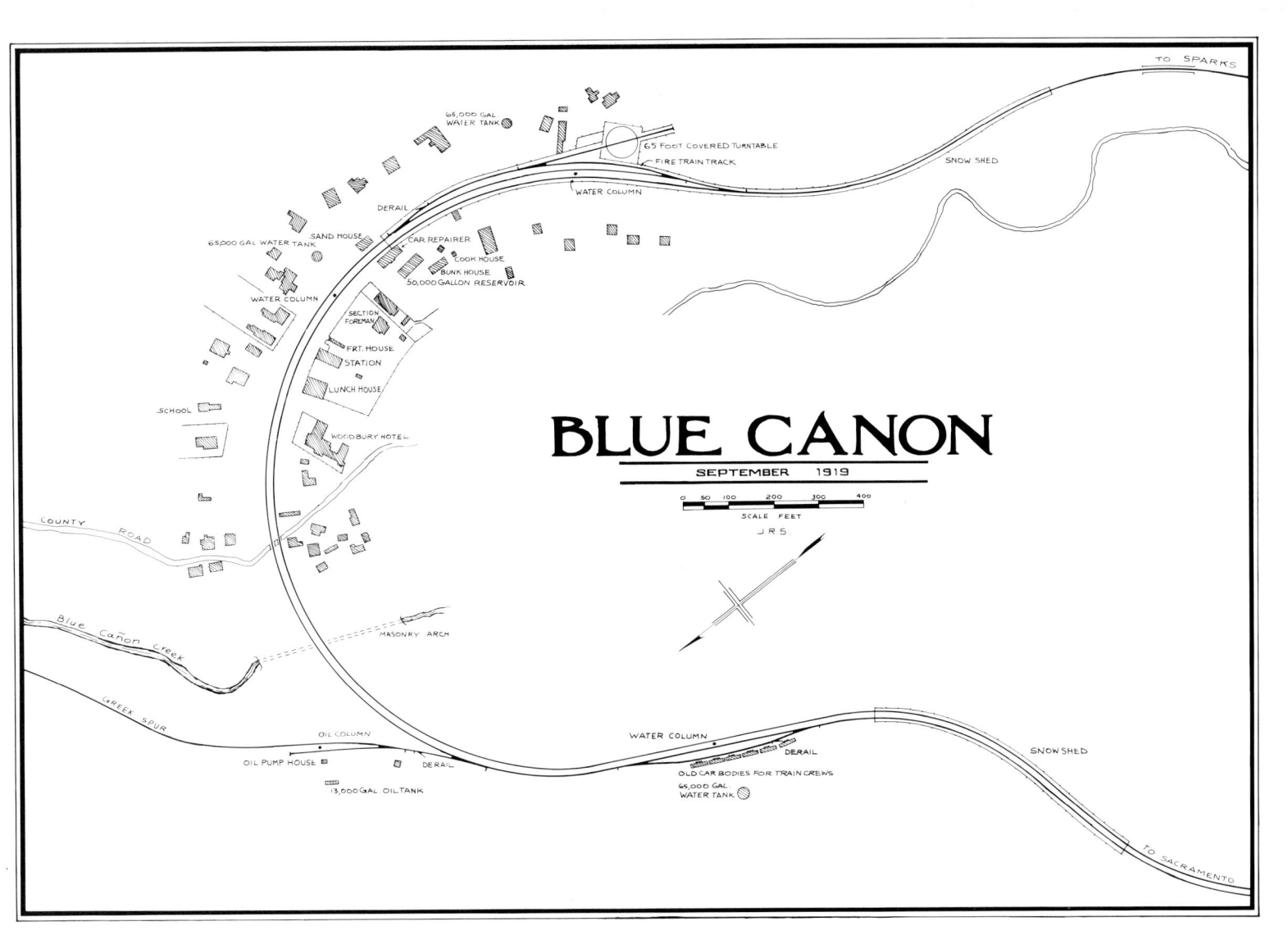

This staff office was located at Fulda, a siding three miles east of Blue Cañon, from 1905 through the summer of 1923. — SOUTHERN PACIFIC COLLECTION (LEFT) Train No. 1, the *Overland Limited,* passes Fulda in March 1920. — ALAN ASKE COLLECTION

From 1902 through 1917, the Reed Lumber Company, utilizing equipment and track from the Towle Brothers' operation, logged Onion Valley, Texas Hill and the surrounding country. (LEFT) Former V&T engine No. 25 was used to haul cars over a standard gauge spur which dropped down from Fulda to Fulda Flat where connections were made with the Reed Lumber Company's narrow-gauge lines. — D.T. McDERMOTT

Emigrant Gap is completely covered with snowsheds in this 1918 view taken from the mouth of tunnel No. 2. — SOUTHERN PACIFIC COLLECTION (RIGHT) During 1912-1914, the Pacific Gas & Electric Company used this diminutive Shay to haul materials from a connection with the SP at Smart, located in the distance, down to the work site at Lake Spaulding. The route was tortuous, utilizing an old spur laid for the firm of Birce & Smart in 1903. This spur was laid on a 3.3 percent grade while PG&E built additional tracks on a 5 percent grade down to the valley floor. — D.T. McDERMOTT

A motorist has attempted to beat the train to the crossing at Emigrant Gap, but with predictable results. A crossing in the shed proved to be very treacherous. — SOUTHERN PACIFIC COLLECTION

Snowshed construction took on many forms in the Sierra. There were designs for single-track (BELOW), double-track (BELOW-LEFT), and also, telescoping sections devised as fire breaks. At one time, there were 17 of these unique sheds in place. The section, at the left, is just west of Crystal Lake, circa 1922. Come fall, a locomotive was hitched to the telescoping section and it was rolled out to form an unbroken line of snowsheds. — ALL SOUTHERN PACIFIC COLLECTION

During 1876 it was discovered that from Red Mountain, opposite Cisco, it was possible to observe almost all of the entire line of snowsheds from Blue Cañon to Summit. A fire lookout was established here and was in continuous use up until 1934. (ABOVE) The view from Red Mountain was spectacular. — BILL FISHER COLLECTION (RIGHT) This substantial stone building at Red Mountain dates from 1909. — ALAN ASKE COLLECTION

The old stone lookout on Red Mountain, now abandoned for over 50 years, has changed very little as this March 1985 view indicates. — S.R. BUSH

The Red Mountain lookout crew poses for the camera in 1914. — SOUTHERN PACIFIC COLLECTION

107

A rockslide delays an eastbound freight near Cisco in 1924. Double-tracking in this section, between Emigrant Gap and Andover, was the most difficult and costly of the entire Sierra double-tracking program. — SOUTHERN PACIFIC COLLECTION

Union Switch & Signal hooded color light signals replace the staff system in shed territory as double-tracking advanced. (BELOW) R-2 style signals are shown east of Tamarack in 1928. — SOUTHERN PACIFIC COLLECTION

Contractor's dinky tracks cross the SP mainline at the site of tunnel No. 36 near Yuba Pass in October 1924. — SOUTHERN PACIFIC COLLECTION

In connection with train No. 9 the *Fast Mail,* overspeed was indicated as the reason it went over the bank at Crystal Lake the night of September 12, 1932. By watching the train's lighted windows, the Red Mountain lookout followed the train's progress as it wound down the ridge, and then sounded the alarm when the lights suddenly disappeared. — SOUTHERN PACIFIC COLLECTION

Oft photographed train No. 5, the *Pacific Express,* drops downgrade at the Butte Cañon bridge near Crystal Lake (RIGHT) in 1911. This place is now designated Shed 10. — A.C. PHELPS COLLECTION

At 7,017 feet, Donner Pass is the highest point reached by Southern Pacific rails to date. However, for a number of years, portions of the Cloudcroft Branch in south central New Mexico held that distinction followed by subsidiary Carson & Colorado's line over Montgomery Pass in southwestern Nevada; both long gone. But it could be argued that Summit, SP's outpost in the upper reaches of the Sierra, experienced the extremes in weather and certainly rivaled the others in isolation. (ABOVE) Completely enclosed in a shed, Summit is distinguished in this general view, taken from the south, by the cantilever support over the turntable midway into the sheds. Off to the right is tunnel No. 6. — TRUCKEE-DONNER HISTORICAL SOCIETY

At the right, a shaft of light catches a young lady operator hooping up the staff deep in shed territory for Extra 4007 East. (BELOW) No. 4007 arrived while shed renewal was underway.
— BOTH SOUTHERN PACIFIC COLLECTION

110

The sheds at Summit, in winter (ABOVE) and summer (BELOW), were normally gloomy indeed, requiring night signals to be displayed 24 hours a day. The Summit "block house," or staff office, appears to the right in the lower view. — BOTH SOUTHERN PACIFIC COLLECTION

The actual apex of the Donner Pass line occurs at the west portal of tunnel No. 6. This point, once known as Summit, was designated Tunnel No. Six when a staff office was installed here in 1918 in order to facilitate the movement of helpers during the busy war years. (ABOVE) The small building built directly into the shed at the right was the staff office at Tunnel No. Six. — GUY L. DUNSCOMB COLLECTION (LEFT) Within the shed, the essential operational features of the Tunnel No. Six office are more apparent. From left to right, they include spare hoops and pouches for delivering the staff, illuminated station sign for identification, and the staff catcher-deliverer. — TED WURM COLLECTION

A shed fire laid waste to Tunnel No. Six on October 15, 1921. (RIGHT) Consolidation No. 2681, consumed in the fire, was essentially in tact, but oddly distorted. (BELOW) The Summit Hotel escaped the costly blaze which burned everything from the east water column to the mouth of Tunnel No. Six. Fires such as this were a strong argument against the use of sheds. — ALL SOUTHERN PACIFIC COLLECTION

NORDEN
AND VICINITY

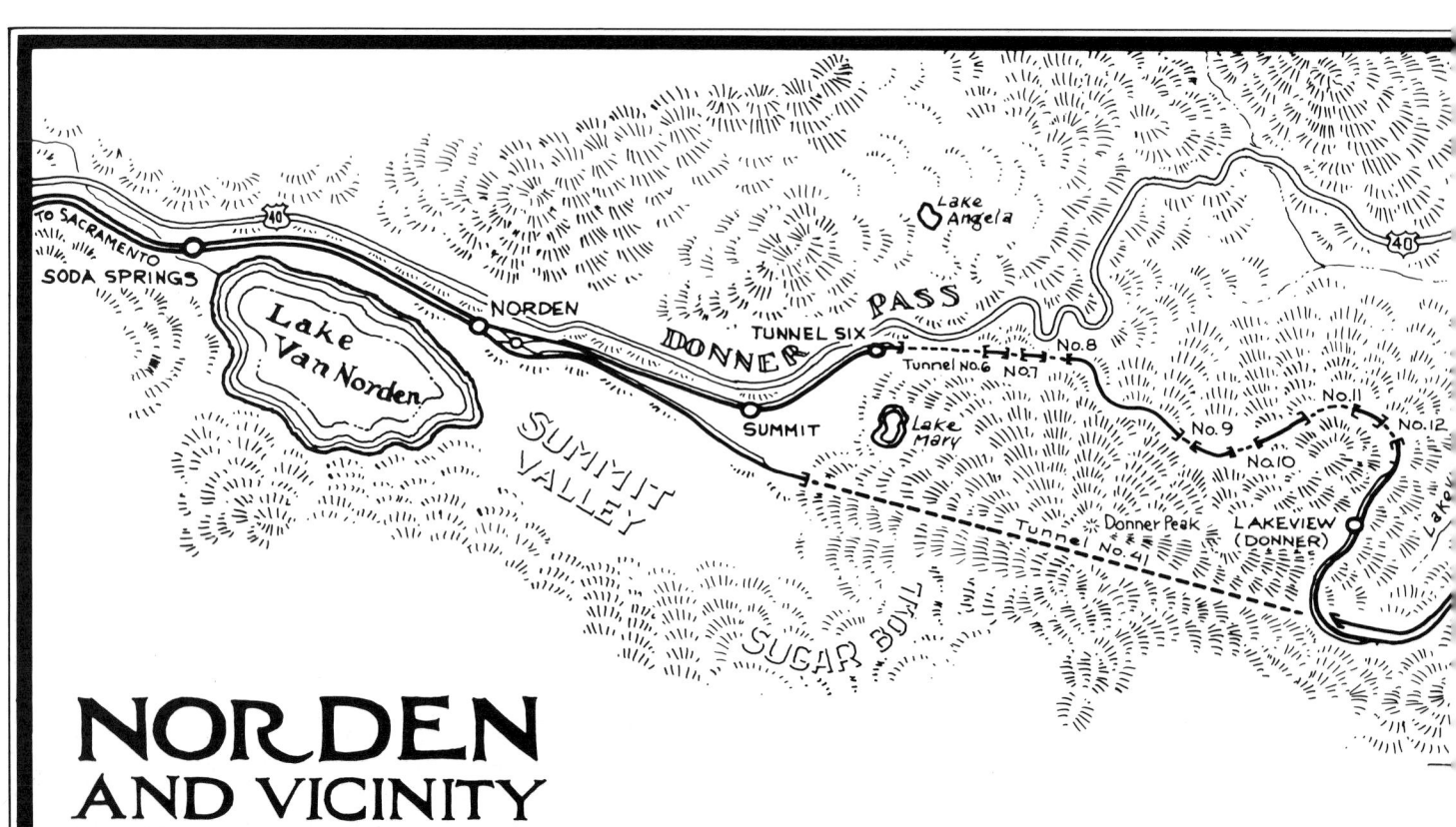

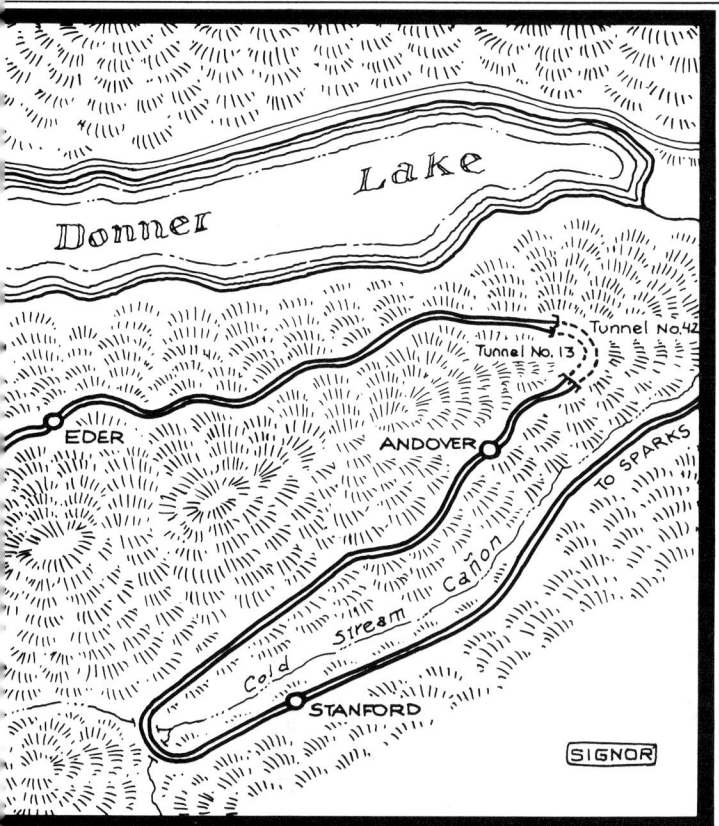

During 1924-25, between a point west of Summit and Eder, a 4.07-mile line change was constructed entirely independent of the existing grade as the final stage of the Sierra double-tracking program. A new summit tunnel 10,320 feet in length was incorporated in this work. New yards, built at the junction of the old and new lines west of the great bore, assumed all the operations formerly carried out at Summit. (ABOVE AND OPPOSITE PAGE) Work is underway on the new 100-foot turntable. Soon all will be covered by sheds including a portion made of a new concrete design which marked the first limited use of this type of shed work on the Mountain. Initially called Summit, and the third location on the Sierra line so named, this yard was soon renamed Norden. — ALL SOUTHERN PACIFIC COLLECTION

Work is nearly complete on the west approach to the new summit tunnel (ABOVE) in October 1924. (BELOW) The east end of the same bore tunneled directly below the old line near Eder. (LEFT) Shed renewal exposes the rugged portal of tunnel No. 8 and the landmark known as the "Chinese Wall." — ALL SOUTHERN PACIFIC COLLECTION

A Truckee helper pauses at Lakeview, on February 1, 1922. This station was changed to Donner in 1928 to avoid conflicting with a station of the same name on the newly acquired Nevada-California-Oregon Railway. — SOUTHERN PACIFIC COLLECTION (RIGHT) Looking east at a time before the second track was installed, the staff office and covered turntable, used principally by snowplows, appears in the middle distance in this view at Andover. Originally called Strong's Cañon, then tunnel No. 13, the place was renamed Andover about 1910. — DONALD DUKE COLLECTION

Despite the fact that all the sheds were abandoned and removed between Truckee and tunnel No. 13 by 1923, it was still deemed advisable to maintain a fire train, under steam, at Andover during the dry season. This set of equipment was formerly located at Truckee. — GUY L. DUNSCOMB COLLECTION

In the view above, a double-headed 49-car freight train rounds the big horseshoe in Cold Stream Canyon between Andover and Truckee, the famous "Stanford Curve." Crown Willamette's pulpwood tramway on the far curve dates the picture to about 1918. — BILL FISHER COLLECTION (RIGHT) Looking to the west, on October 11, 1924, is the new center siding at Stanford. — SOUTHERN PACIFIC COLLECTION

This remarkable sequence of photos, taken in 1918, depict the recently opened staff office at Stanford on a warm August afternoon during the busy war years. The cluttered operator's desk, at the right, is ruggedly built. — SOUTHERN PACIFIC COLLECTION

The staff instruments, shown on the left, resembled a giant oriental "Pachinko" machine. Its job was to govern movements to the east or west and it was electrically interlocked with adjoining offices. (BELOW) Wartime congestion demanded that Stanford, formerly a spur, be extended into a siding. Mallet No. 4003 was assigned to dump ballast on the project. — BOTH SOUTHERN PACIFIC COLLECTION

The staff catcher known as the "Keefe Time Saving Device" is shown (INSET) loaded and ready to be picked up. The staff itself is held in the leather pouch attached to the steel hoop. In operation, using the catcher apparatus mounted below the cab window, the fireman on an eastbound train simultaneously drops off the Andover-Stanford staff and retrieves the Stanford-Donner staff. This device was found on every locomotive assigned to the district. — SOUTHERN PACIFIC COLLECTION

Consolidation No. 2626 pauses at Donner, two miles west of Truckee, on February 1, 1922, while her crew pumps water from the locomotive tender into the station's holding tank. This was a common task which had to be repeated at many offices on the Mountain where wells did not exist.
— SOUTHERN PACIFIC COLLECTION

Train No. 24, the *Tonopah Express,* drops down the main at Donner. In the background on the far ridge is Andover, completely enclosed in a shed. — DENNIS BEEGHLY COLLECTION

For years train Nos. 9 and 10 operated on the Mountain as fast mail and express trains. While No. 9 remained the *Fast Mail* throughout, train No. 10, while basically a mail train, underwent more name changes than any other train on the SP. (LEFT) In the late 1920's, when this photo was exposed west of Truckee, the train was called the *Salt Lake.* —
W.S. PRINGLE COLLECTION

In 1902, train No. 2, the *Overland Limited,* clatters over Cold Stream bridge just west of Truckee. The 422-foot structure was later replaced by a fill and culvert. Highway 89, between Interstate 80 and Lake Tahoe, now passes through this draw. — D.L. JOSLYN, GUY L. DUNSCOMB COLLECTION

As an operating point, Truckee, California, has always figured importantly in the railroad scheme of things. Situated as it was at the foot of the steep climb to the summit of the Sierra, the helper engines would congregate there and trains would crowd the local yards. From the earliest days, through the mid-nineties, the town was the dividing point between the Sacramento and Truckee divisions. The affairs of over 326 miles of railroad extending east to Carlin, Nevada, were administered by the superintendent and dispatchers based there. On May 1, 1895, the Truckee Division was absorbed by the Sacramento and Salt Lake divisions with Wadsworth, Nevada, becoming the dividing point. Crews and engines still changed at Truckee and the dispatchers remained until 1907 when everything was moved to Sparks. During the Harriman years as many as 13 helper crews were assigned there, as well as, a large maintenance of way force and fire and snow service crews. (ABOVE) Extra 4023 departs Truckee for the west in 1923. — SOUTHERN PACIFIC COLLECTION

Truckee looking east on a frosty morning in the spring of 1926. — SOUTHERN PACIFIC COLLECTION

The Southern Pacific station at Truckee about 1940. — A.C. PHELPS

The Tahoe Branch

Lake Tahoe bound tourists, for several decades, had been leaving their SP trains at Truckee and taking the Lake Tahoe Railway & Navigation Company's "Cordwood Express," from the mainline, to the picturesque tavern on the shores of Lake Tahoe. Operated only during the clement months, the 15-mile narrow-gauge railroad followed along the banks of the scenic Truckee River. The railway, constructed during 1898-99 by the Bliss family, was built utilizing the track and equipment of the former D.B. Bliss Lumber Company's logging railroad. The original line had been laid from Glenbrook, on the east shore of Lake Tahoe, to a place called Summit during 1875. The railroad was originally used to supply the Comstock with mine timber. The lumber company dismantled the road, when the mines closed down, and in 1898 they transported it to the north shore of the lake. During April 1899, work commenced on the grading and laying of track down the Truckee River canyon to the Southern Pacific mainline at Truckee. Regular service commenced May 1, 1900, and thereafter, was operated seasonally from May 15th through November 15th, between the SP and the dock on the lake, where connections were maintained with the steamers *Tahoe* and *Nevada*.

The Southern Pacific acquired the lease of the Lake Tahoe Railway & Navigation Company on October 15, 1925 and soon after the line was standard gauged. The work was sufficiently advanced to run trains by May 1926. The first Pullman sleepers, ever to run direct to the shores of Lake Tahoe, arrived at the tavern at 6:20 A.M. the morning of May 15th. Regular scheduled service was instituted on June 6, 1926 with a daily operation each way, consisting of two passenger and two mixed trains. This optimistic schedule was trimmed by fall to a Saturday only train run as an extra. Train service resumed the following season with four trains daily, but encroaching auto roads and the Depression soon stifled the Lake Tahoe tourist business. Intermittent extra service continued through the 1930's. The branch was not operated following the outbreak of World War II and was abandoned on November 10, 1943. Today little trace of the line remains since the present State Highway 89 was built, for the most part, directly upon the old grade.

A passenger extra handled by Ten-Wheeler No. 2301 threads the scenic Truckee River Canyon near Lake Tahoe. — JAMES H. HARRISON COLLECTION

Arriving at the Tahoe Tavern aboard the morning train, the tourists were introduced to the charms of the area by being served a trout breakfast. (ABOVE) The resort, in 1916, accommodated 400 guests and had all the conveniences of a first-class hotel — baths, steam heat, electric lights, telegraph and telephone, casino, bowling alleys, billiard room, barber shop and photographic studio. Lake Tahoe itself, widely regarded as the grandest of mountain lakes, was the principal attraction, however. Lying at an elevation of 6,240 feet, the tourists marveled at the brilliant clarity and intense blue coloration of its waters. Anglers fished its depths for Rainbow, Eastern Brook, Lock Leven and Mackinaw trout. Steel-hulled steamers made the 92-mile circuit of the lake daily pausing at other resorts in the area — Homewood, McKinney's, Moana Villa, Pomin's, Emerald Bay Camp, Al Tahoe Inn, Lakeside Park, Glenbrook Inn and Ranch, Brockaway, Tahoe Vista, Carnelian Bay and Tahoe City. — COURTESY BRUCE PETTY

Standard gauge operations at the Tahoe Tavern pier, in the above views, were photographed in the late 1920's. — BOTH SOUTHERN PACIFIC COLLECTION

127

Traditionally, the Lake Tahoe line or the resorts were open only from May 15th through October 31st or later, weather permitting, but no attempt was ever made to keep them open during the winter until the line was standard gauged. Extra 2338 East poses for the publicity department near Big Chief in 1929. (LEFT) Dog sled races were introduced as part of the Truckee winter sports activities during the season of 1928-29. The route used followed the SP's Tahoe Branch and the SP conveniently provided a pace train for the event. — BOTH JAMES H. HARRISON COLLECTION

During the winter season, Truckee remains the base for snow removal operations on the east slope. (ABOVE) Rotary No. CP 714 pauses in front of the Truckee depot about 1930. — ROGER L. TITUS COLLECTION Two different flanger styles are represented by SP No. 727 (LEFT) and SPMW No. 7341 (LOWER-LEFT). Earlier more rugged designs provided no cabin protection for the crew. (BELOW) An early spreader, No. SP 1527, graced the Truckee yards in the 1920's. Later versions were completely enclosed to afford the crew protection from the elements. — ALL SOUTHERN PACIFIC COLLECTION

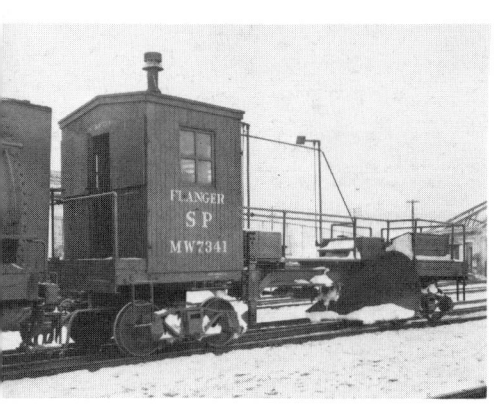

The circular roundhouse at Truckee was covered with a mantle of snow on February 21, 1922. A rotary plow has cleared the balloon track in the foreground. Mallets dose in the drifts. — SOUTHERN PACIFIC COLLECTION (CENTER—RIGHT) During more temperate weather, with its parapet, vaulted roof and massive stone foundation exposed, the Truckee roundhouse resembled a Medieval battlement. The coal handling machinery dates this picture to the first decade of the 20th century. — DENNIS M. BEEGHLY COLLECTION (LOWER-RIGHT) In the off-season, fire train engine No. 2188 was safely stored within the confines of the Truckee roundhouse. This unique portrait was exposed February 21, 1922. — SOUTHERN PACIFIC COLLECTION

ward downtown Truckee are the Southern Pacific's facilities, circa 1926. — SOUTHERN PACIFIC COLLECTION

TRUCKEE

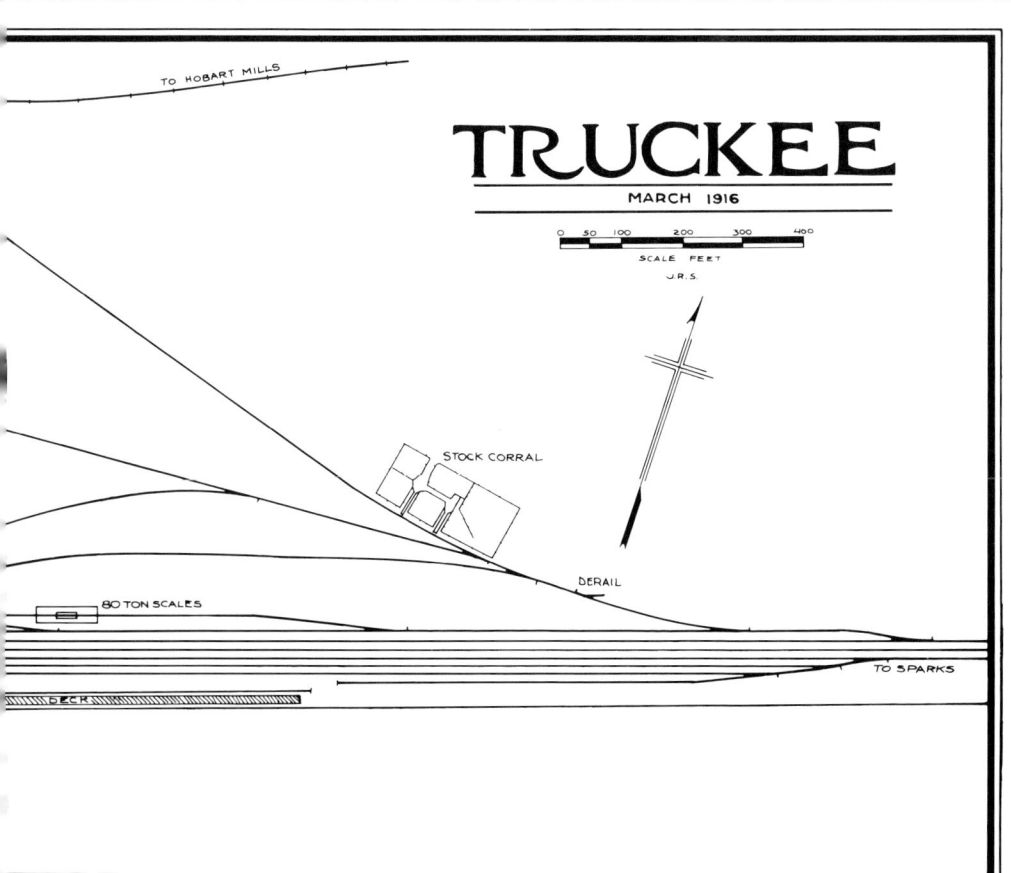

MARCH 1916

TO HOBART MILLS

STOCK CORRAL

DERAIL

80 TON SCALES

TO SPARKS

Looking west t

SCHOOL ST.

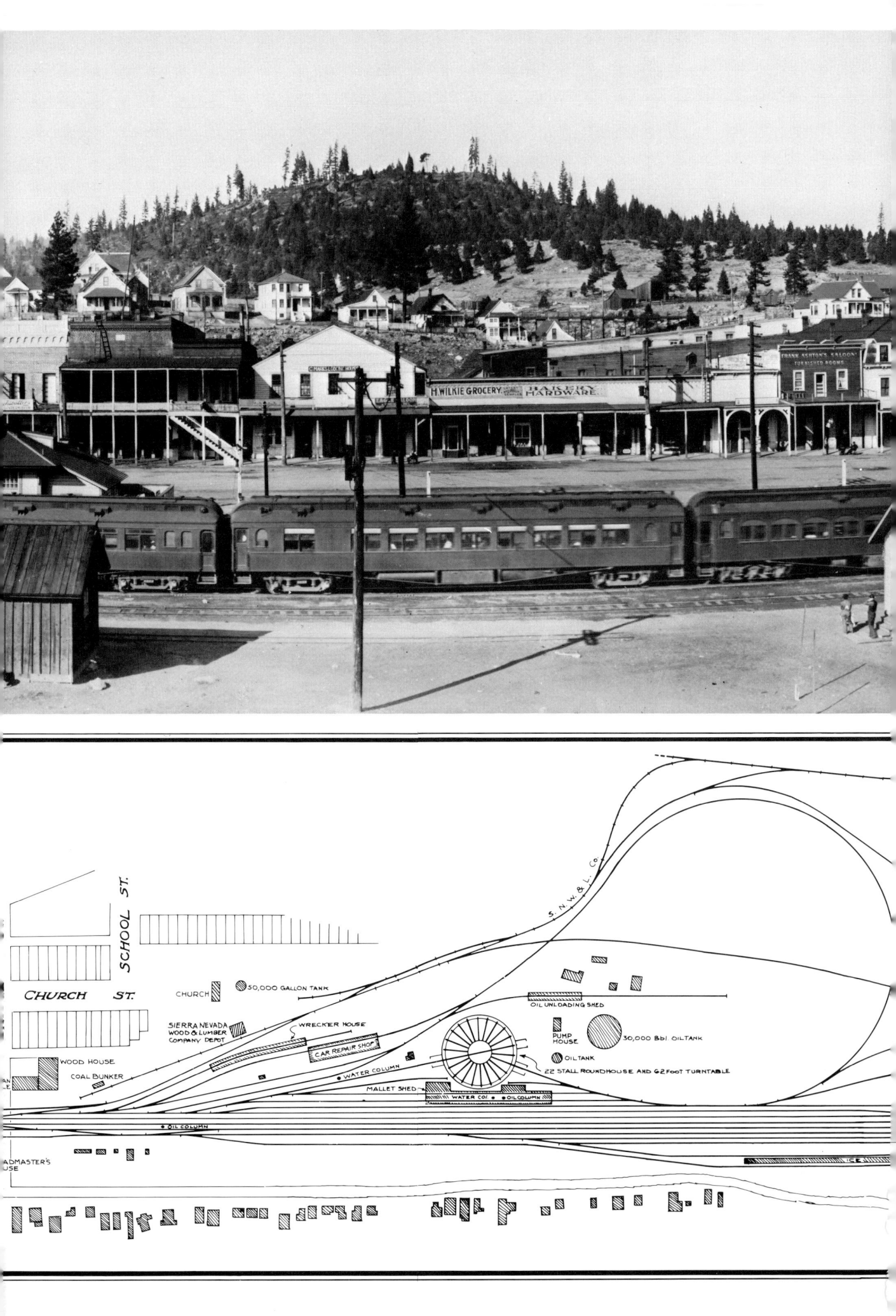

CHURCH ST.

CHURCH   50,000 GALLON TANK

SIERRA NEVADA
WOOD & LUMBER
COMPANY DEPOT   WRECKER HOUSE

CAR REPAIR SHOP   OIL UNLOADING SHED

WOOD HOUSE   PUMP
COAL BUNKER   HOUSE   30,000 Bbl OILTANK

                    WATER COLUMN   OILTANK
                                                   22 STALL ROUNDHOUSE AND 62 FOOT TURNTABLE
                    MALLET SHED   WATER COL. OIL COLUMN

        OIL COLUMN

ROADMASTER'S
HOUSE   ICE

S.N.W. & L. CO.

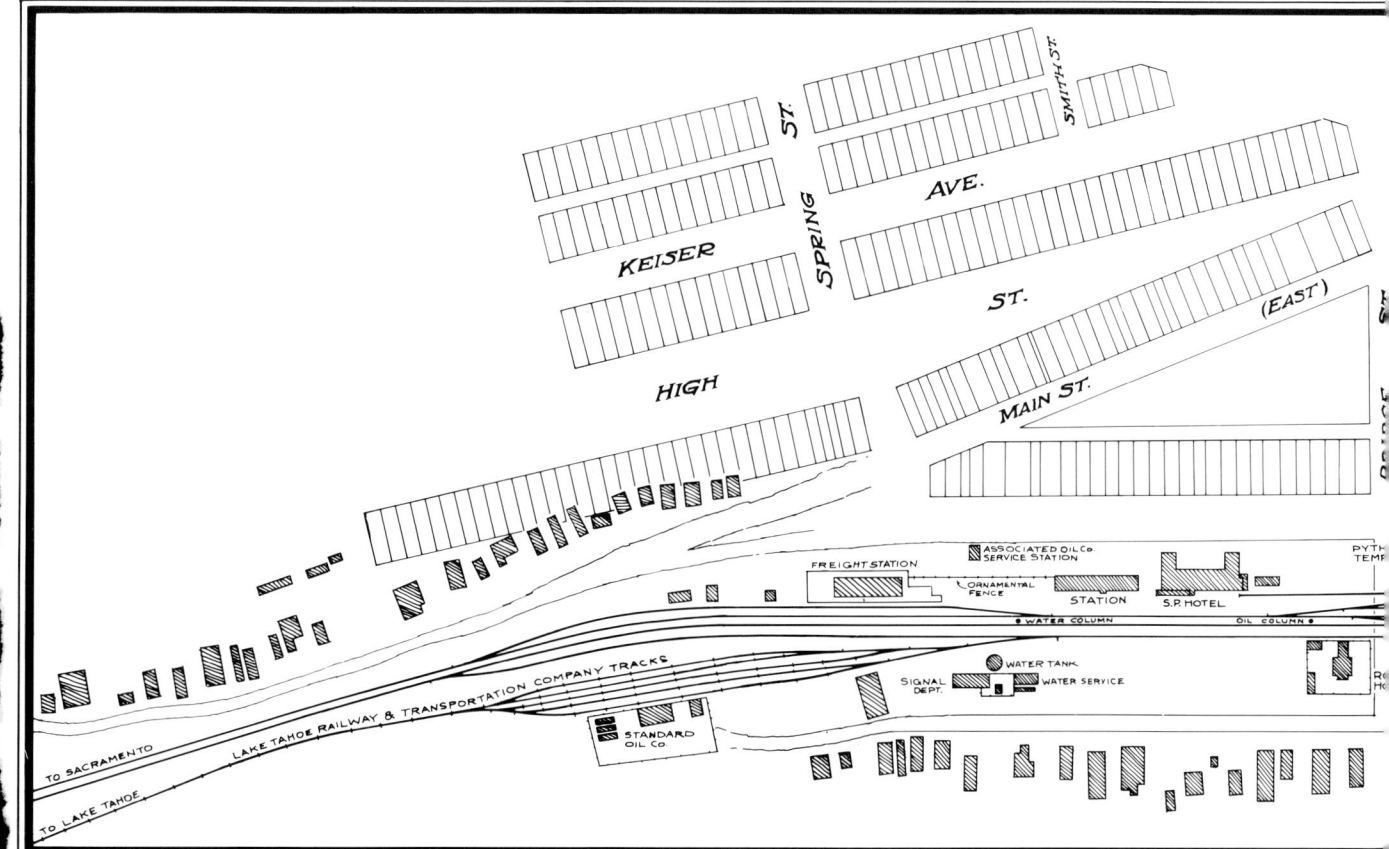

KEISER ST.
SMITH ST.
SPRING AVE.
HIGH ST.
MAIN ST. (EAST)

FREIGHT STATION
ASSOCIATED OIL Co. SERVICE STATION
ORNAMENTAL FENCE
STATION
S.P. HOTEL
WATER COLUMN
OIL COLUMN
SIGNAL DEPT.
WATER TANK
WATER SERVICE
STANDARD OIL Co.
LAKE TAHOE RAILWAY & TRANSPORTATION COMPANY TRACKS
TO SACRAMENTO
TO LAKE TAHOE

By studying the magnificent panorama and accompanying 1916 map in this foldout, some of the Truckee layout can be seen. Spread out across the above picture is the 12-car *Pacific Limited* as evidenced by the through Milwaukee Road cars in its consist. At the upper left, on a distant hill, stands the columned futuristic mansion of local entrepreneur C.F. McGlashan. The narrow-gauge tracks and equipment of the Lake Tahoe Railway & Transportation Co. appear in the left foreground and are a sharp contrast to the Southern Pacific mainline. Stretched out behind train No. 19 is the celebrated boardwalk fronting on what today is known as commercial row. The roundhouse is at the far right. — DONNER MEMORIAL STATE PARK COLLECTION (BELOW) The balloon track dates from 1901. — GUY L. DUNSCOMB COLLECTION

Extra 4038 West pauses in the canyon east of Truckee while brakemen inspect the train. — DR. ROBERT J. CHURCH COLLECTION

At 5,534 feet, Boca experienced extremely cold weather. The record was 22 degrees below during 1875-76 along with occasional heavy snow. (ABOVE) Following an unusually heavy storm in February 1922, snow removal operations were underway. — SOUTHERN PACIFIC COLLECTION (LEFT) The Boca Brewing Company was an important shipper on the Sierra line. The firm produced 30,000 barrels of suds each year. — DONNER MEMORIAL STATE PARK COLLECTION (BELOW) Rotary No. 715 plows out the house track at Boca during February 1922. — SOUTHERN PACIFIC COLLECTION

A Consolidation, with a flanger in tow, races down the eastward mainline at Farad. During such maneuvers, fine powdery snow was sucked into the firebox, thus making it hard to keep the fire hot. As a result, frequent stops were required to build up steam. — W.S. PRINGLE COLLECTION

A rotary clears the siding at Hinton on February 21, 1922 while a Ten-Wheeler and flanger wait. — SOUTHERN PACIFIC COLLECTION

134

An eastbound freight works the yards at Boca, in the above scene, in 1915. At the left, west of town, are cordwood loads destined for the pulp mill at Floriston. The ice house is in the center. The cut on the hill to the right is the line of the Boca & Loyalton Railroad. — COURTESY DONNER MEMORIAL STATE PARK **(OPPOSITE PAGE-LOWER LEFT)** Extra 4038 West pauses for the photographer at the east switch of Boca in the 'twenties. Double-track was completed in this section and automatic signals installed during 1910. — DR. ROBERT J. CHURCH COLLECTION **(BELOW)** A westbound reefer drag works through Boca during the summer. The foundations for the ice plant, abandoned in 1924, appears to the right. — GUY L. DUNSCOMB COLLECTION

A general view of the first crossing of the Truckee River at Iceland in the fall of 1914. Taking advantage of the prevailing sub-zero weather in the area, the natural ice manufacturing district extended from near Floriston through to Stanford. The large sheds stored ice in the more clement months. Modest line changes were developed in this area as the second track was added in the 'teens. (LEFT) This view looks east near Farad. The upper line is the westbound track. — SOUTHERN PACIFIC COLLECTION

A general view looking west at Floriston in October 1914. The lower line is the eastbound track. — SOUTHERN PACIFIC COLLECTION

One of the more important industries in the Truckee River Canyon was the Crown Willamette paper mill (RIGHT) established at Floriston in 1900. Cordwood was gathered at various points up and down the canyon and forwarded to the mill. The mill's principal product was tissue wraps for the California fruit industry. The plant was closed in 1930 partly due to the Depression and partly due to environmental concerns regarding acid wastes. It was reported that it was possible to tell what paper was being made at any given time by the color of the river. This view looks down the "go to hell" track, a moniker derived from the frequent instances of runaway cars. Interstate 80 now occupies the site. (BELOW) The quaint SP depot at Floriston as it appeared October 30, 1914. The structure at the right is a baggage elevator to the eastbound track. Cars of cordwood are parked beyond. — BOTH SOUTHERN PACIFIC COLLECTION

This wooden structure served as the SP depot at Verdi, Nevada, for many years. Snow still dusts the surrounding Sierra in this May 1915 view. — SOUTHERN PACIFIC COLLECTION **(BELOW)** A westbound stock extra pauses for the photographer just east of Verdi. — A.C. PHELPS COLLECTION

A recently delivered 4100 class Mallet storms out of Reno on a westbound run. (RIGHT) Baggage and express carts line the platform at Reno as the *Atlantic Express* waits patiently on the eastbound main. — BOTH W.S. PRINGLE COLLECTION (BELOW) Downtown Reno, in December 1920, was a far cry from today's scene of glitter and high rise buildings. Although legalized gambling was still 11 years away, the city was already firmly established as a divorce mecca. — SOUTHERN PACIFIC COLLECTION

Mirroring the increasing importance of Reno as a regional commercial and transportation center, Southern Pacific built a handsome new station here in the mid-1920's. The fourth to be erected at Reno since 1868, this new structure was greatly enlarged from its immediate predecessor, seen (ABOVE) about 1913. The new station's exterior was composed of stucco enriched with ornamental detail. The interior walls were fashioned of plastered caen stone with marble base and wainscot caps. The floors were of terrazzo and edged in marble, the ceiling was detailed with ornamental beamwork, and all the woodwork was oak. Steam heat was also provided. Opened to the public on February 8, 1926, the structure continues today to meet the needs of AMTRAK. The photos on this and the adjoining page were taken two months after the unveiling. — ALL SOUTHERN PACIFIC COLLECTION

SOU. PAC. FREIGHT OFFICE
MENLO
POSTAL TELEGRAPH

TELEGRAPH
TICKETS
TELEPHONE

In the spring of 1903, work commenced on the new Sparks terminal and, by the summer of 1904, all functions formerly carried out at Wadsworth were transferred here. These two views of the sprawling roundhouse and back shop at Sparks date from March 1908. — BOTH D.T. McDERMOTT COLLECTION

The yard office, along with division headquarters, was moved from Wadsworth to Sparks in June 1904. Passenger trains made two stops at Sparks. One here, to exchange crews and power, and another three-quarters of a mile west (LEFT) at this little depot. — BOTH SOUTHERN PACIFIC COLLECTION

Eliminated by a line change in 1902-1904, Wadsworth appeared busy indeed, in the years just prior to its abandonment. Consequently, many of the structures found their way to Sparks. — BOTH NEVADA HISTORICAL SOCIETY

143

An extra west pounds upgrade toward Truckee in the spring of 1940. On the point, three-year old AC-7, No. 4151 presents an image that was closely identified with the railway operations over Donner Summit for nearly two decades.
— JAMES H. HARRISON COLLECTION

3
The Modern Steam Era 1930-1955

Little did Southern Pacific planners realize, when expending such vast sums to complete the second-track in the high Sierra, that there would soon be a halt to the then seemingly limitless upswing in traffic that had been occurring on the "Overland Route." As a consequence of the Great Depression, the modern plant, that had been completed with such a sense of urgency in the mid-1920's, was destined to lay underutilized for the better part of the following decade. Traffic peaked in 1928, just two years after the Sierra operation had been streamlined. It then took a nose dive, and bottomed out in 1933 with 14,017,483 gross ton miles, a decline of over seven million. The cost cutting and retrenching that occurred in its wake touched every aspect of operations on the Donner grade.

An ambitious expansion program at Roseville, announced during 1923 and placed in operation during June 1927, saw the erection of a $600,000 icing plant (No. 2), the development of extensive PFE shops on a 200-acre site between Antelope and Roseville, and the laying of nearly 77 miles of new track. This much expansion seemed a bit over optimistic in light of the decline in carloadings. Employment in the Roseville shops and yards hovered near 1,360 men during the summer of 1929. Two years later this figure was cut by one-third. The roundhouse at Colfax was closed and 33 men were laid off during January 1930. The rosters of train and engine crews were cut so deep that, ten years later, a man hiring out with a 1941 date followed in line against a 1929 man.

The substantial local business enjoyed by the railroad throughout the first two decades of the 20th century eroded as, one by one, tributary railroads and lumber operators cut back or suspended operations entirely. The ice business in the Truckee River canyon was history by 1927. Even the Floriston pulp mill closed its doors in 1930, a victim of environmental, as much as economic pressures.

Local passenger service was cut to the bone, and on October 9, 1929, Colfax local trains, Nos. 33 and 34, were discontinued. The remaining Colfax motors, Nos. 294 and 295, were cut February 26, 1933 and the service was never revived. Long distance schedules were similarly affected. On May 3, 1931, Nos. 23 and 24, the *Sierra*, were removed from the timetable and on May 31, 1931, Nos. 27 and 28, the *San Francisco Limited*, suffered a similar fate. Even the prestigious *Overland* did not escape cost cutting measures, after June 19, 1932, having coaches added to its formerly all-Pullman consist. September 18th of that year, train Nos. 22 and 23, the former *Tahoe*, were dropped. At its lowest point, employee timetable No. 149 for the Sacramento Division, dated

145

On January 15, 1936, crews worked to free train No. 21, the *Pacific Limited,* caught in an avalanche just east of Eder at 2:40 P.M. Fifty feet of shed was swept away in the incident, turning Pullman sleeper *Aransas* (ABOVE) on its side and derailing Pullman *McGrattans.* (ABOVE RIGHT) By 5:00 P.M., the portion of the train unmolested by the slide was on its way west. — ALL R.A. MILLER JR. COLLECTION

April 16, 1933, listed but three first class trains in each direction across the Mountain District.

The Tahoe Branch service lapsed into a seasonal business during this period. On February 26, 1933, the remaining regular schedules operating over this picturesque line were dropped from the timetable, and the train, thereafter, ran as an extra during the season from mid-June through early fall.

The Tahoe Branch and foothill local passenger business was suffering the pinch of hard times but, undeniably, it was the encroachment of the automobile that caused the demise of these services. In 1910, few roads existed in the region but consistent lobbying by automobile interests and the general populace, in the years immediately prior to and following World War I, led to an extensive program of road construction state wide. During 1918, the Lincoln Highway, extending eastward from Sacramento, was opened over the Sierra to Reno. This forerunner of U.S. 40 and today's Interstate 80 was a primitive two-lane affair, which, during clement weather, met the needs of the motorist of that period. No attempt was made, however, to keep the road open over Donner Summit during the winter. Up until the late 1930's, the road was closed from November through early June, even as many of the Sierra passes are today.

Recognizing the inevitability of the automobile, the Southern Pacific moved to take full advantage of the situation and offered to "ferry" automobiles between Sacramento and Reno. For $15 one's car could be driven aboard a baggage car, attached to the rear of train Nos. 23 and 24, the *Sierra,* and hauled over the mountains. This special service was first offered during January 1929 and was available each way on a tri-weekly basis through June 8, 1929. Records after this date are incomplete, but it is known that auto ferry service was offered again during the winters of 1929-30 and 1930-31.

Along with the automobile, the weather was another inevitable factor that the Southern Pacific had to contend with in its day-to-day operations over the high Sierra. Indeed, it was during the lean years of the 1930's that the elements chose to rise up in a fury that had not been seen since the terrible storms of 1889-90.

The upper reaches of the Sierra had been lashed by storms for days when, at 2:40 P.M. Monday, January 15, 1936, the Southern Pacific's westbound *Pacific Limited,* train No. 21, was caught in an avalanche of serious proportion. Without warning, hundreds of tons of rock and snow crashed through the sheds as No. 21 was approaching Eder station at milepost 198.5. Fifty feet of shed was swept away, pinning beneath it, the train's observation car, *St. Marcy,* and tearing two Pullman cars from the tracks. The third Pullman, *Aransas,* was struck on the forward end, turning it partially on its side. The other, *McGranttans,* was derailed but remained upright. A hastily recruited crew worked for an hour and one-half to release the last of 13 people trapped inside the buried observation car. By 5:00 P.M., that portion of the train, unmolested by the slide, was able to pull away westbound. A second slide near Colfax delayed the train again, but no damage resulted and the track was soon clear.

Snowfall that season amounted to 588 inches at Norden, a respectable figure, even above average. But two years later another storm descended upon the Sierra Nevada that was to shatter all previous records in duration, intensity and total accumulation of snow. A snowfall of 341 inches, the heaviest recorded for any month or part of a month fell at Summit during the storm that settled over the mountains February 1, 1938 and continued unabated through the night of the 14th. Complicating the situation, a gale of hurricane proportion swept in from the Pacific shortly before noon on February 9th burying wires on the three lower crossarms of 25-foot telegraph poles. Snow reached a maximum depth of 234 inches at Norden and in settling, it snapped crossarms and wires which in turn interrupted communications and knocked out signals. During the rest of February, 15 more inches fell. The season total came to 819 inches, 43 more than the legendary storms of 1889-90. This amounted to 68.25 feet, a record that has not been equalled as of this writing. Incredibly, throughout this epic blizzard, railway operations were not seriously hampered. February 11th, during the height of the storm, all passenger trains were moving behind rotary snowplows. The only actual stoppage occurred February 14th, when at 1:45 A.M., a rotary derailed on the westbound track after striking a tree which had been downed in a slowslide at Smart. But trains were moving again by 2:50 P.M. on the same day.

On February 9th, while the blizzard raged in the mountains, the yards and roundhouses at Sacramento and Roseville suffered from a hurricane that descended on the Sacramento Valley, overturning standing equipment, tearing roofs from buildings and causing widespread flooding. After the storm, the roundhouse at Sacramento presented a weird scene. Much of the roof was collapsed or completely blown away and equipment stood in several feet of mud.

The weather may have been unpredictable and severe, but the commercial aspects of it were not overlooked by a hungry Depression-era Southern Pacific management. The snowfields and icy forests of Donner Pass were just a short train ride away from California's growing lowland communities. Since much of the state enjoyed a year 'round Mediterranean climate, snow was a saleable novelty. During the winter of 1931-32, SP began running "Snowball Specials" on a semi-regular basis. Leaving Oakland Pier about midnight, the specials arrived in the Truckee basin the following morning in time for a full day of winter recreation. Excursionists were then returned to Oakland Pier the following midnight.

This was not an entirely new idea. During 1895, the first winter excursion trains had been operated between Oakland Pier and Truckee, in conjunction with local entrepreneur C.F. McGlashin's ice carnivals. Featured winter sports, unavailable in the more temperate cities west of the mountains, included ice skating, tobogganing and good honest snowball fights. The idea caught on. Dog sled racing was added in 1929. The nationally acclaimed Sierra Dog Sled Derby first occurred in February of that year, with the course set along the Truckee River from downtown Truckee to Tahoe Tavern. Southern Pacific provided a special pace train for officials and spectators taking in the event.

A dog sled race was featured in the closing scenes of Jack London's *Call of the Wild,* a motion picture starring Clark Gable, Jack Oakie, Loretta Young and "Buck" the St. Bernard, filmed during February 1935, on location, at Donner Lake and along the Truckee River. The final scene took place in the streets of Truckee. Southern Pacific provided transportation for the actors and film crews. Other films shot in the area, with SP's help, included the 1929 epic *The Storm,* starring Lupe Velez, and Charlie Chaplin's *Gold Rush,* which was shot in April 1924. Chaplin so loved the town of Truckee that he permanently retained six rooms at the Sierra Tavern Hotel for his frequent visits.

Downhill skiing, a winter sport for which the Tahoe-Donner-Truckee region is world famous today, was late in appearing on the scene. Oscar

Prior to the 1938-39 winter sports season, SP's "Snowball Specials" were operated on a comparatively small scale, handling about 2,500 enthusiasts a year, principally in the Truckee area. Following the completion of the Norden "Ski Hut" in 1939, and the development of nearby "Sugar Bowl" ski resort, in addition to an ambitious promotional campaign, train patronage jumped in the 1939-40 season to 8,598 and to 12,750 the following season. So great was the 1940-41 season, that 60 extra trains were operated between January 11th and March 23rd to accommodate the influx of business. (ABOVE AND LEFT) The main room of the "Ski Hut," situated adjacent to the Norden telegraph office, was built in a simple semi-rustic fashion with oiled pine walls and a cement floor. (LOWER LEFT) These stairs led to an overhead passageway above the tracks which connected the resort areas, the "Ski Hut," and U.S. Highway 40. The national emergency of 1941-45 quelled the plans to substantially improve the "Ski Hut" in size and the amenities offered. It was closed for the duration of World War II. In postwar years, the facility was neglected due to SP's lack of interest in the passenger business and it ultimately succumbed to a fire in 1961. Today, looking at the traffic-jammed Interstate 80 on winter weekends, one can't help but wonder if the "Ski Hut" wouldn't still be successful today. — ALL SOUTHERN PACIFIC COLLECTION

Jones and his son Dennis came to the Summit Valley from Blue Cañon in 1923, built the Soda Springs Hotel during 1926 and developed the first ski hill in the region. This attraction opened for business during the 1931-32 season and featured a rope tow lift which wound off the axle of an old Model-T. The Depression years kept a lid on new developments although the "Snowball Specials" returned each winter season. Then, during 1938, with the nation in recovery, clearing began on an ambitious new ski resort near Norden. Located about a mile and one-half southeast of the interlocking office, the new "Sugar Bowl" opened for business in the 1939-40 season, sporting the first chair lift in the area.

Southern Pacific worked closely with the "Sugar Bowl" developers by providing transportation and constructing facilities at trackside to accommodate the skiers. During the fall of 1939, the Ski Hut was built inside the sheds at Norden. A house within a house, the Ski Hut consisted of a room 168 feet long by 28 feet wide, built in a simple semi-rustic fashion with oiled pine walls and a cement floor. Shelter and accommodations, such as ski racks, large restrooms for changing and a lunch counter were provided for the enthusiasts. An overhead ramp led to resort areas. Motor sleighs operated every few minutes between the hut and the resort. Aboard the "Snowball Special," a new Ski Hut car sold mittens, socks and ski apparel, offered toboggan rentals and professional equipment fitting. Arriving at Norden during the early morning hours, skiers were welcomed by the melodic yodels of Hannes Schroll, an authentic Scandanavian, imported for the occasion and employed as the host of the "Sugar Bowl."

Eastbound train No. 210, the *Sierra* and No. 14, the *Pacific Limited,* stopped at the Ski Hut. Westbound daily trains No. 87, the *Challenger,* and No. 209, the *Sierra* were also scheduled to stop here for the convenience of skiers. In addition, No. 295 was scheduled to stop on Sundays and holidays. Southern Pacific and the "Sugar Bowl" looked forward to a long and healthy future.

The mid-thirties saw a dramatic resurgence of passenger service traversing the "Overland Route" in the form of the gleaming autumn brown and armour yellow 11-unit *City of San Francisco* streamliner. This bright star, in a world of black and Pullman green, was built by Pullman Standard Car Manufacturing Company. Two "power cars," equipped with 1,200-horsepower V-16 diesel engines, headed up the consist of a mail-baggage-express car, kitchen-dormitory-baggage car, dining-lounge car, two coaches and four Pullman sleepers. Resembling a huge projectile on wheels, the streamliner was capable of speeds in excess of 100 miles-per-hour and looked it. Weighing one-half as much as conventional trains of the same size, the streamliner was 714 feet long and tipped the scales at 502 tons.

During the early part of June 1936, a series of test runs of the new train were conducted between San Francisco and Chicago by way of the Southern Pacific, Union Pacific and Chicago & North Western. A 39 and three-quarter-hour schedule was established for the run, cutting an incredible 19 hours off the fastest time between the two cities. Commencing on June 14, 1936, the streamliner was placed in service completing five round trips per month. Westbound, the streamliner operated as the second section of train No. 9, the *Fast Mail*. Eastbound, it carried 2-14 in the boards. December 13, 1936, the *City of San Francisco* received schedules of its own, running on the Southern Pacific as Nos. 101 and 102. A new 17-car train supplanted the original 11-car consist on January 2, 1938. A second train was added on July 26, 1941, increasing the frequency to ten round trips per month.

On the Mountain District of the Sacramento Division, No. 101, with only one scheduled stop at Reno, made it from Sparks to Sacramento in four hours and 30 minutes, exactly one hour faster than train No. 9. The gain was achieved primarily between Loomis and Roseville, where the train was allowed to run 70 m.p.h., fully 20 miles-per-hour faster than the regular passenger train speed, and a blistering 95 m.p.h. between Roseville and Sacramento, 35 miles-per-hour over the previous maximum speed.

To ensure the streamliner an unobstructed path, first class trains were required to be in the clear of its time by at least 10 minutes, and all other trains by at least 15 minutes. Although slow speed boards also applied to the *City of San Francisco,* special round yellow boards were placed below the regular speed boards, allowing the streamliner a greater speed at these restricted locations, than conventional trains. In order to allow for these greater speeds, the track was further super-elevated on curves.

With the *City of San Francisco* regularly blistering the rails, there was a renewed interest in the added protection that could be afforded by Automatic Train Stop. This apparatus, employing heavy magnets installed between the rails, provided a fail-safe system by energizing the magnets according to a given signal indication. An engineer, encountering a signal displaying any indication except proceed, would operate the forestalling valve in the cab while passing over the track magnet. A failure to forestall the magnet would result in a penalty, emergency application of the train's air brake system. Automatic Train Stop, manufactured by the Union Switch & Signal Company, was first introduced in 1927 on the 28.8

The *Streamliner* races through Antelope at a blistering 95 miles per hour. Train No. 101 covered the 167 miles between Sparks and Sacramento in 4 hours and 30 minutes. — R.B. TREXLER, ALAN ASKE COLLECTION

A sparkling new autumn brown and armour yellow 14-car *City of San Francisco* streamliner paused for the company photographer just west of Boca in the Truckee River Canyon, in January 1938. The train, introduced two years earlier as a nine-car consist, made headlines with its 39 and ¾ hour schedule between Chicago and the west coast — fully 19 hours faster than the best previous schedule. — JAMES H. HARRISON COLLECTION

In 1942, train No. 102 made an unscheduled stop at Roseville where yard forces added a 4300 series Mountain type to the point. It was a frequent practice to add a helper in order to maintain the *Streamliner's* rapid schedule on the long grade up the west slope of the Sierra. — J.F. OREM (RIGHT) Another day finds beefy AC class cab-forward No. 4174 providing the assist. — R.B. TREXLER, ALAN ASKE COLLECTION

miles between Emigrant Gap and Andover. This was in response to problems over poor visibility encountered in this heavy curve territory which were frequently aggravated by sheds, tunnels and seasonal snow and storm conditions. Starting in July 1937, the limits of Automatic Train Control were extended from Andover to Truckee, 7.4 miles, and from Emigrant Gap on down to Gold Run, 19.6 miles, completing a total protection of 55.08 miles. The 1937 work employed magnets and apparatus released from the retirement of ATS between Pittsburg and Fresno on the Western Division.

An additional magnet was installed following a disastrous wreck during the fall of 1943, protecting movement on the westbound track at a curve at the end of a long tangent west of Colfax. In the incident, which occurred at 5:10 A.M. on November 8th, train No. 1-87, running 15 minutes late with a Mallet and 18 cars, overturned on the 30 mile-an-hour curve 2.55 miles west of Colfax. Government investigators estimated the train, carrying 206 passengers and crew, left the rails at 57 miles-per-hour. The engineer and eight passengers, including members of the Armed Forces, were killed and 194 people injured.

Transcontinental train No. 87, the *Challenger,* and its counterpart No. 88, were new trains on the Mountain that were placed in service on September 15, 1937. Another train to make its debut in 1937 was the deluxe all-Pullman, extra-fare, steam powered flyer, the *Forty Niner.* It operated five times a month between Chicago and San Francisco via the Chicago & Northwestern, Union Pacific and Southern Pacific. The *Forty Niner* acted as a counterpart to the streamliner *City of San Francisco,* featuring such ammenities as a valet, stewardess, shower and barber shop. Each car in the train's eight-car heavyweight consist was named for an important person, place, or symbol of California's rich historic past. The baggage-dormitory-kitchen car was named *Donner Lake* and the diner-lounge *Angel's Camp*. The six following sleepers were named *Joaquin Miller, James Marshall, Capt. John Sutter Gold Run, Bear Flag* and *California Republic*. The *Forty Niner* began operation over the Mountain on July 8, 1937 as No. 49 westbound and No. 48 eastbound. With the delivery of the second 17-car *City of San Francisco* in July 1941, the short-lived *Forty Niner,* whose principal function had been handling overflow from the streamliner, was no longer needed and on July 23rd the train was discontinued.

Another transcontinental train, the nine-car, all-Pullman, heavyweight limited called the *Treasure Island Special,* operated between Chicago and the coast during the seasons of 1939 and 1940. It was run for the benefit of tourists taking in the Golden Gate International Exposition on Treasure Island in San Francisco Bay. The train, alternating with the *Forty Niner*, shared the schedule Nos. 48 and 49 on the "Overland" run, and was operated from May 22nd through September 25, 1939 and from June 21st through September 18, 1940, after which time, the exposition ended and the *Special* was discontinued.

The resurgence of passenger traffic on the Mountain, which occurred in the late 1930's, was not the only encouraging sign that the nation was recovering from the great Depression, freight traffic was also on the upswing. Business on the Roseville-Sparks district had bottomed out in 1933 at 14,017,483 gross tons, but by 1937, this figure had climbed to nearly 22.5 million. War in Europe and the development of defense plants on the west coast benefited the Southern Pacific. Army camps and airfields, Naval land and air stations, shipyards and other military installations, strung out along SP lines, began to expand and new ones were developed. When war was declared on Japan in December 1941, and the focus of hostilities shifted to the Pacific, Southern Pacific, whose principal lines were located in extremely strategic areas, suddenly felt the full force of the national defense and war program. The system's traffic load in 1941 jumped more than 47 percent above 1929, which had previously been the greatest year in the history of the company. During the war, the 780-mile SP leg of the "Overland Route" between Oakland Pier and Ogden, handled the greatest traffic density in its history. During 1944, at the height of hostilities, gross tons on the Roseville-Sparks district approached 55,700,000 — nearly tripling the 1929 figure!

These statistics reflected the rush of troops, war material, armaments and oil feeding the defense effort. But general transcontinental freight traffic swelled as well, with the abandonment of coastal shipping via the Panama Canal. The Pacific Fruit Express Company also experienced its greatest activity during this period. On the Pacific System, Southern Pacific was now averaging 350 special troop or "Main Trains" per month, involving the movement of 5,500 cars. Approximately 2,000 additional car loads of military personnel were accommodated in regular trains. Raw materials, moving west in trainload lots to defense plants, were designated *GOAD's* or government loads. Regular troop trains, hospital trains, Coast Guard trains, Civilian Conservation Corps and alien specials were also handled. On the Mountain, the bulk of this vital extra passenger work fell on train Nos. 87 and 88, the *Challenger*. While every train but the streamliner, *City of San Francisco,* was running in one or two sections daily, frequently the *Challenger* was running in eight! Effective December 31, 1944, a special train began operation for furloughees and members of their families traveling with them. Designated as the *Furloughee Challenger,* the special operated daily between Sacramento and Ogden as the second section of No. 28, the *Overland*. September 9, 1945, the train was assigned schedule No. 14, then on December 23, 1945, it was changed to the *Military Challenger*. April 14, 1946, No. 14 was renamed the *Advance Challenger*.

To streamline its operations, the SP, in 1942, began to discourage unneccessary travel and eliminated 27 passenger trains on the Pacific Lines. On the Mountain, train Nos. 210, 289 and 295, collectively known as the *Sierra,* were discontinued on March 8, 1942. No. 210 had been the last train to routinely operate over the No. 4 track between Rocklin and Loomis, with the last trip being made June 17, 1940. The annual *"Snowball Specials"* were not run during the 1940-41 season or during subsequent winter periods. The rustic Ski Hut inside the sheds at Norden was closed, and the Norden ski resorts discontinued operations for the duration. After the war, when the resorts reopened, the automobile had made such inroads that the *"Snowball Specials"* were not revived and the Ski Hut never reopened.

During February of 1941, Antonio Nencini, an SP track walker, discovered 44 spikes and an angle bar missing from the westbound track at Alta. Less than a week later, three Sacramento youths were arrested for the sabotage. But the vulnerability of the Sierra grade, which was rapidly becoming the principal pipeline for the war effort in the Pacific, was brought to the attention of authorities. Shortly after the Alta incident, the 754th Military Police Battalion was deployed at Camp Placer, Camp Flint, Soda Springs and Norden to guard tunnels, bridges, snow sheds and other vulnerable points along the right-of-way. At Cisco and Verdi, the men were quartered in box cars provided by the Southern Pacific.

Attack from the air seemed inevitable and, after the attack on Pearl Harbor, the Donner grade fell under the blackout and dimout operations of the Civil Defense authorities. It became necessary for all artificial illumination, stretching from the coast 150 miles inland, to be shielded or turned out during emergencies. In the SP shops, many thousands of metal hoods were manufactured for screening locomotive classification and headlamps, marker lights on cabooses, the rear of passenger trains, signals and switch lights. Even locomotive fireboxes were especially shielded to hide the glare of normal operation. During blackouts, cab shades were drawn, white smoke from the engine was changed to black and shades on passenger trains were drawn from sunset to sunrise. The windows of express cars, not equipped with shades, were painted black for the duration. Even lanterns were required to be extinguished, except to give signals.

At the height of wartime activity, the 24-hour office and interlocking plant at Norden hummed with excitement as an incredible parade of trains passed over the Sierra divide on their rush east or west. At Norden, some passenger trains and all freights paused to cut helpers and adding to the congestion, westbound freight crews generally took beans here. The rush of the fall harvest complicated things even more as we present the following glimpse at operations occurring on the mountain during this fascinating period.

24 HOURS AT NORDEN, CALIFORNIA
SATURDAY, OCTOBER 7, 1944
Weather: Clear and calm

THIRD TRICK

X4200 West	11:30 P.M.-1:35 A.M.	2CS5 (Chicago Manifest) 4200 4186 Truckee-Norden 55 loads - 11 empties - 6,508 Ms (1,000 lbs.)
X4159 East	12:25-12:45 A.M.	TAB5 4159 4198 Roseville-Norden 32-37-5885
X4245 West	12:56 A.M.	MAIN (troop train) 4245 28-0-2150
X4198 West	12:58 A.M.	Light engine off X4159 East
No. 9	1:14 A.M.	*Fast Mail* 4170 14-0-2050
No. 27	2:17-2:30 A.M.	*S.F. Overland Limited* 4230 16-0-2600 -Takes siding to be overtaken by following military special.
X4259 West	2:25 A.M.	MAIN 4259 17-0-2400
X4218 East	2:45-6:35 A.M.	R1604 (Roseville Perishable Block) 4218 4289 Roseville-Norden 2788 Colfax-EGap 69-0-6986 -First perishable of the day, the 1,604 such block to run since 1/1/44. Unusual delay explained by air trouble and being held for east passenger traffic.
No. 1-87	3:01 A.M.	The *Challenger* first section 4211 18-0-2640
X4289 West	3:10 A.M.	Light engine off X4218 East
No. 2-87	3:18 A.M.	The *Challenger* second section 4184 17-0-2600
No. 28	3:27-3:31 A.M.	*S.F. Overland Limited* 4185 4340 Roseville-Norden 18-0-2775
No. 3-87	3:45-3:52 A.M.	The *Challenger* third section 4234 18-0-2780
X4340 West	4:05 A.M.	Light engine off No. 28
No. 101	4:25 A.M.	*City of San Francisco* SF-1 SF-2 SF-3 18-0-2680 -The streamliner.
No. 1-88	4:29-4:32 A.M.	The *Challenger* first section East 4176 4349 Sacramento-Norden 18-0-2650
X4169 East	4:41-4:44 A.M.	MAIN 4169 4313 Roseville-Norden 18-0-2650
X2252 West	4:50 A.M.	Fire Train 2252 -Responding to a brush fire at Troy.
X4349 West	4:55 A.M.	Light engines off 1-88 and X4169 East 4349 4313
No. 2-88	5:14-5:16 A.M.	The *Challenger* second section East 4241 2519 Roseville-Norden 19-0-2700
No. 3-88	5:20-6:00 A.M.	The *Challenger* third section East 4271 2811 Roseville-Norden 18-0-2870
No. 4-87	5:23 A.M.	The *Challenger* fourth section West 4210 18-0-2300
X2519 West	5:26 A.M.	Light engine off 2-88 returning to Colfax.
X4252 West	5:45-6:45 A.M.	Manifest 4252 4186 Truckee-Norden 56-7-5634
X4186 East	6:05 A.M.	Light engine off X4252 West
X2811 West	6:10 A.M.	Light engine off 3-88
No. 10	6:24 A.M.	"Passenger" 4294 11-0-1475
X4164	6:55-7:25 A.M.	R1605 4164 4173 RV-Norden 2769 Colfax-EGap 69-0-6882 -The "Cut-off," last originating block at Roseville for the previous day.
X4219 West	7:40-8:30 A.M.	3CS5 (Chicago Manifest) 4219 4153 Truckee-Norden 61-10-6721

FIRST TRICK

X4153 East	8:10 A.M.	Light engine off X4219 West
X4180 West	8:52 A.M.	DHQ (Dead head equipment — passenger) 4180 20-0-1850

X4223 East	9:25-10:15 A.M.	Drag freight 4223 4229 RV-Norden 2785 Colfax-Norden 1-68-3710
X2785 West	9:45 A.M.	Light engines off X4223 East 2785 4229
X4151 East	9:57 A.M.	DHQ 4151 2826 Colfax-EGap 20-0-2749
X2579 East	10:05 A.M.	Shed Local 2579 0-4-230
X4284 East	11:05-11:25 A.M.	R1606 4284 4260 RV-Norden 2788 Colfax-EGap 67-0-6940
X4260 West	11:20 A.M.	Light engine off X4284 East
X4293 West	11:59 A.M.	MAIN 4293 20-0-1960
X4155 East	12:25-12:50 P.M.	R1607 4155 4291 RV-Norden 2715 Colfax-EGap 68-0-7010
X4291 West	12:39 P.M.	Light engine off X4155 East
X4152 West	1:05-2:05 P.M.	1-KSF-5 (Kansas City- San Francisco) 4152 4186 Truckee-Norden 56-13-6460 -Ran alot during the war to P.O.E. Oakland.
X4185 West	1:33 P.M.	Cab hop -Run often to balance crews. No pooled cabooses in those days.
X4186 East	1:35 P.M.	Light engine off X4152 East
X4176 West	2:01-2:50 P.M.	Drag freight 4176 2795 Truckee-Norden 0-82-4573
X2795 East	2:20 P.M.	Light engine off X4176 West
X4169 West	2:25-3:25 P.M.	2-KSF-5 4169 4153 Truckee-Norden 69-2-6584
X4179 East	2:50-3:20 P.M.	1-EM-107 (East Manifest) 4179 4336 RV-Norden 2769 Colfax-Norden 2811 Colfax-EGap 47-23-6476
X4336 East	3:02 P.M.	Light engine off X4179 East to Truckee
X4153 East	3:05 P.M.	Light engine off X4169 West
X4241 West	3:05-4:00 P.M.	4-KSF-5 4241 4160 Truckee-Norden 60-10-6864
X2769 West	3:07 P.M.	Light engine off X4179 East
X4245 East	3:20-3:40 P.M.	R1609 4245 4259 RV-Norden 69-0-6882
X4170 East	3:40-4:05 P.M.	R1608 4170 4268 RV-Norden 2800 Colfax-EGap 54-8-6976
X4259 East	3:05 P.M.	Light engine off X4245 East
X4270 West	3:55-4:45 P.M.	GOAD (Government loads) 4270 4186 Truckee-Norden 30-40-5305

SECOND TRICK

X4268 West	4:10 P.M.	Light engine off X4170 East
X4178 East	4:15-4:35 P.M.	R1610 4178 4198 RV-Norden 42-17-5961
X4198 West	4:45 P.M.	Light engine off X4178 East
X4230 East	4:45-5:40 P.M.	2-EM-107 4230 4292 RV-Norden 33-34-5982
X4292 West	5:00 P.M.	Light engine off X4230 East

No. 22	5:20-5:25 P.M.	The *Pacific Limited* 4289 4349 RV-Norden 18-0-2900
X4248 West	5:25-6:10 P.M.	GOAD/Stock 4248 4153 Truckee-Norden 49-20-5783
X4349 West	5:30 P.M.	Light engine off 22
X4143 East	5:50 P.M.	Light engine off X4248 West
X4211 East	6:00-6:20 P.M.	3-EM-107 4211 4210 RV-Norden 2715 Colfax-EGap 67-6-7056
X4210 East	6:10 P.M.	Light engine cut off X4211 East and run ahead of train to Sparks
X4234 East	7:05-7:30 P.M.	East empties 4234 2785 Colfax-Norden 0-76-3785
X2252 East	7:15 P.M.	Fire train -Returning from brush fire at Troy.
X2785 West	7:25 P.M.	Light engine off X4234 East
X4218 West	7:35-8:25 P.M.	3-KSF-5 4218 4160 Truckee-Norden 70-1-6802
X4164 West	7:47 P.M.	Mail & Express extra 24-0-2480
X4160 East	7:55 P.M.	Light engine off X4218 West
X4180 West	8:25-9:10 P.M.	6-KSF-5 4180 4186 Truckee-Norden 43-27-6148
X4186 East	8:40 P.M.	Light engine off X4180 West
X4173 East	9:15-9:45 P.M.	R1611 4173 4206 RV-Norden 2811 Colfax-EGap 69-0-7052
X4206 West	9:35 P.M.	Light engine off X4173 East
No. 21	9:58-10:03 P.M.	The *Pacific Limited* 4284 2795 Truckee-Norden 20-0-2950
X2795 East	10:10 P.M.	Light engine off No. 21
X4192 East	10:40-11:00 P.M.	R1612 4192 4290 RV-Norden 2800 Colfax-EGap 66-0-6960 -Last perishable block through Norden for the day, making nine in all.
X4290 West	11:05 P.M.	Light engine off X4192 East
X4223 West	11:15 P.M.-12:25 A.M.	5-KSF-5 4223 4153 Truckee-Norden 67-3-6740
X4153 East	11:35 P.M.	Light engine off X4223 West
X4154 West	11:40 P.M.—1:05 A.M.	7-KSF-5 4154 4160 Truckee-Norden 65-3-6885

Eighty-three movements in 24 hours is amazing enough, but absent from the foregoing account were the long strings of empty reefers returning west in blocks of 86 cars. Seven or eight westbound reefer drags, along with the attendent helper moves, could have easily swelled the day's total to nearly 100 movements. Empty reefers, especially as late in the season as this, were occasionally held east of Sparks due to congestion at Roseville or on the Mountain.

As amply demonstrated by the foregoing Norden "OS" sheet, the Mallets, during the war, were holding down just about all assignments on the Mountain. This pattern was broken only by a handful of Consolidations in helper and local service, the Ten-Wheeler on the fire train, the

4300's in passenger helper service and the diesels on the *City of San Francisco*. These Mallets, however, were a far cry from the true compound Mallets which were developed for Sierra service during 1909-1912. Not one of these early designs appeared at Norden on that day in October 1944, for the simple reason that there had been vast improvements made in subsequent deliveries of the engines and the older Mallets were transferred off the district.

The first of the improved Mallets were delivered between 1928 and 1930. These 4-8-8-2 locomotives, numbered in the 4100 series, had 24x32 cylinders, 63-inch drivers and developed 116,900 pounds of tractive effort. All 51 were simple articulateds, but they all operated cab-forward, thus, to the men, they were "Mallets," as were all subsequent classes of these engines. In freight service between Roseville and Sparks, the 4100's outperformed the older 4000's by more than one-third, and in so doing, the Mountain operation was streamlined even more.

The original design of Mallets used water to a much greater degree than the later versions. Whereas, with the 4000's, it was necessary to take on water every ten or 15 miles when working steam out of Roseville. Now it was possible to limit the water stops to Colfax and Emigrant Gap. Truckee was now the only routine westbound water hole. More "Mallets" were delivered during the years 1937 through 1944, bringing the total available to nearly 300 system wide. The last 90 locomotives, Nos. 4204 through 4294, were delivered during the war years of 1942-44 and were pressed into immediate service.

The cab-forwards also held down passenger assignments, although other locomotive designs were experimented with from time to time. First, the 3600 series 2-10-2's were tested on the Sierra passenger run, then, the 5000 series 4-10-2's and finally, the 4400 series 4-8-4's — over a ten year span from the late 1920's through the mid-1930's. All of these classes were withdrawn due to the familiar complaints regarding visibility and smoke accumulation in the sheds and tunnels. The 5000's, however, had even more pronounced trouble. District roadmasters complained that the long and rigid wheel base of this class would knock the track out of line on curves and cause excessive rail wear. The leading pair of drivers of a 5000 class would cut "worms" off the ball of the rail. At night, a 5000's passing would be marked by little glowing curls of hot steel falling away from the wheels. More seasoned crews cautioned "student" firemen to keep their hands off the window cushions when rounding curves in the sheds or they might lose the skin off their knuckles.

Thus for a time, during the Depression, the Roseville-Sparks district was virtually an all-Mallet operation. With traffic increases, however, a few Consolidations were once again placed at Colfax in helper service. During July 1941, their numbers were increased to five. By late August of that year seven Consolidations were being used in helper service at Colfax and the roundhouse force was doubled.

Colfax and Truckee helpers were preferred "old head" jobs. Most of the time, the Colfax helpers were placed on the point and cut at Emigrant Gap. Once cut, the helper returned to Colfax, making a total trip of 58 miles. A "basic day" of 100 miles was allowed each trip, but frequently a crew would help two trains or "double" for another 100-mile day in one shift. On occasion, when conditions dictated, the Colfax helper would work through to Norden accompanied by the grumblings of her crew. On such trips, longer hours were put in for their basic day and more than 98 miles was actually logged, preventing the crew from being used again that shift.

Truckee helpers operated under similar circumstances. The round trip to Norden and back amounted to but 29 miles and doubling or tripling of the crew was a common practice. The custom was to cut the Truckee helper, frequently a Mallet, in ahead of the caboose. Virtually all westward freight trains received a helper but, on occasion, if tonnage warranted, westbound trains could make it to Norden unassisted. In order to speed up cutting in the helper, the practice was to cut the caboose on the fly and stop it short of the crossover, just as the train rolled into the yards at Truckee. With no radio communication on board the caboose, there was no way to warn a crew whether or not a helper would be added. A wise conductor would judge this by studying the tonnage of his train. But in more than one instance, the headend got the "highball" at Truckee and would reach Norden before they realized that the caboose was left standing in the Truckee yards. On these embarrassing occasions, an extra engine had to be called to haul the forsaken caboose up to the Summit.

Roseville freight helpers had the long mileage job. Mallets, used almost exclusively in this service, logged over 167 miles each round trip between Roseville and Norden. No freight helper crews were based at Roseville. The first out-man on the extra board worked through to Sparks and the second out-man worked the helper, as did the third man, if a second helper was called. The SP also maintained a separate passenger helper pool. At Roseville, all passenger trains, except the streamliner, that came in with light motive power from the valley, swapped for Mountain engines in front of the depot. Mallets were used exclusively as the road engine and the versatile 4300 series 4-8-2's were used as helpers, if available. The streamliner, while retaining its diesel locomotives, frequently received a helper on the point.

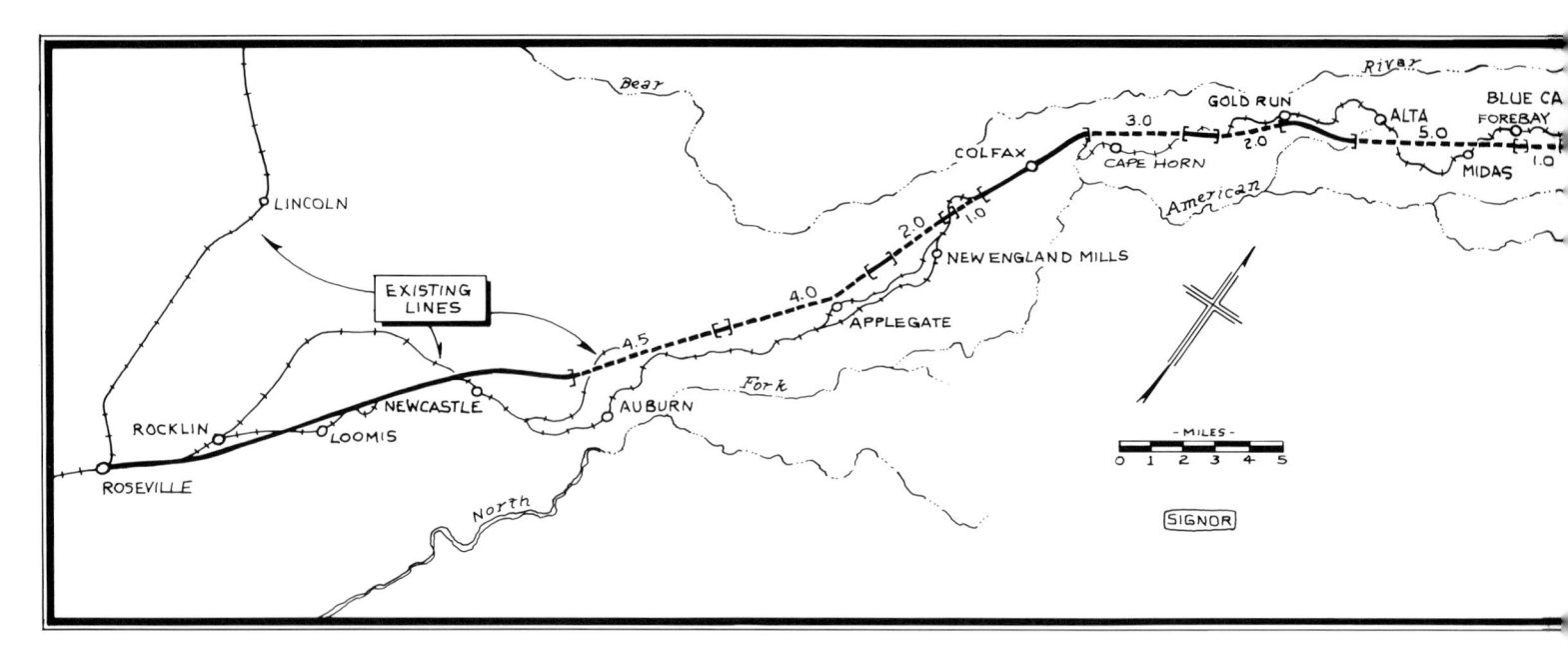

Prior to the elimination of the California Full Crew Law through the California general election of December 15, 1948, Mountain train crews were strictly regimented by the train's length. Three brakemen were mandatory on trains up to 55 cars. On trains consisting of 55 to 74 cars, four were required; 75 to 86 cars, five; over 86 cars, six men, and so on. Regularly assigned Mountain crews consisted of a minimum of three brakemen and a conductor. Extra men filled fourth, fifth and sixth man positions out of Roseville and, upon arrival at Sparks, were called in turn off their own extra board for the return west. Empty refrigerator car blocks, moving west out of Sparks, frequently were long enough to require a seventh man. After December 1948, however, four brakemen per train became the norm. Later, a fifth "swing man" was assigned between Roseville and Truckee.

In freight service, the trip over the hill frequently required the full 16 hours allowed under the law, although 11 or 12 hours was the norm. The time consumed making the uphill run, over the Mountain, was used to clear superior trains at various sidings along the line, adding helpers at Colfax or Truckee, taking water and eating. Eastbound crews took their "beans" at Emigrant Gap, the approximate midway point, after cutting their helpers and taking water. The head end crew ate at the upper cook shack, while the rear crew found sustenance at the lower cook house. In order to free the Emigrant Gap yards for snow service equipment, additional eating facilities for eastward trains were maintained, during the winter season, at Knapp-Blue Cañon. After cutting their helpers, the westbound crews, as previously stated, ate at Norden with the rear end crew getting a ride on the helper down to the cook house located near the turntable. For a time, an additional cook house was maintained at Troy for westbound traffic.

At Norden, all retainers were turned up for the run down to Truckee on the east slope, and also turned down here for the run down the west slope to Loomis. Setting and releasing retainers consumed large amounts of time, as did the frequent stops for cooling wheels and car inspection, but were required by special instructions. It was said that the brakemen rode east to Sparks but, due to the many inspections required on the westbound run, he walked west. A ten minute walking inspection was required at Norden, on the No. 2 track, and also at Stanford and Truckee, on an eastbound run. But westbound, on the descent to Roseville, trains were required to make at least nine separate walking inspections. These inspections occurred at Summit, on the No. 1 track, at Troy, Crystal Lake (during stormy weather) or at Yuba Pass, Emigrant Gap, Knapp, Midas, Gold Run, Colfax and Flint. Brakemen still rode out between Truckee and Loomis. From the head end, tail houses were cut into the train's air system every 20th car, providing an emergency function.

From May 1st through November 1st, locomotives operating west from Norden to Loomis and east from Norden to Truckee, were required to use tie sprinklers on all freight trains and light engines. Also, trains handling empty express refrigerator cars had the additional requirement of taking on water at Blue Cañon, so that the sprinklers could work at full efficiency.

It seems extraordinary that trains could comply with all the requirements and procedures of the

THE KAISER PLAN
OCTOBER 1945

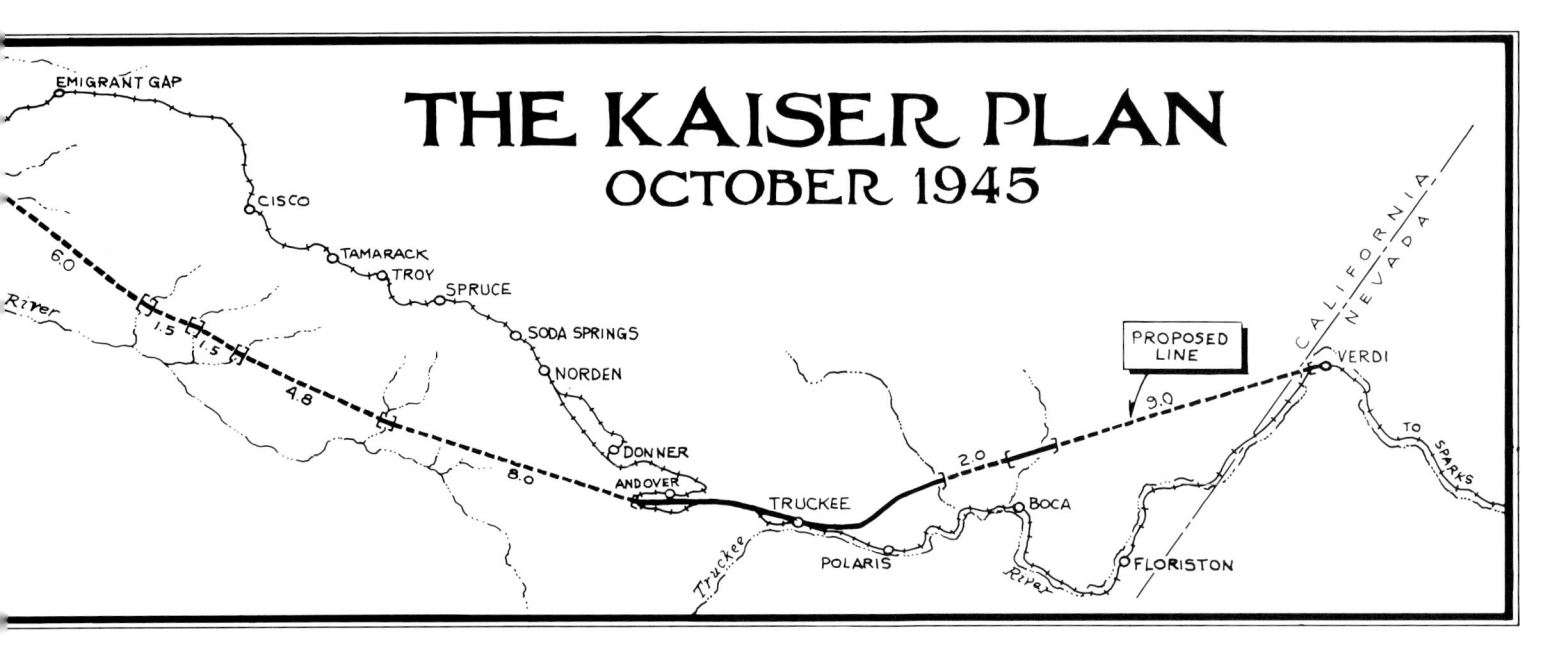

period, especially in the face of a heavy wartime traffic load, and still get over the Sierra divide as quickly as they did. So heavy was the business on the Mountain at this time, that the Kaiser Company was led, on their own initiative, to develop a plan for realigning and electrifying what they determined to be the one great bottleneck on the "Overland Route" — the Roseville-Sparks Mountain District.

Kaiser released, to the media, the details of their proposed relocation of the Donner grade on October 8, 1945. They offered a bold scheme and backed it up by pointing out that the Sierra line was at that time operating under a tremendous strain, and with all probability, postwar traffic would exceed the capacity of the railroad as the West continued to grow. The proposal called for the elimination of all steep grades, as much as possible, and all but 1,600 degrees of curvature. This also included a series of tunnels, with an aggregate length of 57.3 miles, to be drilled through the backbone of the Sierra. The longest tunnel on the double-track line was to be a staggering nine miles in length. The summit elevation was to be reduced to 6,200 feet, with the maximum grade held to 1.9 percent and a total mileage between Roseville and Sparks, cut from 138 to 108 miles. Because of the nature of the work, electrification of the entire district was recommended. It was pointed out that the Central Valley Project and Army Flood Contol dams, then under construction, would provide cheap and plentiful sources of power.

The proposed Kaiser line would be laid out almost entirely apart from the existing grade and, while under construction, would not interfere materially with traffic. Of the existing railroad, only the Verdi-Sparks section was to be retained and utilized. The shorter length of the Kaiser line would provide easier grades and reduced curvature which in turn would allow for much higher operating speeds. It was estimated that the *City of San Francisco,* then operating over the Mountain in four hours 15 minutes, could be expected to cover the distance on the new line in about two hours. Freight trains could save as much as two hours running time.

At the bottom of all this rosy speculation was the price tag. A project of this size entered into the realm of "public works" and, although unspoken, it is almost certain that Kaiser smelled government money in the wind. The tunnels, new track, signal systems, right-of-way, grading and culvert work alone was estimated at a staggering $95.4 million. The addition of electrification, 20 three-unit electric locomotives and other fees and contingencies, including interest during construction brought the grand total to $125 million, more than one million dollars per mile. At best, it was estimated that it would take 27 years to amortize the cost of the venture, and that was if traffic held up according to Kaiser's projections.

Donner Pass, in its present form, was good enough for the SP and the government money was never offered. Consequently, the Kaiser plan never received much serious attention, save for a few articles in the trade press of the period.

In the immediate postwar years, "Overland Route" freight traffic was to experience a sharp decline. Traffic did not exceed the capacity of the railroad as the Kaiser plan had proposed. Cutbacks in military spending was one factor, and the operating policies of the Southern Pacific was another. While efficiency was the order of the day during the war years, and the most expedient routing of traffic was utilized, things changed on the SP in the postwar era. The road returned to its long standing and more lucrative traffic routing policy of favoring the Sunset-Golden State routes which kept the freight on Southern Pacific rails for a greater percentage of the haul.

Military passenger specials declined after the war, but the "Overland Route" regularly scheduled passenger trains increased. By the fall of 1947, the automobile had chipped away at the intrastate passenger business. But there were still ten transcontinental passenger trains regularly picking away the miles on the Donner grade. The *Mail,* having for many years operated as Nos. 9 and 10, briefly ran as Nos. 25 and 26 (the former *Pacific Limited*) before settling down as Nos. 21 and 22 on October 19, 1947. The same day, the *Gold Coast,* a legendary name unused since the Depression, was reestablished using the schedule Nos. 23 and 24. The *Challenger,* having filled these schedules for the previous season, was dropped at this time. A new train, handling baggage and express for Colfax and Truckee and simply known as the "passengers," was placed on the timecard in November 1946 holding down schedule Nos. 25 and 26. Numbers 27 and 28 continued as the *S.F. Overland.*

The *City of San Francisco* had long since displaced the *Overland* as the crack train on the Chicago-San Francisco run. Being the premier train on the route during the postwar years brought little glory, as the traveling public became increasingly infatuated with the automobile and airplane. Holding down schedule runs Nos. 101 and 102, the *City's* frequency had been increased to tri-weekly in each direction as wartime restrictions on non-military travel began to ease up during the fall of 1946. Following the delivery of more new equipment, the trains began to operate daily in each direction over the Mountain commencing September 1, 1947. It was the *City of San Francisco* and its 226 passengers, held in the icy grip of winter, however, that was suddenly thrust into the national consciousness a few years later as the modern Southern Pacific came head to head with an old nemesis in the high Sierra-King Snow.

Snow and the expense of removing or protecting against it had been on the minds of Southern Pacific's operating people since the early days. The road's proven and principal line of defense against the elements had for years been the sheds. These great wooden structures were not only costly to erect, but also extremely expensive to maintain and protect. Many officials felt that the rotary snowplows, backed by a fleet of flangers (and later on spreaders), could handle just about any contingency. No serious interruptions to service had been encountered on the district since the deployment of the rotaries during the 1890's and with the double-tracking in the mid-twenties, shed mileage had been cautiously reduced by 6.4 miles. Studies were made at this time to determine what could be done with them as far as fire protection, removal or conversion to more fire resistant materials.

Southern Pacific examined similar mountain operations in the United States and Canada. First to be examined was Rogers Pass, located in the Selkirks at Glacier, British Columbia. Here, at an elevation of 3,278 feet, the Canadian Pacific encountered a heavy wet snowfall amounting to a yearly average of 396 inches. At the time (1926), the Canadian Pacific found it necessary to maintain 3,624 feet of wooden shed in the area. In the Cascade Mountains of western Washington state, the Great Northern maintained 7.5 miles of wooden and 2,500 feet of concrete shed. At the Cascade Tunnel, at an elevation of 3,381 feet, the Great Northern was experiencing an average of 453 inches of wet heavy snowfall a year.

In the Canadian Pacific and Great Northern operations, neither encountered a particularly long dry season, nor did they have problems with fire, though, the GN had fitted their wooden sheds with a rooftop sprinkler system. As a preventative measure, nearly a half mile of continuous concrete shed had been built immediately following a disastrous avalanche that occurred during the spring of 1910 at Tye, Washington, which carried a passenger train down into the valley. Nevertheless, no plans were being made to increase the concrete footage and, in fact, both roads were moving to reduce shed mileage.

The results of the investigation confirmed SP's plans to gradually reduce snowshed mileage. Some experimental pre-cast concrete sheds had been placed in the new yards at Norden, but no ambitious plans for concreting existing wooden sheds were developed at this time. Instead, with an increased reliance being placed on mechanical snow removal methods, the sheds began to come down in earnest. Those structures not slated for removal were fitted with sprinklers. By March 1940, 8.11 miles of shed remained. As the Sacramento Division braced for the winter of 1951-52 only 5.2 miles of shed were left intact.

The first section of train No. 32, a seldom remarked local mail and express train, arrives at Sparks in 1947. — GUY L. DUNSCOMB (RIGHT) On a July morning at Reno in 1941, the perishable season was in full swing and the action was hot and heavy. No sooner had the rumble of the long westbound reefer drag Extra 4203 West subsided, when AC No. 4180 rolled into town (BELOW) with an eastbound fruit block. — BOTH A.C. PHELPS

Recently delivered AC-6 class cab-forward No. 4144 paused for the camera (LEFT) on a bleak day in January 1931 at Verdi, Nevada. With the AC-6 class in service, the weight of eastbound reefer trains jumped from 3,500 to 4,500 tons. (BELOW) Another cab-forward, No. 4100, the first such engine to be built since the initial deliveries were completed in 1913, wheels a long westbound stock extra into Floriston in the 1930's. The No. 4100 and those that followed, incorporated vast improvements in capacity and design, thus relegating the older 4000 series Mallets to less demanding districts. — BOTH DR. ROBERT J. CHURCH COLLECTION

In 1940, a ten-car *Pacific Limited* winds its way down the Truckee River Canyon near Hinton, 11 miles west of the California-Nevada state line. — DENNIS BEEGHLY COLLECTION

An SP track walker sweeps snow and ice from the points of a switch in the Truckee yards in November 1940. Even with heavy snow removal machinery available at all times, many tasks still had to be done by hand. — SOUTHERN PACIFIC COLLECTION

A Southern Pacific "Snowball Special" prepares to depart Truckee in January 1938. These trains operated throughout the 1930's for the benefit of winter sports enthusiasts, making their last runs during the season of 1940-41. (RIGHT) Truckee, buried under a mantle of snow, may have been a Mecca for tourists, but moving the trains under such severe weather conditions presented many hardships for railroaders. The thermometer registered a bone-chilling seven below zero as a helper, under a canopy of steam, shoved a westbound tonnage train out of Truckee. — BOTH A.C. PHELPS

In the three views below, crews work to open the Tahoe Branch near Deer Park following the epic storms of early 1938. — ALL ALAN ASKE COLLECTION

Train No. 26 pauses at Truckee on May 7, 1954, two days before its discontinuance. (LEFT) By the summer of 1939, the roof of Truckee's celebrated circular roundhouse was being removed. — GUY L. DUNSCOMB COLLECTION (BELOW) Navy landing craft, destined for the South Pacific, rolls through Truckee during the busy war year of 1943. Note the hooded switch lamps. — SOUTHERN PACIFIC COLLECTION

Extra 4282 West charges out of Truckee in the summer of 1940. — J.F. OREM (RIGHT) A Truckee helper, cut in immediately ahead of the caboose, shoves hard against a westbound train as it clatters past the depot. — DONALD DUKE COLLECTION (BELOW) Freshly shopped AC No. 4219 pauses between helper trips at Truckee in 1940. — R.B. TREXLER, ALAN ASKE COLLECTION

An eastbound perishable block, at the left, slows down to make a meet with train No. 27 (BELOW) west of Truckee in February 1952. In the years 1949 through 1953 legions of diesels were assigned to the Sierra run. — ALL SOUTHERN PACIFIC COLLECTION

In February 1950, west of Truckee, Consolidations were still holding down flanger assignments. — W.C. WHITTAKER

At Stanford curve, the action is hot, but its a cold winter day in 1943 as troop sleepers roll east on the No. 2 track. (RIGHT) Presently, a westbound extra "Main Train" charges uphill past the caboose of an eastbound manifest. During World War II, the 780-mile SP leg of the strategic "Overland Route" handled the greatest traffic density in its history. In 1944, gross tons handled on the Mountain was triple that amount of 1929, which had previously been the greatest year in the history of the Company. — ALL SOUTHERN PACIFIC COLLECTION

With placid Donner Lake far below, westbound tonnage snakes upgrade near Eder. The cab-forward helper, added at Truckee, will cut out at Norden. — SOUTHERN PACIFIC, DR. ROBERT J. CHURCH COLLECTION

Newcomer Baldwin AS616 No. 5235 nears Andover, following a helper assignment to Norden, in the summer of 1951. Enginemen referred to these units as "Belly Robbers" because their three-axle trucks had center idlers which not only reduced the weight on drivers, but also the engineer's pay. — DENNIS BEEGHLY COLLECTION

Donner Peak towers over the snowsheds and tunnels on the No. 1 track just east of Summit. — ALAN ASKE COLLECTION

On a late summer afternoon in the 1950's, train No. 28, the *S.F. Overland,* makes its way east near the old station of Eder. — SOUTHERN PACIFIC, DENNIS BEEGHLY COLLECTION

In the winter of 1938, operator O. Rife manipulates the original 48-lever Norden interlocking machine, as the *Pacific Limited* (LEFT) approaches the complex from the west. In later years, the limits of the Norden interlocking were extended to embrace some 36 miles of railroad between Truckee and Emigrant Gap. — BOTH SOUTHERN PACIFIC COLLECTION

For a number of years, an elaborate fire alarm system was maintained within the snowshed district on the Donner grade. In the event of an emergency, alarms out along the line (ABOVE) were actuated by track walkers or passing crews and recorded on a device called the "Gerry Machine" (RIGHT) which was located in the Norden telegraph office. The machine got its name during World War I, when sentries used the system (then located at Summit) during their rounds, to guard against German saboteurs.
— SOUTHERN PACIFIC COLLECTION

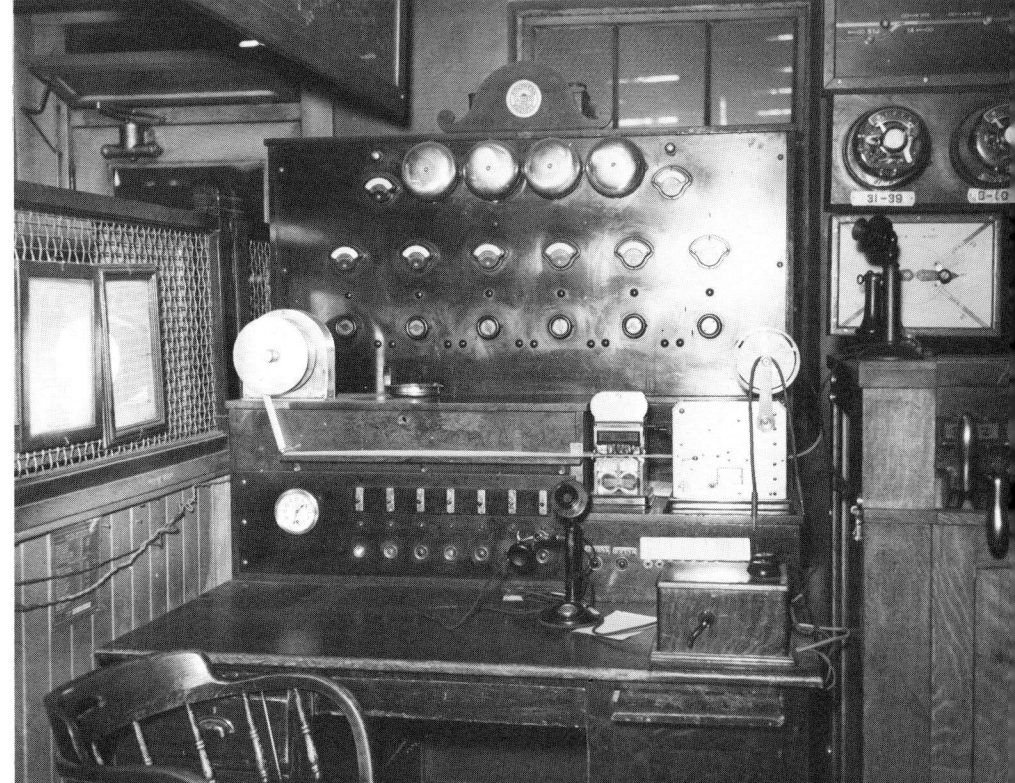

When the alarm sounded, the fire train closest to the blaze was called into play. In later years, two of these unique trains — one at Emigrant Gap, and the other at Norden — were kept hot and a crew was on duty 24 hours a day during the dry season. This fire train, under steam, hisses quietly on its spur in the Norden sheds about 1940. — R.B. TREXLER, ALAN ASKE COLLECTION

171

The Norden fire train is hauled out of the sheds and its gear inspected (RIGHT) and tested. While this was an exciting and dangerous job at times, crews assigned to the train spent a large portion of their time playing Pinochle or Loo, especially in later years with the cutback in shed mileage and the advent of the diesel. — BOTH JAMES H. HARRISON COLLECTION

Once a week the Norden fire train was run down to Soda Springs and back just to keep the rust off. — R.B. TREXLER, ALAN ASKE COLLECTION

The Norden fire train powered by T-8 class Ten-Wheeler No. 2181 swings into action on a brush fire somewhere on the west slope in the early 1930's. — JAMES H. HARRISON COLLECTION
(RIGHT) The fire train races uphill two miles west of Gold Run on June 28, 1955. The train is making its first run from Roseville to Norden at the beginning of the fire season. That fall, with its services no longer needed, the little train was retired. But the engine still survives, and it is on display at the Placer County fairgrounds in Roseville. — BRUCE BLACK, GUY L. DUNSCOMB COLLECTION

The switch is thrown and AC No. 4239 prepares to cut away and hand over the seventh section of train No. 87, the *Challenger,* to the much lighter engine, Pacific type No. 2431, waiting in the wings. (LEFT) Later, the train leaves for Oakland with its load of military furloughees in March 1946. — GUY L. DUNSCOMB COLLECTION

For years the custom was to swap Mountain power, usually the big AC's for the lighter valley power. This was done on the tracks adjacent to the Roseville depot. (LEFT) Train No. 27 receives a stripped down 4400 on May 13, 1950. — JAMES H. HARRISON COLLECTION (ABOVE) By October 1955, the train was running through with brilliantly colored ALCO PA diesels. — ALAN ASKE

Train No. 18, Western Pacific's *California Zephyr*, running as Extra 805 East, departs Roseville for the Sierra in January 1953. (LEFT) "Main Train" Extra 920 East follows closely behind. Slides in the Feather River Canyon necessitated the detours and in each case SP power was on the point to actuate the Automatic Train Stop. (BELOW) The busy auto subway area of the Roseville yards, has changed little from this October 1954 view. — ALL ALAN ASKE

Extra 4334 East, heavily ladened with produce from California's Salinas Valley, pulls into ice deck track No. P4 at Roseville during the summer of 1947. PFE crews swung into action replenishing the ice bunkers on the 100-car train. In the late summer, at the height of the season, six to eight perishable blocks were moved through the facility every day, providing employment for nearly 500 men. — ALL SOUTHERN PACIFIC, R.E. BUIKE COLLECTION

Soon the reefers were iced and the Mallet helpers were coupled up against the 5,000 ton train in order to start it rolling out of the yard. (RIGHT) As the caboose clattered over the switches opposite the Roseville depot, the highball was given and a run was made over the Sierra grade. — BOTH SOUTHERN PACIFIC, R.E. BUIKE COLLECTION

On the first of July, near the outskirts of Roseville, in one of the truly great action photos of Sierra railroading, AC helpers roared around the curve at Enwood with another eastbound fruit block. The long hot summer of 1955 lay ahead and the Mallets were living on borrowed time. (LEFT) Up front, a five unit diesel powered this train all the way through to Ogden.
— BOTH ALAN ASKE

As the caboose markers trailed off towards the mountains, the helpers of Extra 6277 East broke into the sharp syncopated exhaust that characterized the cab-forwards. These engines, perhaps more than any other within living memory, presented the classic image of Southern Pacific steam motive power. — ALAN ASKE

A shortage of crews and cabooses at Sparks prompted this cab hop at Rocklin on May 10, 1949. — A.C. PHELPS (BELOW) In July 1951, four-unit diesel No. 6276 raced up the 1.5 percent grade at Lincoln Ave. Penryn, with eastbound tonnage. Crews sometimes referred to this stretch of track, completed in 1909, as the "Harriman." — ALAN ASKE

Train No. 49, the *49er,* slips down through Newcastle on a spring morning in 1940. This all-Pullman extra-fare flyer operated five times a month between Chicago and the west coast as a counterpart to the *City of San Francisco.* (RIGHT) On the eastbound run, patrons enjoy the amenities offered in the diner-lounge *California Republic* on the rear of No. 48 as it winds up through the Sierra foothills. The short-lived train, inaugurated on July 11, 1937, was discontinued on July 23, 1941 after the second set of the 17-car *City of San Francisco* equipment was delivered. — BOTH JAMES H. HARRISON COLLECTION

181

A hike along the No. 1 track between Newcastle and Penryn, on a warm July morning in 1949, found train No. 101 snaking into view behind E2 No. 6011, about an hour off the advertized. (LEFT) Following closely behind were assembled light engines Nos. 4186, 4231 and 2378, returning from a long night on the Hill. — BOTH A.C. PHELPS

SP Extra 4155 East, a 900-ton 20-car express extra of early season high-value produce, raced up the No. 2 track near Auburn, on July 27, 1952. Normally a single AC could handle the tonnage, but a two-unit diesel insures that the train would make the time. — A.C. PHELPS

Train No. 48 passes the boarded up East Applegate depot on November 5, 1940. — A.C. PHELPS (BELOW) Train No. 28, the famed *San Francisco Overland,* drawn by recently delivered AC No. 4249, rolls through the Sierra foothills just west of Colfax in 1943. — SOUTHERN PACIFIC COLLECTION

Southern Pacific train No. 289, the *Sierra*, makes a stop at Colfax on March 21, 1941. Within a year, the train was discontinued in order to ease traffic congestion caused by the United States entry into World War II. — A.C. PHELPS

By July 1941, as war related traffic increased, five helpers were placed at Colfax; by August seven helpers were in town. (RIGHT) Six helpers are evident in this view taken from the bluffs to the west in 1946. — MANUEL BRAVO (BELOW) Three sturdy Consolidations grace the ready tracks at Colfax in the spring of 1940. — J.F. OREM

An eastbound fruit block, with Colfax helper No. 2579 on the point, eases past the depot on its way out of town in 1940. Ahead lay a hard 29-mile pull to Emigrant Gap where the Consolidation would be turned and sent back down the Mountain light. — J.F. OREM (LEFT) Extra 4214 East sweeps through Colfax on August 2, 1950. (LOWER) Cut deep in the same train is a four-unit diesel urging the manifest onward. The advent of the diesel doomed Colfax helper operations which were shut down for good in December 1949. — BOTH A.C. PHELPS

185

On March 27, 1941, the first section of the *Pacific Limited* slips downgrade near Cape Horn. — A.C. PHELPS (BELOW AND LEFT) The location is Oilville, just outside Colfax, where for years the diminutive Nevada County Narrow-Gauge Railroad maintained a turntable and a fuel transfer connection with the SP. In these two views, Extra 4154 West slows down and then comes to a complete stop as the train waits for traffic to clear at Colfax. By 1940, when these views were taken, time was running out for the narrow-gauge line. — BOTH J.F. OREM

Train No. 14, the *Pacific Limited,* negotiates the big curve at Long Ravine in April 1941. — A.C. PHELPS

Engine No. 5024 pounds upgrade near Cape Horn, entrained as the second of two helpers on an eastbound manifest. In 1953, the big three-cylindered engine was en route to the Modoc Line for testing in helper service. — A.C. PHELPS
(RIGHT) Train No. 22 double-headed for the Sierra run out of Roseville, thunders upgrade near Cape Horn in the summer of 1943. — SOUTHERN PACIFIC COLLECTION

The upper cookhouse at Blue Cañon, established during World War II to relieve the pressure off the Emigrant Gap facility, was about to be dismantled in this October 1945 view. — SOUTHERN PACIFIC COLLECTION

A westbound freight train snakes through the top end of Emigrant Gap in 1953. Company buildings line the tracks at this location which had been the scene of great activity. The large building at the lower left was the Emigrant Gap Hotel. The Tahoe Sugarpine Company planning mill, at the right, still required a spur. — ALAN ASKE COLLECTION (RIGHT) The last vestige of snowsheds, in the Emigrant Gap area, protected an 80-foot turntable and a strategic crossover near the telegraph office. — R.B. TREXLER, DENNIS BEEGHLY COLLECTION

At the west end of the deep snow belt, plows and other equipment were required to turn on the turntable at Emigrant Gap. — SOUTHERN PACIFIC COLLECTION (RIGHT) Delays were experienced here in turning the plows, and it was also a critical factor in the horrible blizzards of 1952. In fact, the storms had barely subsided when work was begun on a "balloon" track two miles to the west, near the old station of Fulda. — S.R. BUSH (BELOW) The "balloon" and the advent of diesel power, like No. 6272 on this fruit block, creeping up the center siding at the Gap in July 1952, was the cause for dismantling the turntable about 1955. — W.C. WHITTAKER

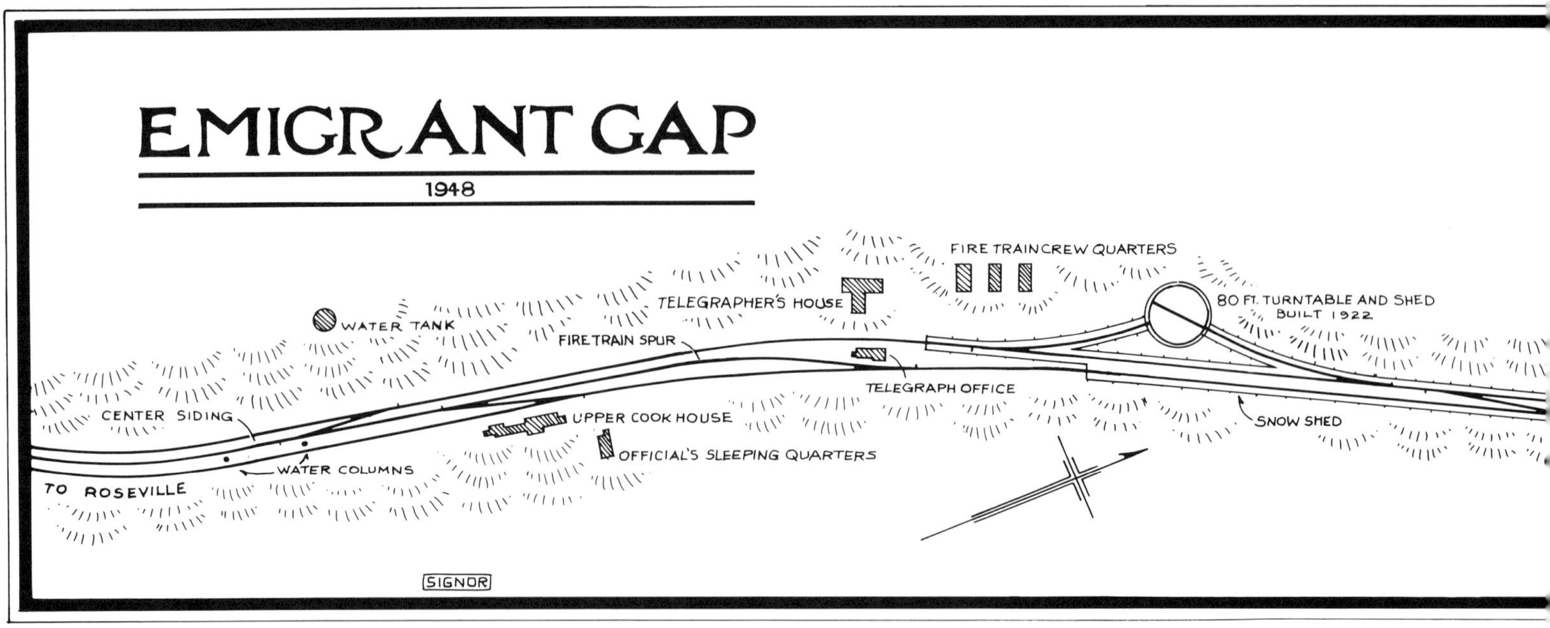
EMIGRANT GAP
1948
FIRE TRAINCREW QUARTERS
TELEGRAPHER'S HOUSE
80 FT. TURNTABLE AND SHED
BUILT 1922
WATER TANK
FIRETRAIN SPUR
TELEGRAPH OFFICE
CENTER SIDING
UPPER COOK HOUSE
SNOW SHED
OFFICIAL'S SLEEPING QUARTERS
WATER COLUMNS
TO ROSEVILLE
SIGNOR

For years, a fire train (ABOVE AND RIGHT) was kept in steam on a special spur just west of the Emigrant Gap telegraph office. By 1950, the train had outlived its usefullness and was pulled off. — BOTH R.B. TREXLER, DENNIS BEEGHLY COLLECTION

The Emigrant Gap station, shown in the two photographs at the right, was little more than a glorified telegraph office. Yet, day and night, the place hummed with activity, until the end of steam. — BOTH SOUTHERN PACIFIC COLLECTION

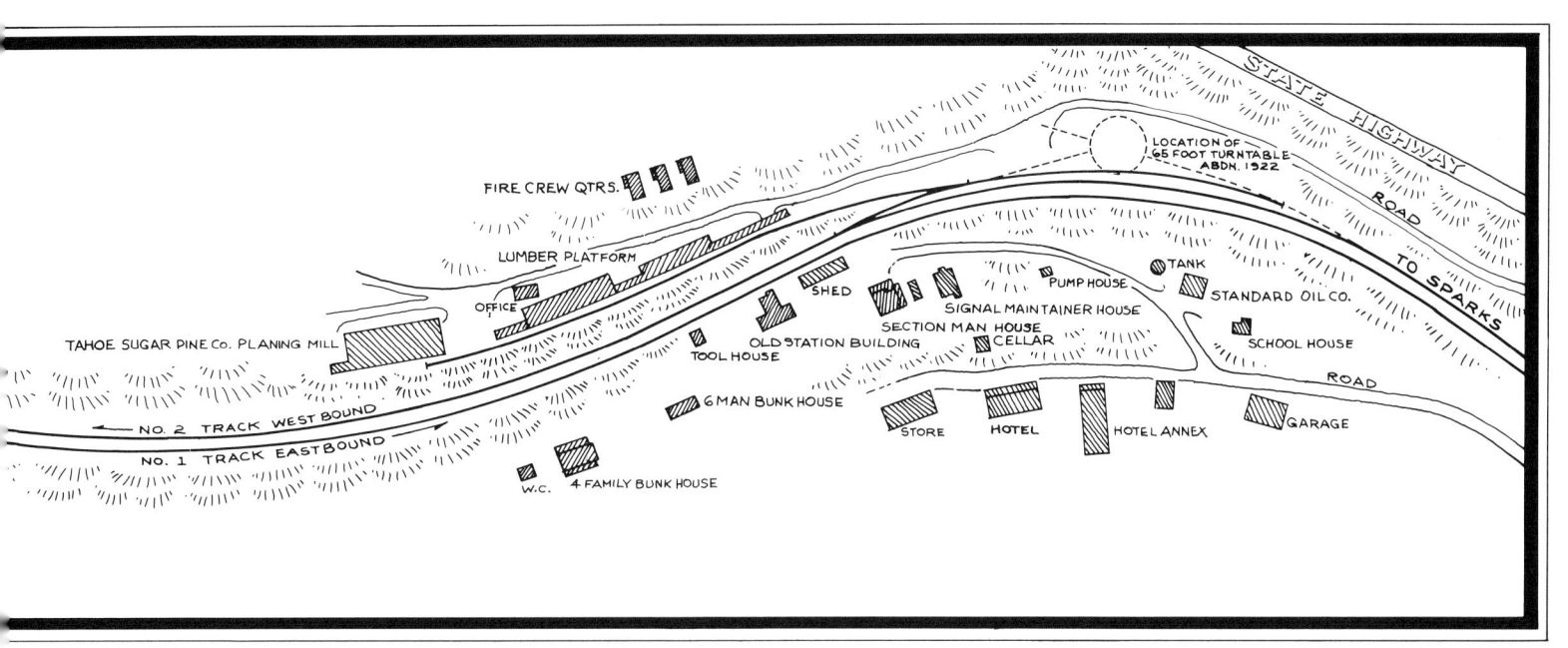

On a glorious winter day, in the hectic war year of 1943, SP lineman Gordon Campbell snapped this engaging photograph of an eastbound drag overtaking another in the Emigrant Gap yards. — BILL FISHER COLLECTION

Near Troy, empty reefers are rolling west behind No. 4158, in July 1950. — A.C. PHELPS (RIGHT) Extra 4178 West paused in the center siding at Troy to cool wheels and allow brakemen to inspect the train. Light engine No. 4258 slipped by on the westbound track. — KEN YEO (BELOW) Train No. 27 passes Crystal Lake on its way west in the summer of 1950. In the Sierra, one AC could handle, unassisted, 14 to 16 passenger cars. — W.C. WHITTAKER

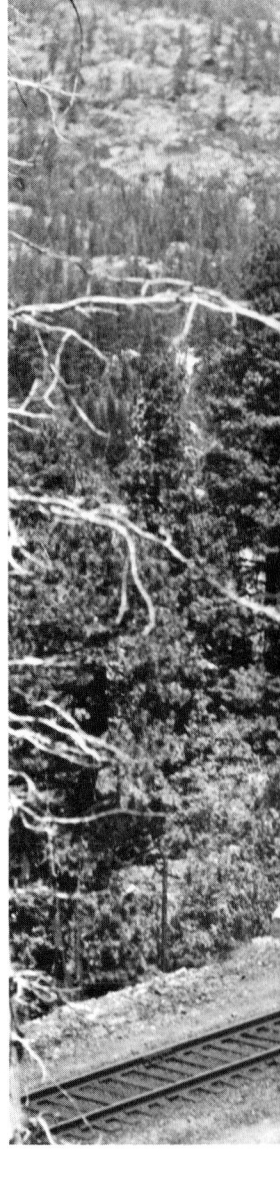

During the second half of the 1940's, more than 40 percent of SP's modern articulated fleet was assigned to the Sacramento Division. Towards the end of the decade, as diesels displaced steam throughout the system, even more cab-forwards came to the Sierra grade. (ABOVE) Two such beasts drift downgrade near Yuba Pass in the summer of 1950. — W.C. WHITTAKER (RIGHT) More light engines drop downgrade at Spruce. In the Sierra, MT class 4300's were frequently seen on the point of passenger and express trains. — KEN YEO

A distant but unmistakable chant builds into a throaty roar as five General Motors diesels of Extra 6311 East hove into view (TOP-OPPOSITE PAGE), then sweep past a location (ABOVE) at the Lower Cascade Bridge on a grey day in 1952. — BOTH JAMES H. HARRISON COLLECTION

The headend crew of an eastbound train mugs for the camera at Yuba Pass. The combination of heavy snows and shiny new diesels proved irresistable to the company photographer. — SOUTHERN PACIFIC COLLECTION

Steam, for all practical purposes, was now history in the Sierra Nevada mountains. On February 3, 1956, train No. 27 whines down through Yuba Pass behind a trio of ALCO PA units with the assistance of a two-unit point helper. — GUY L. DUNSCOMB

195

Standing 13-feet high and 12-feet wide, a steam rotary snowplow was an impressive machine while at rest. But it created a spectacle unequaled in railroading when at work in the Sierra drifts, along with the combination of the bitter cold, the hot steam and the action of the blades. Six such machines, each with an 11-man hand-picked crew, were available. In these two scenes, rotary snowplows clear the mainline over Donner Pass at Blue Cañon (ABOVE) and Troy (LEFT) in the 1950's. — BOTH SOUTHERN PACIFIC COLLECTION

Often run in advance of the rotaries, a spreader (ABOVE) would shove snow into the path of the plow's whirrling blades. (ABOVE-LEFT) Her crew was adept at clearing obstacles by raising and lowering the spreader's wings. At full extension these wings measured some 17 feet. — BOTH DR. ROBERT J. CHURCH COLLECTION (LEFT) By the mid-1950's diesels powered the spreaders and shoved the rotaries too, but the plows themselves (LOWER-LEFT) were still gloriously steam powered. — BOTH SOUTHERN PACIFIC COLLECTION

Tucker Snowcats proved invaluable to Sierra lineman. — JAMES H. HARRISON COLLECTION

The culmination of all the snow removal work now gives the railroad a snow free passage for the trains. (ABOVE) Between storms Extra 4174 East charges upgrade along Smart Ridge just west of Yuba Pass over a railroad recently cleared by the rotaries. — DENNIS M. BEEGHLY COLLECTION

The rotary banks are six feet high in this 1941 view just west of Norden. — JAMES H. HARRISON COLLECTION

An eastbound manifest works steam between Soda Springs and Norden on the last mile of the long eastward ascent to the summit of the Sierra. — J.F. OREM (RIGHT) The barometer is dropping and a steady wind kicks up fallen snow on Donner Peak as another storm brews in the upper reaches of the Sierra. — SOUTHERN PACIFIC COLLECTION

No. 101 stranded in drifts at Yuba Pass. — SOUTHERN PACIFIC COLLECTION

The 1952 Storm

There was no reason to suspect that the upcoming season was to present any more problems than usual. In the decades following the great storms of 1889-90, it had never been found necessary to shut down the Mountain for extended periods due to a storm. This was a record to which Sacramento Division officials looked with pride. SP's operations in the high Sierra remained fluid even during the record storms of early 1938 and had since enjoyed comparatively mild winters. The previous season (1950-1951), at Norden, a scant 327 inches of snow had been deposited.

On Wednesday, January 9, 1952, at 12:01 A.M., the weather at Norden was in no way indicative of an impending storm. The barometer reading stood at 2330, which was above normal, the temperature was 28 degrees above zero, there was 118 inches of snow on the ground, skies were cloudy and a brisk southwest wind was blowing. All the previous snowfalls had been cleaned up and the railroad was in excellent condition. No cause for apprehension was seen in the conditions that existed as Wednesday faded into Thursday.

However, things had changed by 9:00 P.M., Thursday evening. The barometer had dropped to 2308, four inches of new snow had fallen and it continued to do so. Accordingly, tonnage per freight train was reduced and a rotary and two flangers were placed in service between Truckee and Emigrant Gap. Another flanger began working between Truckee and Gold Run. Sacramento Division officials were routinely dispatched to Norden to direct snow removal operations.

At 12:01 A.M. Friday, January 11, 1952, Norden reported that a brisk west wind was causing snow to drift. A "cleanup squad" consisting of a flanger for flagging, a rotary and a spreader, was immediately ordered because the cores (the mound of snow between the main tracks) and rotary banks had begun to fill up and it was the height of the cores that was causing concern. During the day, the barometer continued to fall, reading 2286 at 6:00 P.M. Thirty inches of new snow had now fallen, making for a total of 150 inches packed on the ground.

By Saturday morning, January 12th, it was evident that the storm had reached serious proportions. While the low areas were enduring soaking rains and gale-like winds (Dry Creek in Roseville was overflowing its banks), in the mountains, a hard snow continued to fall steadily throughout the day. Various slides of a minor nature began to occur along Smart Ridge. At 8:15 A.M., a slide of five or six feet deep and 250 feet long came down near Floriston, blocking train No. 27.

At 10:18 A.M., on the 12th, train No. 101 departed from Norden, running several hours late due to the storm conditions. At milepost 182, approximately two miles west of Troy, the streamliner, consisting of cab-forward No. 4205 acting as a point helper, ALCO passenger diesels Nos. 6012, 5912 and 6011 and the train, struck a tremendous slide which extended along the tracks in excess of one-quarter mile. Both the AC, No. 4205 and diesel No. 6012 were completely buried, with the Mallet taking the brunt of the impact. All the windows were pushed inward and broken and the cab was tightly packed with snow. Her crew was badly bruised and cut by broken glass.

While the power was stuck fast in the slide, the bulk of the train was comparatively unaffected. No time was lost in pulling it free and dragging it back to Norden. It took the better part of the day, however, to dig out the locomotives. Early in the evening the ALCO passenger engines were freed. Then, with the assistance of AC's Nos. 4173 and 4155 coupled back to back, the diesels were dragged back in the direction of Norden leaving the cab-forward No. 4205 to the elements. However, at 7:30 P.M., while moving over the west switch at Troy, the trailing AC, No. 4155, derailed, taking all three diesels with it. The remaining AC, No. 4173, was then cutaway and proceeded to Norden to relieve the engine crew of train No. 101 which by now had been on duty for over 20 hours.

By 9:30 P.M. the Sparks relief outfit was on the scene of the Troy derailment. A gang of 30 Bridge & Building department men endeavored to shovel snow from around the units, but it was a losing battle as the storm continued to increase in intensity during the night. Fully nine feet of the stuff covered the siding and surrounding country. Around 7:30 A.M. the following morning a rotary arrived at Troy and proceeded to clean out the track behind the Sparks relief outfit, as well as the passing track. Unfortunately, before the operation was completed, a fuel line broke on the rotary and it was necessary to send it back to Norden before it ran out of fuel, delaying cleanup efforts even more.

Thus, on the fateful morning of Sunday, January 13, 1952, things were not going well on the Mountain Subdivision. The wind was blowing very hard and snow was accumulating at the rate of an inch an hour. During the night, eastbound trains had been held at Colfax and westbound trains at Sparks. Every piece of snow fighting machinery available on the district was now in use. At this point, the westbound track was out of service between Norden and Crystal Lake because AC No. 4205 was still buried in a slide at milepost 182, and the derailment at the west switch at Troy was still to be cleaned up. In another incident, AC No. 4104 was on the ground at Gold Run and all telephone and telegraph wires were out.

Still, some priority trains continued to roll. Train No. 101 of the 12th, left Norden for the second time early in the morning of the 13th and arrived at Roseville without further incident. Later in the morning, at 11:23 A.M., train No. 101, of the 13th, cautiously rolled west out of the Norden sheds into the face of a raging blizzard. To get around the derailed and snowbound equipment, the *City of San Francisco* had to use the eastward main against the current of traffic, for some 15 miles down to the crossovers at Crystal Lake. Although it was tough going and visibility was next to nothing, the train made it to and through the switches at the Crystal Lake crossovers in good order. But a little ways beyond, on the westbound track between tunnel Nos. 35 and 36, the train became mired in a snow slide which was estimated to be between six and 12 feet deep. An attempt to back the streamliner, which was carrying 226 passengers and crew, failed.

The first crews to reach the stranded train were aboard rotary No. 7222, assisted by Mallet No. 4188, which were then in the process of plowing up the No. 2 (eastbound) main. Upon realizing the problem, they continued on to the crossovers at Crystal Lake and then backed down the westbound track towards the stranded train. Stopping short of the last Pullman, inquiries were made as to what course of action could be taken. Before anything could be done, however, the rotary's train line air pumps broke and with snow drifting underneath, it became totally disabled and impossible to move. Since the rotary was on the east end, AC No. 4188 was now trapped between it and the stranded train. The remaining one and one-half

On January 15th, under severe blizzard conditions, signal maintainer Jack Frye clearly illustrates the magnitude of the 1952 storms as he was photographed perched on a buried wig-wag signal at Sugar Bowl crossing. — BILL FISHER

car lengths of track between the Mallet and the train were shoveled out by hand and, cutting away from the rotary, the AC made an unsuccessful attempt to start the streamliner.

At 4:50 P.M., officials aboard westbound light engines Nos. 4220 and 4241 sized up the situation and proceeded down to Emigrant Gap where a call was put out for assistance. At length, rotary No. 7205, accompanied by AC No. 4245, arrived at Emigrant Gap from the east. While turning it on the turntable, three eastbounds; a Western Pacific detour (the Feather River Canyon had been out of service since the 11th), caboose hop X2768 East and No. 28 were let loose. Section foreman Nelson and 35 men were placed aboard the cab hop. Arriving at the streamliner, the men detrained and shoveled all night in an attempt to free the *City of San Francisco*. Presently, rotary No. 7205 and Mallet No. 4245 plowed up to the west end of train No. 101. The lead ALCOs coupler was dug

Army Weasels assemble at Midas on the 15th, from which point an unsuccessful attempt was made to reach the snowbound train. — SOUTHERN PACIFIC COLLECTION

It was during a break in the storms, when rotaries finally reached Emigrant Gap from the west on January 16th. Before the end of the day all the 226 passengers and crew of the snowbound *City* were on their way to safety. — BOTH SOUTHERN PACIFIC COLLECTION

out and coupled to, but it was still impossible to move the train. The rotary then retreated to Emigrant Gap, where a four-unit freight diesel (Nos. 6276-8276-8277-6277) was summoned from Norden to assist in moving the train.

As darkness fell, the snow was falling very hard. Wind, raging with a hurricane velocity, estimated at between 80 and 90 miles per hour, was blowing solid sheets of snow out of the canyon and onto the tracks. In the Emigrant Gap yards, where most of the sheds had been removed some years ago, five men, engaged in sweeping out a single switch, could not keep it clean. At 10:20 P.M., the Chief Dispatchers office at Sacramento was advised to cancel all passenger trains on the Mountain. Three priority westbounds, WP detour Extra 805 (the first section of WP train No. 17, the *California Zephyr),* WP detour X921 (2-17) and main train X6234 West, followed the light diesels down from Norden. Extra 6234 West made it through Emigrant Gap at 12:27 A.M. on the 14th. As it turned out, this was to be the last through train over Donner Pass for 13 days.

Departing Emigrant Gap eastbound on the westbound track, the men and officials aboard the four-unit diesel, dispatched to free the streamliner, got as far as milepost 173. Here a fresh slide, estimated to be from 20 to 30 feet deep and from 100 to 200 feet long, obscured both main tracks. The diesels then retreated back to Emigrant Gap. Once again rotary No. 7205 and AC No. 4245 plowed up to the stalled train and, in so doing, cut through many slides.

Meanwhile, two rotaries with a Mallet sandwiched in between (Nos. 7208-4284-7207) were dispatched west out of Norden about 2:00 A.M., charged with keeping the one remaining line open. While moving west on the eastward track about 300 feet west of tunnel No. 35, yet another slide came down off Smart Ridge, burying the whole affair. All efforts to free the two rotaries failed and, with the possibility of more slides occurring at any moment in the immediate vicinity, the equipment was ordered abandoned. About 6:00 A.M., however, volunteers returned to attempt to free the snowbound rotaries but then another slide came down, striking rotary No. 7208 broadside and turning it over, blocking both mainlines. Engineer Roland Raymond was crushed and rotary No. 7205 and Mallet No. 4245, used to return the men to the disabled equipment, were also completely buried.

Thus, by 6:00 A.M. January 14, 1952, both mainlines of Southern Pacific's Sierra Nevada crossing were hopelessly out of service. Despite the valiant efforts of all concerned, one man had already been killed, the Mountain was down and the lives of 226 people aboard the *City of San Francisco* were hanging in the balance, as the blizzard raged about them in the high Sierra, 89 miles east of Sacramento. At the moment, the railroad was powerless to help them and rescue by other means seemed equally remote. U.S. Highway 40 had been closed since January 11th, after an avalanche had buried a truck and trailer rig near Donner Summit, and it remained closed to through traffic until early February.

These views show the condition of the *Streamliner* on January 17th before the SP crews could free the train, but after her passengers had been safely removed. The location is milepost 177 between tunnels Nos. 35 and 36, just east of Yuba Pass in the shadow of treacherous Smart Ridge. — BOTH SOUTHERN PACIFIC COLLECTION

Rotary No. 7208 and AC No. 4245 are barely discernable in the 18-foot drifts at Yuba Pass. They were caught in a slide just west of the *Streamliner* during its rescue effort. — SOUTHERN PACIFIC COLLECTION

It was January 18th before a path was plowed up to tunnel No. 35. But even then, before the train could be reached, overturned rotary No. 7208, which had been completely buried (LEFT), had to be dug out with the aid of Caterpillar tractors (ABOVE) and moved aside (BELOW) by the Roseville hook. — ALL SOUTHERN PACIFIC COLLECTION

Crews reached the train during the evening of the 18th and through the sheer grit of an army of shovelers, along with the aid of cables and tractors, the massive ALCO PA units on the train were finally broken free of winter's icy grip, at 2:30 P.M. on the 19th. The train itself soon followed. — ALL SOUTHERN PACIFIC COLLECTION

It was January 27th before the line was returned to the dispatchers for normal operation. (ABOVE) Emigrant Gap resembled a war zone as priority mail train No. 22 slipped past ice encrusted rotaries and then worked its way east against the current of traffic (RIGHT) on the No. 2 track. — BOTH SOUTHERN PACIFIC COLLECTION (BELOW) Line crews were busy for weeks afterward, digging through drifts so deep it had buried 20 foot telephone poles. — BILL FISHER

The wire services got hold of the story and in a matter of hours the snowbound streamliner was making headlines nationwide. The newspapers published as background, the grisly details of the dietary habits and untidy end that had befallen the Donner Party, in the same vicinity in the early days. It was left to the reader to speculate as to whether history was, at that moment, repeating itself aboard the upholstered dining car *Chinatown* at milepost 177. That night, No. 101's steam generators gave out and the big Mallet behind the train took over with SP men shoveling snow into her tank to keep up steam.

Rescue efforts were frustrated at every turn. Relief trains reached Colfax at 10:00 P.M., January 14th, but the road was largely impassable from that point on up the line. Troops of the Sixth Army, under the direction of Major G.C. Cotton, loaded Weasels on flat cars and took them to the farthest point of penetration, the west switch at Midas. But once on their own, the Weasels sank hopelessly into the wet snow. State crews were also attempting to open portions of U.S. 40, but with little success. On the morning of the 15th, a more traditional approach was tried when a Truckee doctor and a dog sled team were brought to Norden aboard X6012 West. Setting out for the train about 11:30 A.M., a rendezvous was made with a Pacific Gas & Electric Company Snowcat on the highway which made it up the steep hillside to the train. While this effort brought news of the outside and also medical help, the small vehicle could be of little use in evacuating 226 people.

On the east slope, the wide-wing rotary based at Klamath Falls, Oregon, was summoned. Joining the mainline at Fernley, Nevada, the cumbersome machine reportedly knocked over signals on its way to Sparks. This rotary, however, wound up spending much of its time keeping the railroad open between Sparks and Truckee. With the highway closed, the railroad was the only means of transportation in the area and, throughout the emergency, Southern Pacific used this rotary, along with a locomotive, boxcar and caboose as a daily special supply train loaded with provisions for merchants and resorts in the area. In one case, it was used as an ambulance to speed a sick woman to a hospital in Reno.

Tensions were running high aboard the *City of San Francisco*. A break in the storm allowed a Coast Guard helicopter to get close enough to drop medical aids, supplies and food, yet no rescue was immediately in sight. In one case the anxiety was too much. The third cook bolted through the dining car galley door and ran screaming into the drifts. A party of men tracked him down and cajoled the man into returning to the train.

Despite the blockade, transcontinental traffic had to keep moving and on Tuesday, January 15th, steps were taken to initiate a great detour. Train No. 102, of the 15th, following Western Pacific's lead, operated with all light-weight equipment, except the baggage car, and made the eastbound run by way of Tracy, Tehachapi Pass, Mojave, Barstow and over the rails of the Union Pacific from that point to Ogden. In the days that followed, a number of "Overland Route" schedules were to take this circuitous route. Train Nos. 24, 26 and 28 were annulled out of San Francisco and on the 15th, only stub trains Nos. 23 and 24 operated between Sparks and Ogden. Freight traffic was divided between the Union Pacific detour and a more northerly course via Roseville, Klamath Falls and the Modoc Line to Fernley, Nevada. With signals nonexistent on a large portion of this route, the point at which no more trains could be accepted was quickly reached.

Wednesday, January 16th broke calm and clear. Rotaries, working steadily throughout the night, had reached Emigrant Gap and following close behind them were the rescue trains. With a break in the storm, highway crews were successful in hammering a path from Nyack Lodge at Emigrant Gap to a point on the highway below the stranded train. The 72-hour ordeal of the passengers and crew of train No. 101 was over, and just in the nick of time. Conditions aboard the train were deteriorating. Fuel aboard the Mallet had run out, eliminating the remaining source of steam heat. Toilets were freezing up and pipes were rupturing. It was the women and children first, wrapped with blankets and wearing pillow cases with eye-holes cut out, who were led down the steep path to the highway. Here, a fleet of hastily assembled automobiles ferried the victims back to Emigrant Gap. By 8:50 P.M., the transfer was complete and rescue train Extra 6192 West departed for lower elevations.

Officials breathed a sigh of relief as the last of the trapped passengers reached safety, but the job was by no means over. The entire district, from Blue Cañon to Truckee, had been molested for days by heavy snows and driving winds. Virtually nothing, including snow removal equipment, had moved in the area for at least 48 hours and there was a lot of snow to move. West of Norden, well packed snow never was less than eight feet on the level and in certain instances approached 22 feet in depth. The loss of four rotaries compounded the problem. It was Friday the 18th before a path was plowed to the *City of San Francisco*. Caterpillar tractors, belonging to Sacramento area contractors, did the lion's share in extricating the snowbound equipment. Rotary No. 7208 was shoved off the eastbound track early in the morning of January 19th and by 2:30 P.M., the stricken streamliner was wrested free of winter's icy grip. Snowsheds and tunnels, which had blown full of snow, were slowly dug out. Dynamite was used by both railroad and highway crews to break free of the solid ice formations. Just when things were beginning to open up, another blizzard struck on January 22nd, closing the pass down once again. It was January 27th before the Donner grade was returned to the dispatchers for normal operation.

After this, steps were taken to improve the snow removal situation. A great deal of time had been lost in turning plows and engines on the old Emigrant Gap turntable. That spring, a balloon track, much like that in use at Truckee, was authorized and quickly built about two miles west of Emigrant Gap near the site of the old station of Fulda. This provided quick turning facilities at both ends of the deep snow belt. Rotary snowplows were fitted with much larger tenders so they could plow for longer distances without having to take on fuel. Cuts were widened to provide more room to throw snow.

The great blizzard of January 1952 was one that legends are made of. While certain "authorities" and the press were blaming the unusually severe weather on everything from ozone accumulation to A-Bomb tests in Nevada, the SP wisely recognized that such weather comes with the territory, licked its wounds, and refrained from such speculation.

Diesels played major roles in the events of mid-January 1952. They were in the front lines throughout the ordeal, on the point of the stranded streamliner and later, powered the rescue train that led the trapped passengers to safety. Although the diesel locomotive was a recent innovation, their use in Sierra service had been proposed to E.H. Harriman by Rudolph Diesel as far back as the St. Louis Exhibition of 1909. The implementation of internal combustion equipment, of sorts, did occur soon after, when self-propelled McKeen cars, equipped with 200-horsepower gasoline motors, began taking assignments in Mountain District local passenger service. The bulk of these units later burned distillate fuel. The diesel-powered streamlined *City of San Francisco,* arriving in the summer of 1936, demonstrated the economies inherent in their operation but, to a railroad firmly entrenched in the steam age, the five-times-a-month passage of these early Electro-Motive units was nothing more than a novelty. During World War II, when other western roads were ordering four-unit freight diesels, the Southern Pacific was taking delivery of Mallets. Throughout World War II, 16-drivered AC's formed the backbone of Sierra service, but after VJ Day things began to take a turn.

The first large orders of SP freight diesels began to arrive on the west coast during late 1949. Delivered to the SP through El Paso, this vanguard of the future first found assignments on the Tucson, Rio Grande, Los Angeles and Salt Lake divisions. Units slated for Nevada-Utah operations were forwarded east over the Mountain. In this manner, four-unit freight diesel No. 6139, departing Roseville at 4:25 A.M. March 31, 1949, on the "Cutoff" R block No. 102, became the first to operate over the Mountain. From Roseville to Sparks, the train consisted of 79 loads of fruit, one caboose and 8,715 M's.* The trip was accomplished in eight hours 25 minutes, with 25 minutes lost at Colfax, watering helper No. 4191 and 19 minutes more cutting it out at Summit. By July, a set of diesels was moving east over the Mountain every day to assignments on the Salt Lake Division.

While diesels were not assigned directly, opera-

RATINGS OF ENGINES* — MOUNTAIN SUBDIVISION
OCTOBER 24, 1952

TYPE	CLASS	ROS-COLFAX No. 2 Track	COLFAX-SPARKS No. 2 Track ROS-COLFAX No. 1 Track	SPARKS to TRUCKEE	TRUCKEE to SUMMIT
PA (2-unit)	DP-8,9	2,750	1,650	4,075	2,150
F3 (4-unit)	DF-1,2	4,425	3,100	6,400	4,150
F7 (4-unit)	DF-3-7	5,500	3,175	7,900	4,150
AS616	DF-101-108,112	1,450	900	2,150	1,125
2-8-0	C-5,8,9,10,26-29	850	575	1,300	650
4-8-8-2	AC-4,5	2,225	1,400	3,400	1,775
4-8-8-2	AC-6-12	2,400	1,450	3,650	1,850
4-8-2	MT-1,3-5	1,075	700	1,700	925
4-8-2	MT-2	1,200	725	1,875	950
4-8-4	GS-1-2	1,125	725	1,800	975
4-8-4	GS-3-6	1,175	775	1,850	1,025
4-10-2	SP-1-3	1,625	1,025	2,525	1,325
2-10-2	F-1	1,275	825	1,875	1,050
2-10-2	F-3-5	1,375	975	2,150	1,800

*Ratings in units of tons.

tions on the Mountain began to reflect their presence elsewhere. They replaced the 4100 and 4200 series Mallets on the Tucson and Los Angeles divisions and many of these locomotives found their way to the Sierra operation. Now, three Mallets worked a train east out of Roseville where formerly two had held sway. With three Mallets on a train, the addition of a Consolidation at Colfax was entirely unnecessary and during December 1949, the helpers stationed at Colfax were removed and the roundhouse closed forever. The facilities at Truckee suffered a similar fate. Seldom seen models of steam power, which had been displaced by diesels elsewhere, worked through on their way to new assignments. The 5000 class 4-10-2's, absent from the Mountain for decades, once again pounded the rails above Emigrant Gap en route to the Modoc Line in northeastern California. The 3800 class 2-8-8-2's, conventional articulateds which were displacements from the Rio Grande Division, pursued a similar course. It was late December 1949 or early January 1950 before the Sacramento Division was assigned its first diesels.

From this point, the slow process of dieselization began in the Sierra Nevada Mountains. Much fanfare accompanied the newcomers arrival. Crews had to be trained and the capabilities and liabilities of the engines determined. Of particular interest was the dynamic brake feature which proved to be a great time and labor saving device on the long descending grades of the district. At first the diesels were used primarily as helpers with AC's on the point but it wasn't long before the situation was reversed. In the years 1949 through 1953 legions of "F" units were delivered. Those assigned to Sierra service were fitted with Automatic Train Stop and steam locomotive-type pilot plows. Gradually the "Black Widows" or "Covered Wagons," as they came to be called, began to dominate the operation. Baldwin diesel road switchers filled in as Truckee helpers and also in Mountain local service.

On the passenger side of things, American Locomotive Company delivered the first three sets of its beautiful PA series passenger diesels to the Southern Pacific during 1948. Nine more sets came in 1949. Oakland was set up as a maintenance point and these diesels began to hold down priority Shasta and Overland route schedules. In the Sierra, ALCOs were common on trains like the *City of San Francisco* and the *S.F. Overland.* Gradually the boiler-equipped F7's took over other schedules.

By the summer of 1955, the decision was reached not to run any more steam than was absolutely necessary north and east out of Roseville. Business was unusually heavy that season, however, and the big AC's were called to fill Mountain assignments anyway. On eastbounds, headed up with a four or five-unit diesel, two of the Mallets would be cut in. There was limited use of Mallets as a single engine on express specials of five to 20 cars of priority perishables, like asparagus or strawberries. Upon reaching Sparks, these trains were turned over to diesels and the AC's were dispatched back to Roseville light. The last express specials ran during late September and soon after the perishable rush itself subsided. In late October 1955, the Mallets made their last runs in Mountain helper service. This was supposed to be the end but, due to unusually heavy winter storms, AC's were used intermittently in flanger service during January 1956.

During the spring of 1956, the Southern Pacific beefed up its Tehachapi Freight Pool with 44 SD9's. This in turn freed F7's assigned there to dieselize the Modoc Line. This task was accomplished during April and May 1956. Sparks was the maintenance point for the Modoc Line and it was here that the displaced AC's congregated. In early summer, these steamers were transferred to their final resting place on the Western Division. In this manner, 17 Mallets worked light west from Sparks over a two-week period during June 1956.

It was a year and a half later that a Mallet made the final run on the hill. An excursion, the *Sierra Express,* operated for the benefit of rail enthusiasts and well wishers, was handled by Mallet No. 4274, over the weekend of November 30-December 1, 1957. The official last run of a steam locomotive on the district occurred October 19-20, 1958 when GS 4-8-4 No. 4460, along with a two-unit diesel, hauled a special from Sacramento to Sparks and return, closing the door on nearly a century of revenue steam locomotive operation in the high Sierra.

The last cab-forward to operate in the Sierra, AC No. 4274, attracts a crowd at Truckee on November 30, 1957 while en route to Sparks on a farewell excursion. — ALAN ASKE

Southern Pacific Extra 8463 East looms out of the mist at Andover on December 4, 1966. — RICHARD STEINHEIMER

4
Contemporary Operations 1956-1985

Increased efficiency has characterized the last several decades of Southern Pacific operations in the high Sierra. The end of steam brought about a number of sweeping changes. The backshops and roundhouses at Sparks were closed and the facilities changed to a fueling and sanding point only for Mountain helpers, yard and local engines. At the same time, Roseville assumed added importance as the regional diesel maintenance center for those engines used south to Bakersfield, north to Eugene and east to Ogden. Across the district, water tanks, water plugs, turntables and other landmarks of the age of steam were abandoned and removed. Even the time honored tradition of the Sierra fire train came to a close. This unique steam train was discontinued after the 1955 season.

With the coming of the diesel, vast improvements were made in running time. Delays at Sparks, due to the changeover from desert to Mountain power, were drastically reduced as the diesels began to run through. Helper operations were simplified or eliminated entirely. Water stops became a thing of the past. But the real time saver was the diesel's dynamic braking system. With dynamic brakes in operation, the time consuming practice of working retainers, the many related stops for wheel heat radiation and train inspection were gradually eliminated saving hours in over the road time. The long trip "over the hill" just didn't seem quite as long anymore.

Modifications were also made to the signal system. Between 1949 and 1954, "G" signals were set up on the eastward track between Colfax and the limits of the Norden interlocking plant. These were simply automatic block signals to which a round yellow plate with the letter G was attached. Trains encountering a "G" signal with a red aspect could continue past it at restricted speed without stopping thus saving the time and energy of restarting on the grade, reducing the risk of break-in-twos and other complications. The Norden interlocking plant itself was extended in stages to encompass over 26 miles of double-track in the deep snow belt between Truckee and Switch 9, one mile east of Emigrant Gap, allowing for even more flexibility.

The physical plant was trimmed. Between 1955 and 1965, the sidings at Newcastle, Auburn, East Applegate, Gold Run (westward), Midas, Knapp, Yuba Pass, Crystal Lake, Troy, Donner, Hinton and Verdi were retired and taken up. As the pace of the railroad quickened, the importance of wayside agencies and offices of communications in the mountains diminished, especially after the implementation of the two-way radio. The first such installations, beginning in 1952, provided radio communication between the Truckee, Norden, Emigrant Gap and Colfax stations, the Mountain dispatcher's office at Sacramento, mobile snow fighting equipment and diesel locomotives assigned to passenger trains. In succeeding years, radio coverage was expanded to all aspects of the operation. During 1952, train order offices were maintained at Truckee, Norden, Emigrant Gap, Gold Run, Colfax, Auburn and Newcastle. But steady attrition has left the office at Norden standing alone since July 1, 1978 and, as this book goes to press, there are rumors in the wind that this office may be closed and the Norden interlocking machine be moved to the Mountain dispatcher's office at Roseville. As each station closed, demolition of the structure soon followed.

Cook houses at Knapp, Blue Cañon and Troy have been closed since World War II. Those at Emigrant Gap ceased to operate after helper operations were completely dieselized. Even the Norden cook shack, once open year 'round, was affected. The right to eat was in labor agreements, but it was entirely at the discretion of the crews who were now frequently running "beans" to maintain their standing in the pool. Those men, electing to eat at Norden, were often "run around" by non eating crews which cost them time and money. It wasn't long before the Norden cook house was closed during the summer due to lack of interest. From the 15th of November through April, however, it has remained open, primarily for the convenience of the Maintenance of Way Department and crews manning snow removal equipment.

Clearances can be a problem on any mountain division, with tunnels being the primary offender.

A Caterpillar tractor lowers the floor and the approaches of summit tunnel No. 6 in the summer of 1967. — RICHARD STEINHEIMER

In the Sierra, the bulk of the tunnels were developed as a part of, or reworked in conjunction with, the double-tracking program pursued in the early decades of this century and, as such, were built to modern standards of clearance. After 1926, the only nonstandard tunnels to be found on the line occurred on the westbound track between Andover and Norden. If something didn't fit here it could usually make it through parallel tunnel No. 41. But in later years the trend was toward larger rail cars, starting with the vista domes of the early 1950's and continuing with today's jumbo reefers, woodchip gons, piggyback, auto rack and hi-cube cars, which accentuated the inadequacy of the old tunnels. Of necessity, more and more trains began to take tunnel No. 41. In the mid-sixties, with the advent of higher horsepower diesels, problems began to develop with westbound trains stalling out in the long bore- especially during the summer months. The grade peaks at very nearly the west portal of the tunnel and, with the prevailing westerly winds, heavy trains that slipped below 14 miles per hour would experience engine overheating and shut down, especially on the helpers, which would in turn cause the train to grind to a halt.

In order to make full use of the No. 1 track between Andover and Norden, tunnel Nos. 6 through 12 were the subject of an ambitious program that was designed to bring them up to current clearance standards. Work commenced on this project in mid-June of 1967 and was completed seven months later. These century old bores, enduring monuments to the skill and tenacity of the Chinese, had been, with one exception, largely untouched since the 1860's. The only modifications done were to tunnel No. 10 which was enlarged and concreted in the 1930's. Bits used in the original construction effort were still embedded in the vaulted ceiling of tunnel No. 6. This, the original Summit Tunnel, was enlarged by lowering the floor 3.5 feet. All others were enlarged by raising the ceilings. Tunnel No. 7 was daylighted with one carefully planned blast and reroofed with a concrete snowshed. This, and other snowsheds in the same area, was brought up to current standards at the same time.

The era of the wooden snowshed was drawing to a close, as more concrete sheds replaced timber construction each summer. This program has escalated in recent years, but the real commitment to concrete the sheds came after the disaster that befell Norden one crisp fall night in 1961. On the night of November 14th, an assistant track foreman left his long johns unattended drying over the cookstove, in his company cottage just south of the sheds. No one noticed when the underwear caught fire. The flames spread rapidly and by 8:00 P.M., the house itself was burning and soon the adjoining sheds were ablaze. Frozen fire hoses stifled the first attempts to quell the flames and by midnight, despite the efforts of a small army of Forest Service and county fire units, much of the complex at Norden was an inferno. An eerie orange glow, visible from as far away as Cisco and Truckee, illuminated the sky. With the old fire train long gone, three trains of water cars and 200 men were hastily assembled and rushed to the scene. It was morning before things cooled down enough to assess the damage. As the snow fell softly on smoldering embers of the last great shed fire, officials began to take stock of the situation. Fully 4,300 feet of track, shed and ties had been destroyed. The Norden interlocking office, together with all signal and communication circuits, radio equipment, several tool houses and five company houses, were ashes. Only those sections, protected by the experimental concrete work installed in 1925, were spared. The turntable also escaped major damage, but the message was painfully clear. Even as a tribunal of officials, fire marshals and other investigators was grilling the errant assistant foreman, plans were being made to rebuild Norden. In the reconstruction, all shed work was replaced with fireproof concrete and as this is written, only 3,000 feet of timber shed remains in service on the entire Mountain Division.

Despite these setbacks, the Donner grade has emerged, in the present day, as a lean and efficient artery capable of handling expeditiously vast amounts of traffic over the Sierra divide. Unfortunately, along with this streamlining of the physical plant has come an alarming decrease in the number of trains regularly using the railroad. The first to go were the passenger trains, thinned down in the postwar era due to mounting apathy of the traveling public, competing airlines and the independence of the family automobile, to today's minimal AMTRAK schedules. Of the ten regularly scheduled first-class trains operating over the Sierra in 1950, Nos. 25 and 26 were the first to be cut. Exclusively steam powered to the end, these unnamed trains were discontinued May 19, 1954. Eight months later, on January 9, 1955, the *Gold Coast,* Nos. 23 and 24, were removed from the schedules. Seven years later, on July 16, 1962, the final incarnation of the long running and prestigious *Overland Limited* succumbed. Considerably downgraded from its original deluxe status, the *S.F. Overland,* holding down schedule Nos. 27 and 28 at the last, was at 63 years the longest continually operated passenger train on the Mountain. The loss of federal postal contracts spelled doom for yet another "Overland Route" schedule, No. 21 and 22, the *Mail.* This left the *City of San Francisco* as the only surviving regular first-class train on the route. Southern Pacific, sighting mounting losses, lobbied without success for abandonment of these trains. But Nos. 101 and 102 were permitted to be cut back to tri-weekly operation after March 29, 1970. The bottom in "Overland Route" passenger service had been reached.

A ray of hope was shed on this discouraging state of affairs when the National Railroad Passenger Corporation (AMTRAK) took over most of the nation's passenger service on May 1, 1971. Since that time, conditions have improved somewhat. While only one regular passenger train continues to cover the route, the service has been upgraded. The train, renamed the *San Francisco Zephyr,* and renumbered 5 and 6, was operated daily from June 11th through September 17, 1972. The following June, daily service was again offered and the trains have continued at this frequency ever since. New *Superliner* equipment, incorporating electric heating and air conditioning, was substituted, in the spring of 1980, for the older unreliable steam heated equipment. Effective April 24, 1983, train Nos. 5 and 6 were renamed the *California Zephyr,* reflecting a new routing of the trains over the Rio Grande between Denver and Salt Lake City. Patronage has increased.

Extra and unscheduled movements have not fared as well in the postwar era. At one time, specials in many sections were operated for the benefit of such organizations as the Boy Scouts, Shriners and Elks. During the Christmas season, holiday mail and express specials rushed this priority traffic east. Troop and other military trains, once a common sight on the "Overland Route," gradually dwindled to nothing with the last movements occurring in the early years of the Vietnam conflict. The one bright spot in this gloomy picture has been those specials operated for the benefit of gamblers and pleasure seekers en route to Reno.

Reno, Nevada, widely recognized as a "den of iniquity" of the highest order, was launched on the road to notoriety in 1906, when the wife of U.S. Steel's President William Alles Cory, obtained a "quickie" divorce there. This created quite a sensation and established Reno as the divorce capitol of the world by the 1920's, a distinction the town has clung to despite vigorous challenges from Paris and Mexico City. Another milestone came in 1931, when Reno's city fathers convinced state legislators to legalize gambling. Harold Smith built the first big casino, "Harold's Club," at Reno during 1935. This was upstaged in 1937, when former bingo parlor operator, William Fisk Harrah, came to Reno and established a northern

Nevada gambling empire unparalleled until recent years. The gaming industry boomed in post World War II years and the town grew with it.

Reno came to rely heavily on California and the cities west of the mountains for a large portion of their casino business. Legendary "Harold's Club or Bust" roadside signs sprung up along every major highway in the west. During the summer months, the trek over the Sierra was generally made by automobile, but during the winter many deserted their cars for the comparative safety of the train. The *S.F. Overland,* the secondary train on the route, was frequently used. But this train was discontinued during the summer of 1962, which left a void in the scheduling, especially westbound. The remaining full-service passenger train, the *City of San Francisco,* was timecarded west out of Reno at a brisk 3:36 A.M.

The Reno Chamber of Commerce, noticing a drop in off-season patronage, considered ways to increase business and eventually took steps to organize a special coach train between Oakland and Reno to take up the slack. The special, christened the *Reno Fun Train,* was unveiled on November 6, 1964 with a scheduled Friday night departure from the San Francisco Bay area. The all-expense fee of $38.00 (plus gambling losses) included food, drinks and dancing on board the train, as well as, lodging in Reno. After unloading at Reno, the train was turned at Sparks and tied up on a yard track with a steam connection until an 11:00 A.M. Sunday morning departure. The first season, the trip was offered for eleven weekends from November 6, 1964, through May 5, 1965. Each succeeding season, the *Fun Trains* have returned. In the mid-1970's, midweek departures

Inaugurated by the SP in the fall of 1964, the *Reno Fun Train* **continues to this day under AMTRAK. In this scene, a** *Reno Fun Train* **bound for Oakland, gets underway at Truckee on January 30, 1972.** — T.O. REPP

were even offered.

From the outset, the *Reno Fun Trains* were a favored assignment among railroad crews. Unlike conventional trains, the passengers were composed entirely of adult (over 21) pleasure seekers. Liquor flowed freely aboard the cars and an air of excitement accompanied their journey. The eastward trip was nothing less than a prolonged and roaring party on wheels. On occasion, railroad special agents were stationed aboard the train to keep the peace, although some maintained they were there primarily to discourage the crew from joining in on the spirit of things. But on the return trip, after a full 24-hours of excitement in Reno, the party quieted down considerably. While a few lucky souls revelled in their winnings, the majority of the passengers were either dog tired, sick, broke, or a combination of all three.

Over the years, a sort of folklore has grown up around the train. Rumors fly and stories are told about chance encounters with attractive and unattached females on board; of high rollers and down-and-outers; of drunks making their way up through the units to instruct the engine crew in their duties. One of the most amusing stories concerns a well-upholstered older lady with several drinks under her belt. While the train paused at Reno on the westbound trip, she tottered up to the head end and cautioned the crew... "You boys drive safely now!" to which the fireman remarked, "Drive? They took the steering wheels out years ago." Well, this remark did not sit well with the woman who, joined by others, refused to board the train and it was an hour before the partiers could be cajoled back aboard. It turned out that the woman was a substantial stockholder and as a result, a big flap ensued when she called San Francisco the next day to lodge a complaint. The following morning, the superintendent called the engine crew into his office and requested that they keep such witicisms to themselves.

As of this writing, the *Reno Fun Trains* still run, but a Bay Area concern has taken charge of the operation. Friday night departures from Oakland are now limited to just a few months in the early spring. The AMTRAK schedules are now more convenient for the Reno trade and during the summer months it is common to see a few extra coaches tacked on to the rear of No. 6 which are then removed at Sparks and placed on the rear of No. 5 the next morning.

Even though passenger traffic on the Mountain experienced a steady decline in the postwar years, the parade of colorful orange reefers continued unabated over Donner Pass for some time after the varnish had been cut to a trickle. Freight traffic was, of necessity, becoming the main emphasis of Southern Pacific management. Commencing in the early spring and rising to a peak in the late summer of each year, the perishable business was, as always, the mainstay of the "Overland Route." During the season, six to eight 100-car *R Blocks* originated each day on ice deck tracks Nos. 71, 72, 73 and 74 at Roseville for movement east over the Mountain. *RFRS,* empty reefer blocks received off the UP at Ogden moved west, frequently bypassing Roseville for Salinas or points in the San Joaquin Valley. A considerable amount of meat was also handled, in addition to the fruit and vegetable business.

The perishable business was not immune to the broad reforms sweeping the railroad industry in the postwar years. Individual car capacity had increased from a scant 15 tons in 1906 to an average of 60 tons in 1955. Another significant change came with the development of the PFE mechanical refrigerator car. A diesel powered cooling plant built directly into the car allowed for more accurate temperature control. As more and more mechanicals came on line, perishable schedules were speeded up since stops for re-icing became less frequent. From the first experimental orders in 1950, the mechanical reefer fleet grew steadily. The last new ice bunker car was purchased by PFE in 1957 and, by the summer of 1965, 8,217 mechanicals, out of a fleet of 21,000, were in operation. At Roseville, some 740,000 tons of ice were produced in 1966 and ice was available in succeeding years. But after the 1972 season, the Roseville plant stood idle. This ice plant, the largest in the world, was eventually torn down in the spring of 1974.

Throughout, whether cooled by ice or mechanical means, the perishables continued to roll. But it was a seasonal business, and in the dead of winter traffic on the Mountain was light. During the early 1960's, however, this began to change. A number of new, decidedly non-perishable trains began to crop up on Mountain lineup sheets. New scheduled trains catering to fast freight forwarders, TOFC (trailer-on-flat-car) shippers, and containerized mail and express trains were created. In the vernacular of the railroad, these became known as symbol trains. Among them was the *BAX* (Bay Area Extra) eastbound and the *FMS* (Forwarder Merchandise Special) westbound. *Advance FMS* trains were regularly operated as were *FMS-RG* and *FMS-UP* trains, which reflected the originating carrier for the train at Ogden. Long standing trains *OVE* (Overland East), *OVW* (Overland West), *WCM* (West Coast Merchandise), *BCW* (Bay Cities West) and *CS* (California Special) continued to run, but the fabled *NM* (Nevada Merchandise) fell by the wayside.

New trains, dedicated to one commodity exclusively, began to make an appearance. "Unit trains" comprised entirely of coil steel, loaded in specially constructed cradle flat cars, moved west from Geneva, Utah, en route to U.S. Steel at Pittsburg, California. For a time, solid trains of low grade iron ore, originating at Wabuska, Nevada, on Southern Pacific's Mina Branch, were shipped over the Mountain to the Port of Stockton for export to Japan. Later, in the 1970's, Standard Oil required a unit train to move bulk crude oil between Utah and its Richmond, California, refinery. Solid trains of grain, perhaps the heaviest movement to occur in the Sierra, moved west for export or distribution to feedlots in California. Certainly the most lucrative unit trains to operate on the Mountain were those operated in conjunction with General Motors and Ford Motor companies.

Early in 1962, finding their modest facility in East Oakland overtaxed, General Motors placed in operation an elaborate auto and truck assembly plant complex at Warm Springs, California, on the Western Division. A huge Ford plant sprung up close by at Milpitas. While the Ford plant enjoyed connections with both Southern Pacific and Western Pacific, Warm Springs was served exclusively by SP. The plants generated a tremendous amount of traffic. Solid trains of auto parts moved west in trains like the *Advance FMS* (later *UPWSA* and *UPMIA*) along with empty auto rack cars. Empty auto parts cars moved east in *XAPs* while new autos, moving east, were included in the consist of the *BAX*. The start of a new year's production run at the plants would result in what amounted to a "parts rush" on the Mountain. This traffic swelled the number of *FMS* trains to as many as five sections a day.

Thousands of people and millions of dollars of machinery were tied up in the production effort and a continuous flow of materials was essential. On occasion, the need might arise for a critical part, without which the plant would grind to a halt. In those instances, the needed component would be rushed west in a special movement, consisting of the locomotives, one or two "hot" cars and a caboose. These "shutdown" trains were handled as expeditiously as possible. While on other districts, shutdown cars frequently moved at speeds higher than normally authorized, the severity of the Sierra grades dictated a more cautious approach. While the best they were allowed between Sparks and Roseville was column one speed (passenger), every effort was made to move them without delay.

The early 1960's were interesting times indeed. Along with the new and different trains plying Mountain District rails, came novel developments in diesel motive power. By 1958, it was apparent that there was a need for locomotives of greater capacity to supplement and eventually replace the fleets of "Covered Wagons" which had originally dieselized the railroad. In the Sierra operation it was found, as it was on other districts, that the four-unit concept was too restrictive and before long these sets were broken up and locomotive consists were built according to the power requirements of a given train. Frequently nine units were employed to boost a 5,000-ton perishable block over the divide, four on the point and five cut in.

Units developed after 1960, in addition to steadily increasing horsepower, employed new ideas in mechanical and electrical components, as well as in exterior details. Virtually all were delivered with cabs and operating controls. Although booster units were cheaper to build, they were an inconvenience in day-to-day operation. The first of the so-called "Second Generation" units were assigned to Sunset Route schedules. Of those F units not traded into the builders, most were reassigned to Roseville. At its greatest concentration, in March 1966, 340 cab and booster units were based at Roseville for service north and east, including 19 especially equipped for multiple-unit operation with ALCO passenger engines. The "Covered Wagons" were still firmly in the saddle on the Donner grade.

The General Motors stronghold on Donner Pass was suddenly threatened on November 10, 1961, when an advanced contingent of German-built diesel-hydraulic locomotives arrived at Roseville to begin tests on the Mountain. These units were as radically different from an F unit as night and day. Numbered in the 9000 series, they were built by Kraus-Maffei of Munich and employed two high-compression 12-cylinder diesel engines coupled to hydraulic transmissions to develop tractive effort. Reversing was accomplished by an air-actuated mechanism. The carbody, in principal a "Covered Wagon," reflected continental design standards and appeared grotesque by comparison. Mountain trials began immediately with a small army of officials, German mechanics and an interpreter aboard each trip. As a consequence of these tests, ratings of 1,200 tons between Colfax and Summit on the No. 2 track and 1,625 tons between Truckee and Summit on the No. 1 track were established for the German newcomers. This amounted to an increase of roughly 1.8 percent over a conventional single American built F unit.

These ratings were scoffed at by the crews who, having lost their initial curiosity over the "Krauts," had to deal with them in daily service. In the demanding 24-hour-a-day Sierra Mountain operation, these precision machines never did measure up, even after reboring the cylinders so they would accept the lower grade SP diesel oil.

Experimental Kraus-Maffei ML-4000 diesel hydraulic Nos. 9000, 9001 and 9002 use their hydro-dynamic brakes to hold back a test train on the east slope of the Sierra, three miles west of Truckee, on December 15, 1961. Resembling "covered wagons," these units reflected continental design standards and, in comparison, appeared grotesque. — ROBERT MORRIS, TRAINS MAGAZINE COLLECTION (LEFT) By July 1964, when KM hood version No. 9007 was photographed on the departure tracks at Roseville, the hydraulic's days in the Sierra were numbered. — KEN YEO

217

Domestic builder, American Locomotive Company, developed a diesel-hydraulic locomotive of their own. The SP purchased three of these locomotives which were tested in the Sierra during September 1964. It was their only appearance on the Mountain in revenue freight service. — KEN YEO

General Motors test beds the SD40 near Newcastle in the spring of 1964. These locomotives set the standard for a new generation of motive power on the Mountain. — KEN YEO

Upon arrival at Sparks, the SP turned each Krause-Maffei locomotive set for a return run, much to the horror of the German mechanics who wanted to service units after each use. With all axles universally coupled, serious wheel slip problems began to develop. There was uneasiness about the giant cardan shaft housing located under the middle of the cab. One shaft failed in heavy Mountain service east of Crystal Lake, tearing the cab up badly. Luckily it was a trailing unit and no one was aboard at the time. The consensus of opinion was, that had anyone been aboard they would have been "hamburger" for sure. Within the long tunnels and sheds encountered on the Mountain, the K-M's would starve for cool air. Then there was an ugly incident occurring in the spring of 1964, in which the No. 9021, while moving through tunnel No. 1 between Midas and Knapp, caught fire and burned.

All in all, 21 of these unusual locomotives were delivered, including three units obtained secondhand from the Denver & Rio Grande Western. Invariably, the Krause-Maffei locomotives couldn't move the tonnage they were rated for, because there were just too many problems encountered in trying to operate them on the Mountain. The simple solution was to relegate them to the San Joaquin Valley where there was little grade and no tunnels or sheds. Their remaining days were spent in valley drag service.

The American Locomotive Company developed three prototype hydraulic locomotives of their own for Southern Pacific. These were tested in the Sierra during September 1964. But ALCO's principal contribution to the Mountain freight pool was 29 six-axle Century-628 and 15 Century-630 diesel-electric road engines delivered in the years 1964 through 1966. Assigned to Roseville, all 44 came equipped with Automatic Train Stop for Sierra service. These were powerful locomotives which could outperform an F unit nearly two to one but spread over the Overland and Shasta routes their impact on the F unit fleet was minimal.

Commencing in early February 1966, the arrival of the General Motors SD40, a 3,000-horsepower, six-axle design, was the turning point in Mountain District operations. The SD40 replaced two of the older F7's in drag service. It also had twice the range with the capacity for 4,000 gallons of fuel on board. By March 1966, 40 were assigned to Roseville and by the end of the year a significant order of 79 more were on the property. These were the vanguard of a fleet of immense proportion. While the covered wagons, Krauts, and Centurys are now history, these early SD40's, now rebuilt and joined by others of several variations, today number 315 units system wide and are frequently seen in the consists of trains plying the Donner

RATINGS IN TONS — MOUNTAIN

UNIT	ROS-COLFAX No.2 Track	COLFAX-SPARKS No. 2 Track	SPARKS-TRUCKEE No. 1 Track	TRUCKEE-SUMMIT No. 1 Track
F7 -62/15 gear ratio	1,225	675	1,800	900
ML-4000	2,100	1,200	3,050	1,625
C-628	2,100	1,150	3,100	1,550
GP9	1,550	875	2,225	1,150
C-630	2,350	1,275	3,450	1,725
SD40	2,250	1,225	3,300	1,650
SD45	2,300	1,275	3,400	1,700

grade.

The SD40 was quickly followed, in the fall of 1966, with an initial order for 135 SD45's, a 20-cylinder, 3,600-horsepower improvement on the SD40 idea. While none of these were actually assigned to Sierra service, their impact on Mountain operations was substantial. With the arrival of the SD45, Southern Pacific now had what amounted to a universal locomotive, much like the F7 had been two decades before. Over the ensuing years, 587 SD45's of two different variations were acquired and assigned system wide. In the face of this onslaught, the age of captive pool units rapidly came to a close. Large capacity fuel tanks allowed a locomotive consist to remain with its train across vast distances. Indeed, the era of interchanging locomotives, along with the trains they pulled, between foreign line railroads was fast approaching. Union Pacific power was run through on a limited basis from North Platte, Nebraska, to the west coast as early as 1962 or 1963. This may well have been the first instance of what is today a wide-spread practice, although Rock Island power commenced running through on the Golden State Route at about the same time. The dismantling of the Automatic Train Stop system in the Sierra during 1968 removed the last physical barrier to the use of foreign units, and today locomotives of the Rio Grande and Union Pacific often outnumber those of the SP in the high Sierra on a given day.

It was partly due to their operating experience over Donner Summit, that Southern Pacific was led to request the one major external modification of the SD40/45 that has occurred since their introduction. Some evolutionary developments to electrical and mechanical components were brought about by General Motors, but the distinctive air intakes of later units was a decidedly Southern Pacific invention. Early on, trouble was experienced with the big units overheating in the sheds and tunnels on the Donner grade. Mechanical curtains, designed to eliminate troublesome back drafts, were set up at some locations, most notably at the west portal of tunnel No. 41. Special housings were fabricated and placed on several units to evaluate the effects of drawing cooler air from lower on the flanks of the locomotive. Both ideas were successful to some degree and, as an outgrowth of this, new units built after 1972 came with air intakes of greatly increased size located low on the flanks. Such units, loosely referred to as "Tunnel Motors," came in two versions, SD40T-2 and SD45T-2, and now number 482 units system wide.

Veteran "covered wagon" No. 6432 trails behind a new "tunnel motor" at Roseville in 1972. Certain conditions in Sierra operations led to the "tunnel motor" idea. — RICHARD STEINHEIMER

In the last decade, "Overland Route" traffic volumes, on a gradual decline since the peak war year of 1945, have dropped off dramatically. A number of problems have contributed to this sorry state of affairs. The demise of the "Overland Route's" once vigorous passenger traffic has already been discussed. But in the early 1970's the time honored tradition and indeed, the very life blood of the railroad, the perishable trade, began to suffer in the face of strong competition. Agricultural production in California was on the increase, but Southern Pacific's market share was diminishing. Airlines began to skim such high value business as strawberries and early-season vegetables like asparagus. The unregulated independent trucking industry, encouraged by the growth of the federally subsidized interstate highway system, undercut railroad rates and offered faster scheduling. A May 1979 I.C.C. ruling, deregulating rail transportation of fresh produce, led to a resurgence in business that summer. But many loads, trucked to Richmond and Fresno, California, TOFC terminals, found their way into the consists of trailer trains heading east on the Santa Fe, who had also benefited from deregulation.

In 1974, 700 separate fruit blocks departed Roseville for the Mountain. By 1978, the last year in which consecutive numbers were applied to fruit blocks, the count had dwindled to 427, a decline of over 76 percent from the peak year of 1945. Even after making allowances for increased car and train capacity, this was a discouraging figure. During the final years of solid perishable train operation east out of Roseville, the practice was to kill the first block at Sparks and have following sections filled to 140 cars for the run across the Great Basin.

For the last several years, solid perishable trains have been rare on the Mountain. The *RVNPP* (or *RVOGP*), frequently called the "Cut-off," still originates at Roseville in season with what perishables that may be on hand, but the bulk of the train is comprised of miscellaneous Ogden traffic. A new train, the *RVKCP*, originating at Roseville and operating south through the San Joaquin Valley, gathers perishable traffic and forwards it over the Tehachapi Mountains and east over the Golden State Route to Kansas City.

A crippling recession in the years 1974-75, brought on in part by an Arab oil crisis, cut deeply into other traffic on the "Overland Route." A general decline in warehousing and consumer buying occurred. Bay Area auto plants trimmed production. Another recession in 1981-82, the worst since the great Depression of the 1930's, forced a complete shutdown of GM's Fremont plant resulting in the loss of as many as four trains a day in the Sierra. Even though GM and Toyota planned to reopen the plant in 1984, most essential materials, including steel sub-assemblies, were to be imported from Japan. As the Bay region drifted irrevocably toward a computer and service industry economy, competition for the remaining rail traffic became intense. Contracts for such traffic as the mail, operated on the SP as the *OAOGF* (former *BAX*) eastbound and the *UPOAM* west, the Pittsburg, California, unit coil steel train, *OGPIL* west and *PIOGN* east, and the Ford Fast train *UPMIA*, bounced back and forth between the SP and the Western Pacific.

Southern Pacific's relationship with Union Pacific, throughout its historic partnership in the "Overland Route" operation, began to deteriorate. SP tended to favor its own more lucrative Sunset Route when routing traffic. This occurred in spite of a traffic agreement, hammered out in 1923 known as the "Central Pacific Conditions." It was imposed as a component part of the merger of Central Pacific and Southern Pacific, requiring the latter road, when soliciting traffic, to ask shippers to route traffic between certain areas of the country via the Ogden gateway.

The rift between the two roads widened as they fought over the remains of the bankrupt Rock Island Lines in the midwest. The 72-year partnership between Union Pacific and Southern Pacific in the Pacific Fruit Express Company was dissolved in April 1979. PFE is now a wholly owned Southern Pacific property. In 1980 Southern Pacific successfully bid for the Tucumcari-Kansas City segment of the Golden State Route and announced plans to revitalize it. Union Pacific, in retaliation, abruptly declared its intention to acquire the Western Pacific Railroad, deep in SP territory. While hearings about the case dragged on, the Southern Pacific, almost as if in protest, began the short lived operation of super hot pig trains *CPEFF* and *CPWFF,* emphasizing the historic ties with the "Overland Route." Despite bitter opposition from Southern Pacific and other roads, the "MOP UP" a combination of Union Pacific, Missouri Pacific and Western Pacific was approved December 22, 1982. No time was lost in implementing the merger and, as the Union Pacific shield was hoisted in downtown San Francisco and the Western Pacific disappeared under a coat of yellow and grey, SP's Ogden Route suffered an estimated 30 percent loss in traffic.

In the wake of the merger, the SP and the Rio Grande moved to form a stronger alliance. A traffic agreement was announced between the two roads on February 15, 1983, and, even though Rio Grande's operations were hampered by severe weather that spring, the pact has held, and today fully 75 percent of the transcontinental trains operating over the Mountain reflect the new policy. Destinations or origins at Kansas City, East St. Louis and Chicago appear in such Rio Grande interchange trains as the *BAESF, BAEST, CHOAT, ESBAA, ESBAF, KCBAY, OACHF, OACHT, RGBAT, RGOAF, RVCHT,* and *RVRGT*. Trains *RVNPE* and *UPSFF* handle virtually all of what traffic is interchanged with the UP at Ogden. Seasonal grain movements are handled in trains *OGFRL* and *RVNPN*. Not all these trains operate at all times, but usually four east and four west transcontinental trains operate over the Mountain in a 24-hour period.

Mountain local work was handled in later years by the Truckee Local, which frequently worked over the Hill as far west as Colfax, and the Bowman Turn which did the foothill work. Still later these two were consolidated into the Colfax-Truckee Local based at Roseville. Frequently, this local only worked as far east as Bowman. The Truckee-Colfax Local was pulled off late in October 1984, with the "Sky Train" *(SKRVY)*, a Sparks-Roseville junk train picking up the slack. The Anita Turn, a Sacramento Valley local freight, now goes to Colfax on Tuesday, Thursday and Saturday, if needed.

Recent new trains include the *SKSQL*, operated for the benefit of the Nevada Cement Company. A short and heavy solid hopper car unit train, the *SKSQL* operates from Fernley, Nevada, to Sacramento. A recent example required a five-unit road engine and a one-unit helper to handle 49 cars over the Mountain. Cement empties move east in the consists of other trains. In December 1984, a long-term contract was signed with Kerr-McGee Chemical Company to move two million tons of coal from Sunnydale, Utah, to Trona on SP's San Joaquin Division. An 84-car unit train is employed moving west over the Sierra as the *RGMJL* and east as the *MJRGN*.

Over the years, sweeping changes have come to the railroad operation over Donner Summit. So much so, that little remains today which has a common bond with the Central Pacific in the high Sierra of a hundred years ago, save the gauge and basic alignment of the track, and the weather. Men, machines and techniques can be improved upon, but so far there has been little success in taming the elements. The Pacific storms that crippled the railroad in the early days still come periodically to haunt the upper reaches of the pass. Since the epic storms of January and February 1952, many of the seasons have passed uneventfully, yet there were some that will also leave their mark in memory. Past experience has shown that total seasonal snowfall is not necessarily a factor when problems arise, but the intensity and duration of an individual storm is. Thus, during the winter of 1966-67, in which 629 inches of snowfall was recorded at Norden (not even placing it in the top ten in that statistic), the railroad was paralyzed by a brief but severe storm that swept into the mountains on Saturday, January 21st, dumping nearly ten feet of heavy wet snow at Donner Summit in just two days. Cleanup efforts were frustrated by a derailment which occurred inside Shed 10, blocking rail traffic in both directions. No passenger trains were on the Mountain at the time. No. 101 was held at Sparks until the afternoon of the 24th and No. 102 was annulled. During the storm, an eastbound freight stalled out on the Butte Cañon bridge just east of Crystal Lake, and portions of the train were subsequently buried by snow slides. It was days before the train was dug out and the No. 2 track restored to service. The winter of 1974-75, in which a scant 425 inches was recorded, also created problems. In recent memory, perhaps the most prolonged disruption due to a storm occurred during the spring of 1982.

On Saturday, March 27, 1982, an already unusually wet season had deposited a total snowfall of 433 inches at Norden with 97 inches still on the ground. During the next several days, a series of intense storms swept in off the Pacific which made the 1981-82 season one to remember. An incredible 194 inches of snow fell in the area over a seven day period, beginning just after midnight March 28th and ending at noon April 3rd. On Sunday the 4th of April, 237 inches stood on the ground at Norden, just three inches shy of 20 feet! High winds which accompanied the blizzard created even deeper drifts and contributed to SP's old nemesis in the high Sierra — avalanche.

At the first sign of trouble, Southern Pacific responded and by mid-morning of the 28th, the first of five flangers based at Roseville were called, with others following at staggered intervals throughout the day. Just after midnight, Monday, March 29th, the flangers began to reach their effective limit, and two Truckee-based spreaders were pressed into service between the balloon tracks at Truckee and Emigrant Gap. As a precaution, a set of rotaries was assembled and tested at Roseville. Tuesday morning, March 30th, temperatures dropped and snow began falling below Colfax. Interstate 80 was closed due to poor visibility and blowing snow. After being reopened briefly during the evening, the highway was again closed, this time until April 4th. Conditions on the Mountain worsened and on Wednesday, March 31st, the first set of rotaries, consisting of plow No. 207, power unit No. 8207, power unit No. 8211, rotary No. 211 and operating back-to-back with units Nos. 9361 and 9363 sandwiched in between, departed Roseville at 5:15 P.M. Once on the hill, it took this set eleven hours and 30 minutes to plow the 17 miles from Emigrant Gap to Norden on No. 2 track. Meanwhile, touble developed elsewhere. A westbound flanger, running at speed on the No. 1 track, struck a 12 foot deep by 250 foot long slide at MP 182.5 east of Cisco, derailing the lead truck of the lead unit. Because of this accident and the steadily worsening conditions, the Mountain was shut down at 5:15 P.M. to all traffic but snow removal equipment. AMTRAK No. 6, having been stopped at Roseville, was wyed and run back to Sacramento where it was annulled until further notice. Train

In locating the Sierra line, Judah's concept of a continuous ridge is perhaps nowhere more evident than at Emigrant Gap. Here, the railroad passes from the American River drainage (to the left) to that of the Bear and Yuba rivers (on the right). In this scene, AMTRAK train No. 6, bound for Reno, negotiates this stretch of track in the early 1970's. — RICHARD STEINHEIMER

No. 5 had already been annulled at Ogden.

At 4:00 A.M. April 1st, another set of rotaries consisting of plow No. 209, power unit No. 8209, "Tunnel Motors" Nos. 9289 and 9165, power unit No. 8221 and plow No. 221, joined the frey. With the Western Pacific having their hands full with slides, washouts and heavy snow in the Feather River Canyon, an elaborate detour was staged for backlogged freight traffic. Most of it moved north on the Shasta Route to Klamath Falls and over the Modoc Line to points east, although some traffic was diverted south to Los Angeles and east on the Union Pacific. Snow, driven by high winds, continued unabated throughout Friday the 2nd and on Saturday, so as a precaution, the Sparks rotary was set up for standby use. As things developed, its services were not required.

Finally, on Sunday afternoon, April 4th, the skies began to clear. But high winds continued, and it was not until the following morning that the first train in over five days, the *RVNPY* X9302 East, was let loose at Roseville. It was April 7th before train Nos. 5 and 6 were back on track. Another chapter, in the continuing saga of the Southern Pacific versus King Snow, had come to a close. The snowfall at Norden, for the season of 1981-82, eventually totaled out to 680 inches.

The following season a staggering 796 inches fell at Norden, a record second only to the legendary storms of 1937-38. While California reeled under the onslaught of all this precipitation, heavy snow was falling in the Sierra, but in more measured doses. During those first terrible days in March, when portions of SP's Oregon, Coast and Western divisions, WP's Altamont Pass and Feather River Canyon lines and the Northwestern Pacific were knocked out, Sacramento Division crews managed to keep ahead in the battle with the snow. While a sizeable portion of the strategic joint-track Tehachapi line was being flushed out to sea, trains continued to roll over the Sierra and while repairs were under way elsewhere, many rerouted trains moved east over Donner summit.

As this volume goes to press, Southern Pacific is bracing for yet another winter on the Mountain. Flangers and ice breaker equipped SD9's, line the outbound tracks at the Roseville shops. Last minute repairs are under way on the rotary fleet. Spreaders are being inspected at Truckee. New this season is G38-2 No. 4843, set up for flanger service, complete with breaker bars, storm windows and horn heater. As the clouds gather in the mountains and the first flakes softly fall at the summit, one wonders if this season will be the big one that rails will talk about for generations to come, or so mild that the rotaries are never fired up. Only time will tell.

For decades Roseville had been an important steam locomotive servicing point, and this function continued as the railroad entered the diesel age. A new diesel shop, seen in the aerial view (LEFT) about 1955, was erected on the site where much of roundhouse No. 1 had been located. The facility has grown in size and complexity in the succeeding years. — ALL ALAN ASKE COLLECTION

By the early 1960's, some 550 engines were assigned to the Roseville pool and several dozen engines were assigned to local and switching chores. Frequently, over 100 locomotives could be seen at Roseville shops at any given time, and maintenance and servicing work was carried out day and night. — BOTH ROBERT HALE (BELOW) ALCO DL701 demonstrators 701, 701A and 701B pause at the Roseville facility on June 17, 1956. The SP went on to purchase a number of these locomotives but they were rarely seen in the Sierra. — ALAN ASKE

For years it was the custom for Southern Pacific President D.J. Russell to journey to Truckee at New Years. The move was always made by rail and here, one finds the Russell special returning from the east near Penryn in January 1962. — KEN YEO (BELOW) The quiet stillness of a winter forest is disturbed momentarily by the howl of dynamic brakes as Extra 6410 West drops down around Blue Cañon curve in the 1960's. — R.R. ASZMAN COLLECTION

An early spring Arctic storm has deposited snow as low as Dutch Flat. In these two scenes, train No. 101, the *City of San Francisco,* rolls west through countryside befitting a Christmas card. — BOTH RICHARD STEINHEIMER

227

Working between Oakland Pier and Ogden, the beautiful ALCO PA diesels held down "Overland Route" passenger schedules without incident for nearly two decades. But in later years the engines tended to run hot on the Sierra grade. A foot or two of fire roared steadily from their stacks as a PA worked uphill, and chunks of red hot carbon, the size of quarters, would blow out and land on the ground, setting fires. (ABOVE) At the mid-point in their career, four of these units cut an impressive figure as they led train No. 102 upgrade through the Sierra foothills near Newcastle in the early summer of 1960. (LEFT) By 1966, however, age was taking its toll on the fleet and unit No. 6029 presents a shoddy appearance as it drops below the No. 2 track at Rocklin with the westbound *City of San Francisco*. — BOTH RICHARD STEINHEIMER

An odd assortment of power waits in the helper spur at milepost 111.73 just east of the Rocklin flyover. During the 1960's, helpers were cut in here in order to avoid delays and yard expenses at Roseville. But when it was argued, and successfully so, that the spur was within the yard limits of the old Rocklin yard and that switchmen would get penalty payments anyway, the helpers were moved back to Roseville and the spur was torn up. — DAVE STANLEY COLLECTION

The passenger business, like the perishable traffic on the Mountain, fluctuated widely with the season. (ABOVE) The normally moderate consist of mail train No. 21, seen near Newcastle in December 1963, had swollen to at least 19 headend cars of great variety, requiring a two-unit point helper for the Sierra run as holiday mail and express was rushed west. (LEFT) Summer crowds lengthened the consist of other trains such as the *City of San Francisco*. Seen here at Enwood in 1964, train No. 102 had just received a point helper for the run over the Mountain. — BOTH KEN YEO

Holiday Mail & Express Extra 6236 growls through Newcastle in December 1962. — A.C. PHELPS (RIGHT) Due to slides in the Feather River Canyon, Western Pacific's *California Zephyr* detours over the Mountain. The most spectacular portions of the Donner grade were denied No. 17's passengers, as clearance problems prohibited the occupancy of the train's five Vista Dome cars between Truckee and Emigrant Gap. SP unit No. 6261 is on the point to actuate the Automatic Train Stop. — W.S. PRINGLE COLLECTION (BELOW) A ten-unit cab hop clips through Colfax in the mid-1960's. — KEN YEO

230

A decade separates these two shots of eastbound tonnage being lugged upgrade. (LEFT) A "covered wagon" rounds Cape Horn in the late 1950's on a rainy afternoon. (ABOVE) Sixteen miles farther up the hill, is the site of the viewing platform at American. The view of the North Fork of the American River, as afforded from the Southern Pacific's right-of-way, is as breathtaking as any in the west. — BOTH RICHARD STEINHEIMER

Penninsula commuter Geep No. 3009 is second out in the consist of this returning weekend *Reno Fun Train* at Troy on November 16, 1969. — T.O. REPP (RIGHT) Joe A. Ward set up his camera at Yuba Pass, on May 30, 1968, to photograph the westbound Pacific Locomotive Association "Truckee Limited," featuring ALCO hydraulic No. 9151, but *Advance FMS* Extra 8859 West (BELOW) ran ahead of the special. (RIGHT) Later at Emigrant Gap the excursion met an eastbound perishable block. — JIM EVANS COLLECTION

232

The rugged glacial geology of the upper Sierra frames train No. 101 on a summer day near Crystal Lake in the mid-1960's. Red Mountain looms in the distance. — RICHARD STEINHEIMER

SP Extra 6469 West meets an *OVE* at Soda Springs in 1967 (ABOVE) just as the skies open up with an early September thunderstorm. (LEFT) Five throaty F's are cut deep into this eastbound train. — BOTH JOHN SHAW (BELOW) Ice encrusted F's drift through Yuba Pass following a stormy night on the Mountain in 1959. — RICHARD STEINHEIMER

Priority eastbound traffic rolls through Soda Springs in the early 1960's behind five "covered wagons." — RICHARD STEINHEIMER, SOUTHERN PACIFIC COLLECTION

For nearly two decades, the "covered wagons" held sway in the Sierra. Even after the second generation hood units arrived, like Century 628 No. 4852, seen at Norden in 1965, the aging F units held preference among the men. They were simpler to keep operating. A bit of ingenuity with a paper cup or a piece of string frequently did the trick. And all work on the engine was done inside the carbody, affording protection from the elements. — G.M. BEST COLLECTION

235

Since Southern Pacific clerk Mike Kashiwahara snapped this panoramic view of Sparks yard, and those on the opposite page, from a vantage point of the yard office tower in 1956, a lot of changes have been made. The ALCO yard goats in the foreground and the PFE ice deck tracks appear in the left middle distance, with Reno and the Sierra range beyond. — ALAN ASKE COLLECTION

As the old saw goes, Reno is so close to hell you can see Sparks. The reader could see a lot of Sparks from up in the yard office tower. Much of this structure had come from Wadsworth in the big move of 1904. — TED BENSON

By 1956, much of the former steam facility at Sparks had been razed, including about half of the roundhouse. (ABOVE) The large wooden building to the right was the SP train crew's "club house." (BELOW) The view looking east from the tower stands in stark contrast to today's abundance of warehouses and hotels. Is that another train "comin in off the sand" from the Salt Lake Division? — ALL ALAN ASKE COLLECTION

At the left, hooked up to the yard steam lines is the *Reno Fun Train,* comprised of an SD40 and four F7's, idling away the hours in sub-zero darkness at Sparks. It is Saturday night, January 29, 1972 and the train's patrons are off in nearby casinos on one last fling before a Sunday departure back to California. (ABOVE) Tucked away on another track is leased Rio Grande F7 No. 5731 awaiting a different morning run to the east on the Mina local. — ALL TED BENSON

While all the routine chores of railroading are accomplished in the Sparks yards, Reno 3.3 miles to the west is the more well-known location. The glaring neon of Reno's casinos illuminate the boxy front end of train No. 27, the *S.F. Overland*, as it paused in town in the early morning hours of New Years Day 1963. — W.S. PRINGLE COLLECTION (BELOW) A long and heavy No. 21, the westbound mail train, paused at Reno on a winter's eve about 1960, while station forces work the head-end cars. A two-unit helper had been added at Sparks for the run west across the Sierra. — RICHARD STEINHEIMER

In the summer of 1967, six "covered wagons" growl across the Nevada-California border, east of Mystic, with westbound tonnage. — RICHARD STEINHEIMER (BELOW) Train No. 27 winds up the Truckee River Canyon near the old station of Union Mills just after dawn on February 12, 1960. — DONALD DUKE COLLECTION

The westbound *City of San Francisco* rolls into Truckee in December 1970, as the rear brakeman of a westbound freight sprints to catch his caboose. (ABOVE) The freight, which has just crossed over to the No. 2 track, will soon be overtaken by the *Streamliner* on the big curve at Stanford.
— BOTH RICHARD STEINHEIMER

One can almost smell the coffee and bacon being served in the diner as train No. 101 sweeps past the location at Stanford curve (LEFT AND BELOW) in the upper reaches of Cold Stream Canyon on a fine summer morning in the early 1960's. At dawn, frost on the ties was evident even at that time of the year and all too soon snow will once again come to the high Sierra. (OPPOSITE PAGE) On a wintry day in early December 1966, from a vantage point at Andover a bit farther up the grade, the roar of a heavy westbound manifest, four track miles away, disturbs the solitude of the surrounding forest. — ALL RICHARD STEINHEIMER

Before the train has a chance to reach us, an eastbound freight (RIGHT) pops out of tunnel No. 42 and whines downgrade past our location. A two-unit helper (BELOW) tacked on behind the caboose assists in holding back the train. — BOTH RICHARD STEINHEIMER

6307 SOUTHERN PACIFIC

Yet another eastbound, with shiny new SD40's up front, glides by as the Extra 6213 West finally achieves Andover. Following close on its markers (RIGHT) is Extra 8454 West. — BOTH RICHARD STEINHEIMER

A westbound *City of San Francisco* slips through what remains of shed No. 26 on the No. 2 track at the east end of the Norden complex (ABOVE) in the mid-1960's. This area had been enclosed in wooden sheds but a disastrous fire, started by a pair of long johns drying over a cookstove, leveled much of Norden on the night of November 14, 1961 and these sheds were never rebuilt. (RIGHT) Later, a double-ended spreader passes the same location on the No. 1. track. — BOTH RICHARD STEINHEIMER

For years it was the custom for crews on westward trains to take "beans" at the Norden cookhouse. Operated by the San Francisco based J.V. Moan Commissaries, known to the railroaders as "Moan & Groan," the Norden cookhouse was open 24-hours a day, year 'round. (RIGHT) In the 1950's, Fong Quong, whose distant ancestors had carved the first right-of-way for the rails through the granite barriers of the Sierra, now served up steak and eggs to hungry rails. — D.T. McDERMOTT

At the Norden cookhouse, where the crews chowed down in 1957, basics like meat, potatoes and coffee were the staples. — SOUTHERN PACIFIC COLLECTION (RIGHT) The cookhouse escaped the terrible inferno of 1961 but the old frame structure was eventually consumed in another fire later in the decade. It was rebuilt in concrete adjacent to the No. 2 main just down from the new depot. — RICHARD STEINHEIMER

On a warm moonlit night, just east of the Norden complex, power on an eastbound freight drums quietly outside tunnel No. 41 (ABOVE), waiting for a slow moving westbound to vacate the long bore. — RICHARD STEINHEIMER (RIGHT) The classic profile of Extra 6300 West emerges from shed No. 25 at the west end of Norden on a snowy day in the winter of 1957. The eastward Norden train order signal stands adjacent to No. 2 track. — SOUTHERN PACIFIC COLLECTION

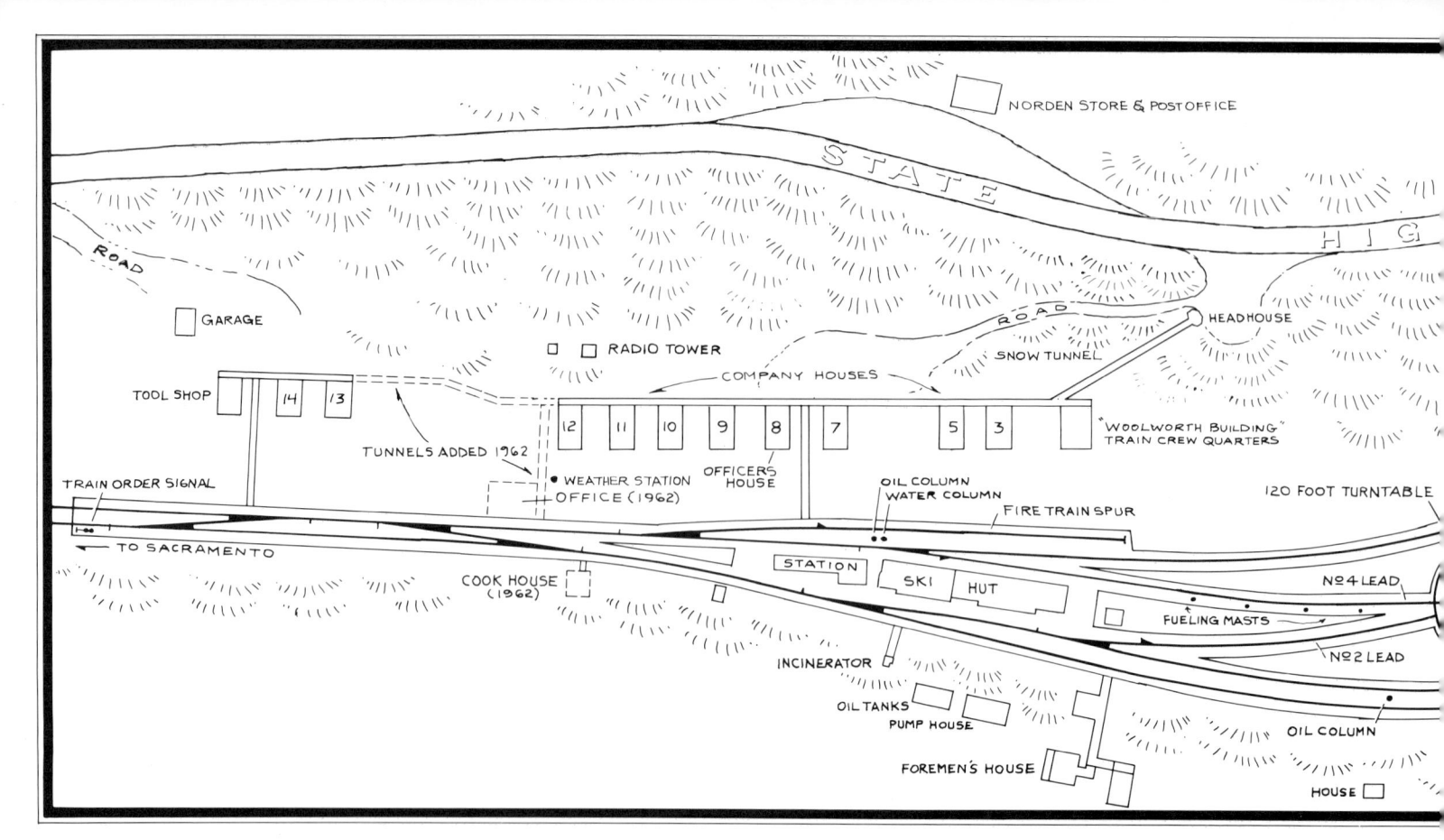

The helper is cut away from the caboose of SP Extra 6311 East inside the protection of the Norden sheds during the winter of 1957. — BOTH PHIL HASTINGS

NORDEN COMPLEX 1952

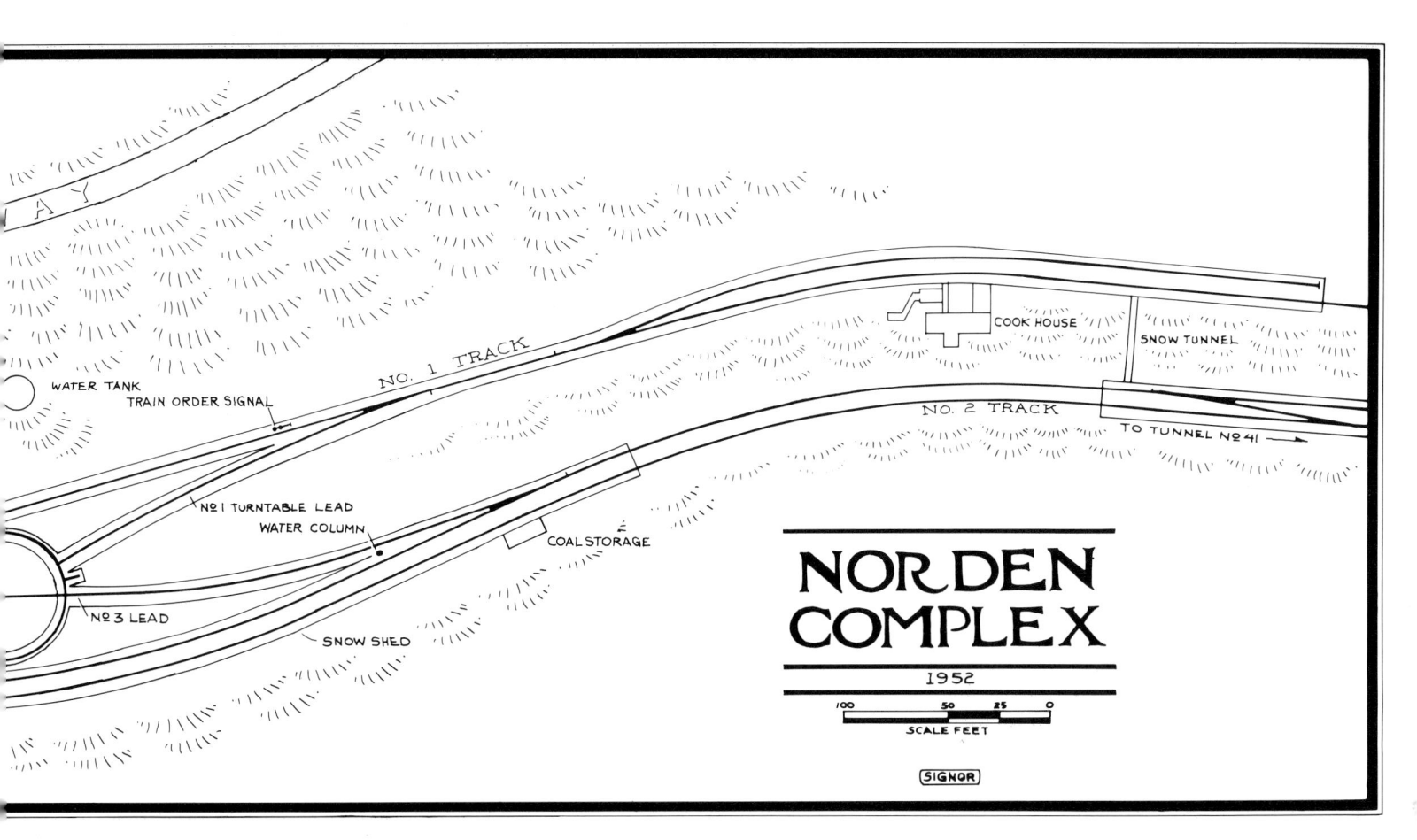

SD9 helpers pause on the No. 4 turntable lead at Norden in 1957. — SOUTHERN PACIFIC COLLECTION

The years have brought about many changes to the Sierra operation, but throughout, it was always a purely Southern Pacific enterprise. This was to change, however, when, on May 1, 1971, the Unites States Government assumed responsibility for the nation's rail passenger service. In the Sierra, the initial effects of the takeover were slight — a change in schedule numbers and names and an increase in the frequency of operation — and one year later there was little to distinguish AMTRAK train No. 5, the *San Francisco Zephyr* (LEFT) seen dropping down into tunnel No. 18 at Newcastle, from a *City of San Francisco* of a decade earlier. — TED BENSON By 1975, however, the AMTRAK presence was more conspicuous. Train Nos. 5 and 6, now sporting red-nosed SDP40F's and foreign line cars decked out in gaudy red, white and blue AMTRAK livery, meet at Rocklin on March 30th. — TIM ZUKAS

In the remarkable sequence of photos across the top of this and the adjoining page, exposed in December 1973 by Ted Benson, the excitement of SP's Mountain operation comes to life as a westbound *BCW* whines downgrade on the No. 1 track near Applegate. Scarcely had the clatter of the freight subsided when No. 6 erupted from tunnel No. 26 on its way east.

An extra west with Rio Grande pool power on the point, pops out of tunnel No. 23 between Clipper Gap and Applegate in March 1983. Off in the weeds, to the left, is the east portal of former tunnel No. "0." Cut through in 1873 to eliminate the spidery trestle over Deep Gulch, tunnel No. "0" reportedly couldn't accommodate Navy landing craft and was abandoned in favor of a line change in 1942. — S.R. BUSH

Having made the stop at Colfax, AMTRAK No. 6 roars off towards the east in the soft light of a winter afternoon. Superliner equipment was introduced on the "Overland Route" in the spring of 1980. (RIGHT) The train order signal at Colfax came down in the fall of 1984 as SP closed their office to all but originating trains. — BOTH DICK DORN

On a chilly moonlit night at Colfax, in December 1973, the helper crew off a westbound *OMW*, aboard Cotton Belt No. 8967, change ends and prepare to cut into a heavy *OVE*, Extra 9019 East, which waits patiently on the eastbound mainline. Caught in the middle are two Geeps waiting for traffic to clear so they can crossover to the westbound track and head for Roseville.
— TED BENSON

Brake shoe haze drifts up from the wheels of Extra 9214 as the train approaches Gold Run. A Union Pacific SD40 is second out in the locomotive consist. — CLINT NESTELL

An empty coal train, powered by Rio Grande locomotives, winds upgrade through Gold Run in March 1983. With the Union Pacific-Missouri Pacific-Western Pacific merger, SP and Rio Grande are doing more business together and the latter's road power is an everyday sight on Donner Pass. — S.R. BUSH

255

The labored exhausts of an eastbound drag, backlit by the summer sun, fill the canyon at Cisco. — DICK DORN

In recent years, eastbound trains have regularly been held to 5,000 tons with five units on the point and a single unit behind the caboose. (ABOVE) This helper seen at Cisco in 1972, will turn at Norden. — T.O. REPP (LEFT) Penninsula based commuter engines were frequently seen in the Sierra on weekends. — CLINT NESTELL (BELOW) Train No. 5, emerging from tunnel No. 38 on the No. 1 track, overtook a westbound train near Cisco in the summer of 1980. The Norden interlocking limits now extend down the hill to Emigrant Gap. — T.O. REPP

Summer was fleeting in the high country and traditionally the first snow comes in October. Substantial pilot plows, found on most Southern Pacific road locomotives like SD40 No. 8449, (LEFT) are sufficient to sweep the first light accumulation from the rails. — G.N. FLANDERS (BELOW) But the storms continued and soon the flangers were called. Drawn across the district at speeds between 37 and 45 miles per hour, and kicking snow from the rails, the flangers are Southern Pacific's first line of defense against the snow. — CLINT NESTELL

Drawn by classic ice-breaker equipped SD9's, the flangers constantly pass over the line between the balloon tracks at Truckee and Emigrant Gap. (ABOVE) A flanger set pauses at the latter point between runs. — CLINT NESTELL (LEFT) Engines assigned to flanger service received a number of modifications besides the distinctive ice-breaker bars. Special controls were fitted to raise and lower the flanger blade, and a heater melted snow and ice from the horns. Unique motorized circular windows, first used aboard ships at sea, spin continuously, preventing snow and ice from accumulating. (BELOW) Traditionally, big units have not been used on flangers, but recently GP38-2 No. 4843, seen at Truckee in December 1984, was introduced in this service and has gained acceptance from the men. — S.R. BUSH

When the "core" or mound of snow between the two mainline tracks reaches three feet in depth, the flangers reach their effective limit and a spreader is then called in to shove the core off to the side. March 1983 found double-ended spreader Extra 4319 East plowing up the No. 2 track near Yuba Pass during a break in heavy storms. — S.R. BUSH

Caterpillar tractors (BELOW) clean up odds and ends at Troy, but the results of their work are far less appealing (LEFT) than are the even banks left by rail equipment. — BOTH CLINT NESTELL

The Truckee local plows through Emigrant Gap (ABOVE) in March 1979 while shovelers look on. — CLINT NESTELL (RIGHT) When conditions would deteriorate to the point that flangers and spreaders could no longer keep the railroad open, SP would then call out the heavy artillary — the rotaries. It was raining hard at Baxter in April 1983 as a "super set" of rotaries rumbled toward the front. — S.R. BUSH

At Soda Springs, the rotaries, once at work, made an impressive sight as they plowed through the snow which had been shoved on to the No. 2 track by a preceeding spreader. The arc, made by the thrown snow, is called a "rooster tail." (RIGHT) At Norden, the baffles have been reversed so that the snow will be thrown to the opposite side of the tracks. The rotary engineer controls the speed and direction, the fireman operates the spinning blades and the maintenance of way personel manipulate the wings. — BOTH DICK DORN (BELOW) Between storms crews work to free ice and snow from a rotary at Colfax. — CLINT NESTELL

With a turn in the weather and the railroad open, a double-ended rotary set drops downgrade near Troy on its way back to Roseville. — RICHARD STEINHEIMER (LEFT) In March 1983, Extra 9216 East, the *OACHT*, passes over a carefully cleared right-of-way where, some 31 years earlier, the *City of San Francisco* had been snowbound for days. — S.R. BUSH

Snow still lingered on the ground at Norden in the spring of April 1972. In this scene an excursion train pops out of wooden snowshed No. 26 at the east end of the complex (LEFT), but at the west end all the sheds are concrete. Company houses in the distance are inter-connected by a series of enclosed passageways or tunnels, like this stairwell (BELOW) which leads from the "head house" at street level down to the tracks. — ALL TED BENSON

Within the sheds themselves, cathedral lighting accentuates the hot exhaust of a light helper set that has paused for orders. — TED BENSON (BELOW) In the age of steam, a 16-drivered cab-forward would just fit on the Norden turntable, if the crew remembered to close both coupler knuckles. But an SD45 had room to spare as it made its turn where missing chunks of supporting pillars bore mute testimony to the giant AC's that preceeded it. — CHUCK FOX

It's all business on a cold winter's eve at Norden as 3rd trick operator A.D. "Shorty" Teal types orders for a westbound train approaching on the No. 1 track. (RIGHT) Stepping outside into the numbing cold, "Shorty" hoops up three sets of orders for the advancing train which had a helper entrained. — BOTH DICK DORN

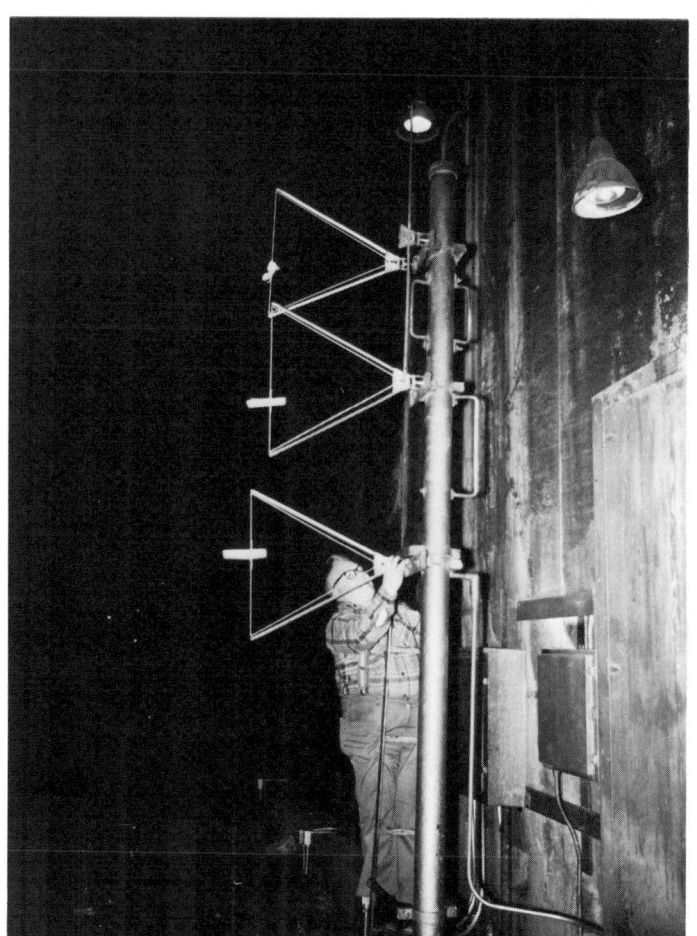

The roar is deafening and it is punctuated by the hot exhaust of Extra 8851 West as it rumbles through the sheds at Norden, with the headend first (RIGHT) and then the helper (BELOW) each snaring their orders. — BOTH DICK DORN

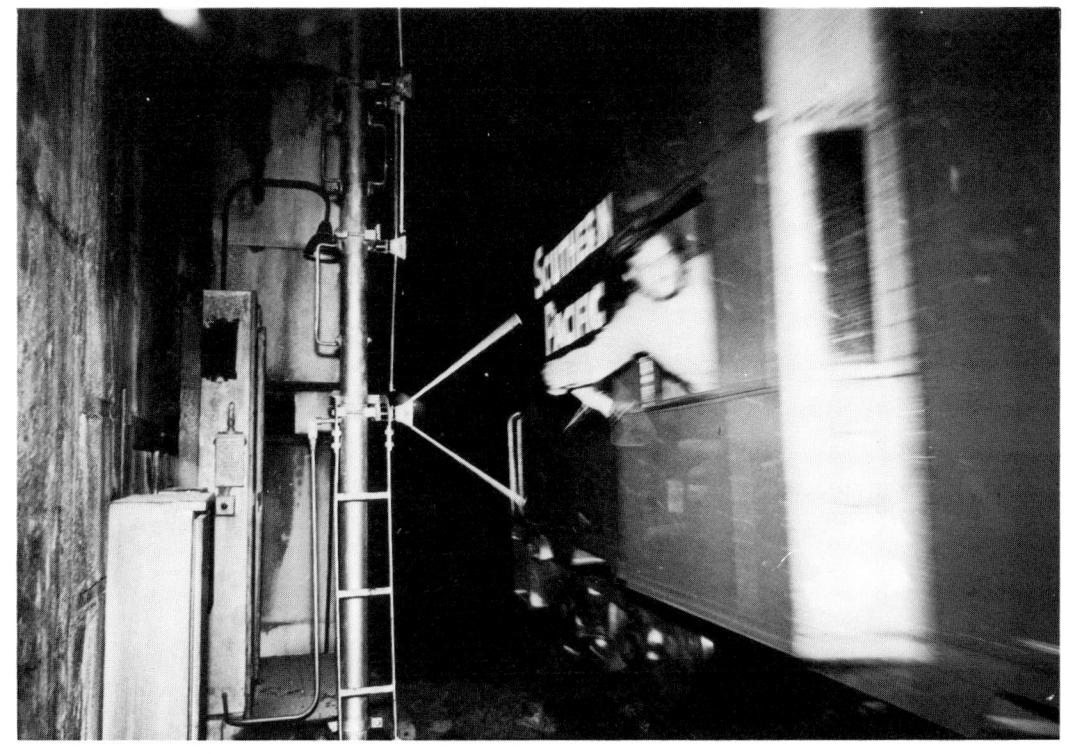

At length the caboose rolls by, the orders are snared, highballs are exchanged and the train disappears into the night. The clatter of steel wheels on distant switches soon gives way to the hollow dripping quiet that is peculiar to the Norden sheds. — DICK DORN

267

From the vantage point of a buried telegraph pole, photographer S.R. Bush captures a flanger passing from one shed to another (ABOVE AND TOP OF OPPOSITE PAGE) on the eastward siding at Norden in April 1983.

A detoured Western Pacific freight train slips into the Norden sheds on March 2, 1983. Slides in Feather River Canyon had forced the detour of four WP trains over Donner Pass. (RIGHT) In this interesting bird's-eye view of the Norden complex taken from the southwest in the spring of 1985, Mt. Judah looms in the distance.
— BOTH S.R. BUSH

A heavy *Reno Fun Train* winds upgrade on the No. 1 track at Andover, on the east slope of the Sierra, on its way towards Norden, on March 3, 1974. Two SD45's, three FP7's and an E9 power the 19-car train. — TIM ZUKAS

A train of perishables drops down the 1.8 percent grade above shed No. 47 during the late afternoon in May 1980. In the distance, sheds, protecting the No. 1 track, are wet from the spring runoff. — RICHARD STEINHEIMER

By the summer of 1980, reefer trains, once the mainstay of the "Overland Route," were becoming few and far between as a long empty drag (ABOVE AND RIGHT) works up through Eder. — BOTH RICHARD STEINHEIMER

An all-Budd equipped AMTRAK train No. 5 negotiates Stanford curve (BELOW) on September 14, 1972. — T.O. REPP

The caboose has not yet cleared, but RVOGP, ladened with vegetables from California's Salinas Valley, emerges from tunnel No. 41 on its way east. The Yellow Union Pacific Fruit Express reefer No. 457696 (LEFT) is indicative of the recent breakup of the 72-year partnership between the SP and UP in the Pacific Fruit Express Company. — BOTH RICHARD STEINHEIMER

In the early 1970's, a new unit oil train was inaugurated on a run between storage areas in Utah and Standard Oil's Richmond, California, refinery. The train, seen here at a scenic bend in the Truckee River east of Truckee, was designated the *UPRML* westbound, but it was commonly referred to as the "cans." Seven locomotives were required to boost the 8,000 ton 70-car train to the summit, but equally important were the seven sets of dynamic brakes which held the train back on the long descent into Roseville. At 112 tons per operative brake, the "cans" exceeded published ratings, forcing their revision. — BOTH JOHN SHAW

In the summer of 1984, expedited trailer train *OACHT* rolls east near Boca behind Rio Grande power. In the break with long time "Overland Route" partner Union Pacific in the early 1980's, the Rio Grande influence on Donner Pass became stronger with each passing season. — DICK DORN

Yet another westbound rumbles out of Sparks at dusk headed for the Mountain. In an era of megamergers, where the soundness of Judah's "continuous ridge" or the wisdom of Harriman's "grand transcontinental highway" are scarcely considered, it seems safe to assume that, whatever the outcome, the granite ridges of the Sierra will echo the passage of trains for sometime to come. -- G.N. FLANDERS

An "Overland Route" tradition - loaded refrigerator cars rolling east near Eder. — RICHARD STEINHEIMER

Epilogue

As of this writing, the 120-year legacy of Southern Pacific operations in the high Sierra faces an uncertain future. Conceived in the true pioneering spirit by Theodore Judah, nurtured by the "Big Four" and brought to full efficiency under the guiding hand of visionary Edward H. Harriman, this strategic segment of the legendary "Overland Route" fell short of its true potential in transcontinental commerce with the breakup of Harriman's Associated Lines, especially the Union Pacific and Southern Pacific systems. Even though legally separated, the two roads continued to operate in close partnership for years. Their jointly-owned Pacific Fruit Express Company virtually made the western fruit and vegetable industry what it is today. As an essentially orphaned segment of a southern transcontinental road, the Ogden Route was sustained for years by the heavy movement of perishables from the valleys of California to markets in the East. Other trains came and went, but the long strings of yellow reefers were at the heart of the operation.

In recent times, a number of problems have come to haunt the "Overland Route." First and foremost has been the loss of the perishable traffic, primarily due to the interstate highway system, deregulation and the rise of the independent trucking industry. The gradual demise of this business over the last 15 years has left a void that has yet to be filled.

Another blow came in 1980, when the Union Pacific announced that in order to solidify its position in the west, it would seek to weld the single-track Western Pacific into its system. That the Interstate Commerce Commission allow traffic to be diverted to this slide-prone sidehill pike, at the expense of the solidly-built double-track Donner grade, is one of the travesties of the age. It is estimated that as the merger was implemented, Donner Pass lost 30 percent of an already greatly diminished traffic load.

Traffic alliances, sought with the Denver & Rio Grande Western Railroad in retaliation, were undermined by heavy weather in the Great Basin. In the early months of the agreement, Rio Grande's line at Thistle, Utah, was severed by a slide of gargantuan proportion. At the same time, record high water levels threatened Southern Pacific's causeway across the Great Salt Lake. While the Rio Grande's mainline was ultimately restored at great expense, a million-dollar battle is still being waged to keep the Salt Lake fill above water.

Rumors are rampant over the ultimate fate of the Mountain and the entire line from Roseville to Ogden. Analysts predict even slimmer business levels over the district in the wake of a southern transcontinental oriented Santa Fe - Southern Pacific combination. For a time it seemed likely that inclusion of the Rio Grande in the merger was being sought as a logical extension east from Ogden to outlets in the midwest. But Rio Grande trackage rights or an outright purchase of the Roseville-Ogden segment now appears more certain. Whatever the outcome, it seems assured that the granite walls of Cold Stream Canyon and the American River Gorge will echo the rumble of passing trains for some time to come.

Appendix

Appendix A
Mountain Passenger Trains 1899-1984

Compiled by Albert C. Phelps
All trains operate(d) daily except as noted.

OVERLAND LIMITED

Train No.	Effective	
1-2	October 15, 1899	Inaugurated. Prior to this known as the *A&P Express*.
	December 17, 1909	Name changed to *San Francisco Overland Limited*.
	April 4, 1913	Name changed to *Overland Limited*.
	October 17, 1922	Name changed to *S.F. Overland Limited*.
	June 9, 1929	Name changed to *Overland Limited*.
27-28	May 31, 1931	Numbers changed to 27 and 28 and becomes *San Francisco Overland Limited*.
	June 19, 1932	Adds coaches to previously all-Pullman consist.
	July 10, 1947	Name shortened to *S.F. Overland*.
	July 16, 1962	Nos. 27 and 28 discontinued and train consolidated with Nos. 101-102, the *City of San Francisco*. After this date, the *Overland* became a part-time train operating during peak summer months and Christmas holidays. Trains were shown in employees timetables, but were annulled on a day to day basis by train orders except when operated as noted.
	October 27, 1963	Employee timetable no longer shows train Nos. 27 and 28. Last run occurred during the summer of 1963.

ATLANTIC & PACIFIC EXPRESS

Train No.	Effective	
3-4	October 15, 1899	*Pacific Express* westbound, *Atlantic Express* eastbound. The trains were established November 13, 1887.
	April 1, 1906	No. 3 became *China & Japan Fast Mail*. No. 4 became *Express*.
	April 4, 1913	No. 3 became *California Mail*.
	May 20, 1914	Nos. 3 and 4 discontinued.

NEVADAN

Train No.	Effective	
17	December 16, 1917	*Nevadan* established Ogden to Reno. West of Reno through cars from Ogden are handled on No. 23 to San Francisco.
	June 2, 1918	No. 17 discontinued.

ST. LOUIS EXPRESS

Train No.	Effective	
21-22	November 16, 1920	New train established.
	November 14, 1926	Discontinued.

PACIFIC LIMITED

Train No.	Effective	
19-20	April 4, 1913	New train established with through Milwaukee Road cars. Up until WWI, operated on Milwaukee. During first World War, operated over C&NW at which time train reverted to Milwaukee Road and continued until 1931.
	May 3, 1931	Adds local stops on Mountain and eastbound operated via No. 4 track Rocklin to Loomis then against the current of traffic Loomis to Newcastle.
20-21	June 19, 1932	Train No. 19 changed to No. 21.
10-21	February 26, 1933	Train No. 20 changed to No. 10. No longer operated against the current of traffic.
14-21	April 1, 1935	Train No. 10 changed to No. 14.
21-22	March 8, 1942	Train No. 14 changed to No. 22.
	June 2, 1946	No. 22 operated as *Advance Pacific Limited*. Train 3-24 operated as the *Pacific Limited*. Train 1-24 was the tourist car section and 2-24 the coach section of the *Challenger*.
	October 1, 1946	Train No. 1-22 becomes the *Advance Pacific Limited* and 2-22 the *Pacific Limited*.
	November 10, 1946	Operations back to normal.
	May 14, 1947	Name shortened to *Pacific*.
	October 19, 1947	Name *Pacific* dropped and trains renamed *Mail*. See section on *Fast Mail & Express*.

GOLD COAST LIMITED
GOLD COAST

Train No.	Effective	
27-28	November 14, 1926	New train established as *Gold Coast Limited*.
21-22	June 9, 1929	Name shortened to *Gold Coast* and numbers changed.
10	September 21, 1930	Eastbound schedule number changed to No. 10. Westbound train discontinued.
	May 31, 1931	Train No. 10 became *Mail & Express*.
23-24	October 19, 1947	*Gold Coast* reestablished with new numbers.
	January 19, 1955	*Gold Coast* discontinued.

SAN FRANCISCO LIMITED

Train No.	Effective	
5-10	January 4, 1914	New train established.
	June 2, 1918	No. 5 became *SF Passenger* and No. 10 discontinued.
27-28	June 9, 1929	Reestablished as *San Francisco Limited*.
	May 31, 1931	Discontinued-see section on *SF Overland Limited*.

276

ATLANTIC EXPRESS
PACIFIC EXPRESS
WESTERN EXPRESS EASTERN EXPRESS
CHINA & JAPAN FAST MAIL
SAN FRANCISCO LIMITED
NEVADA EXPRESS

Train No.	Effective	
5-6	October 15, 1899	Third transcontinental train added began running as *Pacific Express* westbound and *Atlantic Express* eastbound. Two trains on run with the same name.
	May 14, 1904	No. 5 became *Western Express* and No. 6 the *Eastern Express*.
	April 1, 1906	No. 6 became the *China & Japan Fast Mail*.
	January 5, 1908	No. 6 changed back to *Eastern Express*.
	January 4, 1914	No. 5 became *San Francisco Limited*. No. 6 became *Atlantic Express*.
	June 2, 1918	No. 5 became *S.F. Passenger*.
	November 14, 1920	Both trains named *Atlantic & Pacific Express*.
	September 18, 1921	Name changed to *Nevada Express*.
21-22	April 17, 1927	*Nevada Express* received new numbers.
	September 25, 1927	*Nevada Express* discontinued.

FAST MAIL

Train No.	Effective	
9-10	December 31, 1905	New fast mail and express train established.
	November 25, 1906	Passengers were carried on No. 10. Prior to this consist the train had headend cars only.
	January 5, 1908	No. 10 became *China & Japan Fast Mail*.
	May 1908	No. 9 began carrying passengers.
	April 4, 1913	No. 10 became *California Mail*.
	January 4, 1914	No. 10 became *San Francisco Ltd*.
	June 2, 1918	No. 10 discontinued due to war restrictions.
	January 5, 1919	No. 10 restored as *Express*.
	March 21, 1920	No. 10 became *Mail & Express*.
	September 18, 1921	No. 10 became *Atlantic Express*.
	September 25, 1927	No. 10 became *Salt Lake*.
	September 21, 1930	No. 10 became *Gold Coast*.
	May 31, 1931	No. 10 became *Mail & Express*.
	February 26, 1933	No. 10 became *Pacific Limited*.
	April 1, 1935	No. 10 discontinued.
	September 15, 1937	No. 10 reestablished as *Fast Mail*.
	March 8, 1942	No. 10 became *Passenger*.
	-	Note: Train No. 10 had more name changes than any other on the Southern Pacific System.
25-26	June 2, 1946	No. 9, the *Fast Mail*, continued as No. 25 and No. 10 continues as No. 26.
	May 10, 1946	Both trains known as *Fast Mail*.
	July 6, 1947	No. 25 became *Mail* and No. 26 became *Passenger*.
21-22	October 19, 1947	Nos. 25 and 26 assume new numbers and both became *Mail*.
	November 16, 1967	Train Nos. 21 and 22 discontinued.
	-	Note: Train No. 9 consolidated with No. 27 and No. 10 with No. 28 between Ogden and Sparks from February 26, 1933 through May 27, 1934 and again from February 6, 1938 through June 1, 1946.

RENO PASSENGER
TONOPAH EXPRESS
SIERRA SPECIAL
SIERRA

Train No.	Effective	
13-14	April 5, 1903	*Reno Passenger* established.
	November 22, 1903	Discontinued.
	May 15, 1904	Re-established.
	October 1, 1904	Discontinued.
	October 23, 1904	Re-established.
	September 3, 1905	Became *Tonopah Express*.
23-24	November 19, 1906	*Tonopah Express* receives new numbers.
	June 2, 1918	Discontinued on Mountain due to wartime restrictions. Continues run Sparks-Mina.
	June 1, 1919	Restored as *Tonopah Express*.
	March 21, 1920	No. 23 became *Sparks-SF Passenger*.
	May 3, 1925	Trains became *Sierra Special*.
	October 1, 1925	No. 23 became *Sparks-SF Passenger*. No. 24 became *Tonopah Express*.
	June 6, 1926	Trains once again became *Sierra Special*.
	November 14, 1926	Trains once again became *Sparks-SF Passenger* and *Tonopah Express*.
	March 4, 1928	Name changed to *Sierra*.
	May 3, 1931	Trains 23 and 24 discontinued.
224	February 26, 1933	*Sierra* reestablished eastbound only.
210-211	April 1, 1935	No. 224, the *Sierra* renumbered 210. No. 211 established westbound.
211-289	February 2, 1936	No. 211 renumbered No. 289.
210-289 -295	August 1, 1939	No. 289 operated daily except Sunday and holidays, No. 295 Sunday and holidays.
	March 8, 1942	Nos. 210, 289, 295 discontinued.

ADVANCE S.F. OVERLAND LIMITED

Train No.	Effective	
30	April 1, 1935	New train established. Operated eastbound only.
30-287	December 13, 1936	Westbound train established. Operated as part of No. 9 Ogden to Sparks and No. 287 through to San Francisco.
88-30	June 13, 1937	Operated as No. 88 SF to Sparks and No. 30 Sparks to Ogden.
9-87	June 13, 1937	Operated as No. 9 Ogden to Sparks and No. 87 Sparks to San Francisco.
	September 15, 1937	Discontinued.

UN-NAMED TRAINS

Train No.	Effective	
31-32	November 10, 1946	Established as passenger setting out and picking up baggage and express at Colfax and Truckee.
25-26	October 19, 1947	Renumbered Nos. 25 and 26.
	May 19, 1954	Nos. 25 and 26 discontinued.

CHALLENGER

Train No.	Effective	
87-88	September 15, 1937	New train commenced operation.
23-24	June 2, 1946	Changed train numbers.
	October 19, 1947	Discontinued when renamed *Gold Coast*.

277

COLFAX LOCALS — NEWSBOY MOUNTAIN EXPRESS TRUCKEE PASSENGER — SF PASSENGER

Train No.	Effective	
25-26	July 1, 1892	Sacramento-Colfax locals established with even Nos. west and odd Nos. east.
33-34	April 9, 1899	Numbers changed.
	October 15, 1899	Schedules reversed — evens east, odds west.
	February 26, 1900	Schedules extended from Colfax to Towle.
	November 7, 1900	Schedules cut back to Colfax.
37-38	May 29, 1908	Sacramento-Colfax passenger added in addition to Nos. 33 and 34.
109-110	August 20, 1911	Nos. 37-38 changed to Nos. 109-110.
	May 1, 1913	No. 109 became *Mountain Express* and No. 110 became the *Newsboy* both operating Sacramento to Sparks.
109-110 35-36	September 21, 1913	Train Nos. 109-110 discontinued from Colfax to Sparks. Also, add Nos. 35-36 making a total of three Sacramento-Colfax local trains — Nos. 33, 34, 35, 36, 109 and 110.
35-36	October 5, 1913	Train Nos. 35 and 36 discontinued.
109-110	January 4, 1914	Nos. 109-110 becomes 209-210.
209-210	June 2, 1918	No. 209 became *SF Passenger* and No. 210 *Sparks Passenger* operating between Sacramento and Sparks.
	June 1, 1919	Nos. 209-210 discontinued. Nos. 33-34 remained.
	June 27, 1920	Nos. 209 *Colfax-SF Passenger* and No. 210 the *Newsboy* restored Sacramento to Colfax.
	February 27, 1921	Nos. 209-210 discontinued.
	May 28, 1922	Nos. 209 *Colfax-Sacramento Passenger* and No. 210 *Sacramento-Colfax Passenger* restored.
	September 17, 1922	Nos. 209-210 discontinued once again.
	June 10, 1923	Extra train operated on schedule of Nos. 209-210 Sacramento to Colfax.
	January 13, 1924	Extra train discontinued.
	June 25, 1924	Extra train restored between Sacramento-Colfax.
	July 17, 1924	Extra train discontinued.
	May 3, 1925	Nos. 209-210 restored between Sacramento and Truckee. No. 209 *S.F. Passenger.* No. 210 *Truckee Passenger.*
	October 1, 1925	Nos. 209-210 discontinued.
35-36- 33-34	June 6, 1926	Nos. 35 and 36 added Sacramento-Colfax. These were steam trains. At this time Nos. 33 and 34, in service continuously since 1899 are first shown as *Motors,* meaning McKeen cars.
35-36	November 14, 1926	Nos. 35-36 discontinued.
534-535	April 17, 1927	Nos. 34-35 renumbered 534-535.
33-34	May 29, 1927	Nos. 33-34 (steam trans) added between Sacramento and Colfax.
	September 25, 1927	Nos. 33-34 discontinued.
	June 1, 1928	Nos 33-34 restored.
	September 2, 1928	Nos. 33-34 discontinued.
	June 9, 1929	Nos 33-34 restored.
	October 6, 1929	Nos. 33-34 discontinued.
291-294	April 24, 1932	Motor Nos. 534-535 renumbered 291-294.
294-295	June 19, 1932	Motor Nos. 291-294 renumbered 294-295.
	February 26, 1933	Motors 294-295 discontinued ending all Colfax local service. The last run of No. 295 utilized McKeen car No. 45 and an R.P.O. trailer.

FORTY NINER TREASURE ISLAND SPECIAL

Train No.	Effective	
48-49	July 11, 1937	New train established operating five times a month in each direction.
	May 22, 1939	*Treasure Island Special* established. Operated as Nos. 48-49 five times a month alternating with the *Forty Niner.*
	September 25, 1939	*Treasure Island Special* discontinued.
	June 21, 1940	*Treasure Island Special* reestablished.
	September 16, 1940	*Treasure Island Special* discontinued.
	July 23, 1941	*Forty Niner* discontinued.

CITY OF SAN FRANCISCO

Train No.	Effective	
2-9 2-14	June 14, 1936	New streamlined train inaugurated, making five round trips per month with a diesel-powered 11-unit consist.
101-102	December 13, 1936	Train numbers assigned.
	January 2, 1938	New 17-car train supplants original 11-car train.
	July 26, 1941	Second train established increasing frequency to 10 round trips per month.
	October 1, 1946	Operates tri-weekly each direction.
	September 1, 1947	Train now operates daily.
	March 29, 1970	Train cut back to tri-weekly.
	May 1, 1971	AMTRAK assumes operation. Shown as *California Zephyr* in public timetables and *NRPC* in employee timetables.
5-6	November 14, 1971	Change numbers and name to *City of San Francisco.*
	June 11, 1972	Renamed *S.F. Zephyr* and frequency increased to daily.
	September 17, 1972	Cut back to tri-weekly.
	June 10, 1973	Increased to daily operation.
	April 24, 1983	Name changed to *California Zephyr.*

FURLOUGHEE CHALLENGER MILITARY CHALLENGER ADVANCE CHALLENGER

Train No.	Effective	
1-248 2-28	December 31, 1944	*Furloughee Challenger* established eastbound only operating as 1-248 San Francisco to Sacramento and 2-28 Sacramento to Ogden. Train operated for furloughees and members of their families traveling with them.
14	September 9, 1945	Assigned train number.
	December 23, 1945	Became *Military Challenger.*
	April 14, 1946	Became *Advance Challenger.* Also handled civilian passengers.
	June 2, 1946	No. 14 discontinued.

278

TRUCKEE-SPARKS MOTORS
FISHERMAN'S MOTORS

Train No.	Effective	
98-99 100-101	September 12, 1909	*Truckee-Sparks Motors* placed in service marking the beginning of McKeen Motorcar service on the Mountain.
526-527 528-529	February 12, 1911	Train Nos. 98-99 changed to 526-527. Train Nos. 100-101 changed to 528-529.

TAHOE

Train No.	Effective	
21-22	September 25, 1927	New train established and operated San Francisco to Klamath Falls via Sparks and Modoc Line.
	June 9, 1929	Discontinued.
	September 21, 1930	Reestablished.
	September 15, 1931	Name changed to *Passenger*.
22-23	June 19, 1932	No. 21 became No. 23.
	September 18, 1932	Train Nos. 22 and 23 discontinued.

Appendix B
Seasonal Snowfall at Summit 1878-1926, Norden 1926-1985

Source: Southern Pacific Transportation Company

Year	Snowfall	Year	Snowfall	Year	Snowfall	Year	Snowfall	Year	Snowfall	Year	Snowfall
1878	-445*	1896	-560	1914	-361	1932	-428	1950	-327	1968	-639
1879	-783	1897	-262	1915	-480	1933	-247	1951	-741	1969	-322
1880	-153	1898	-481	1916	-365	1934	-661	1952	-270	1970	-538
1881	-492	1899	-406	1917	-290	1935	-588	1953	-264	1971	-449
1882	-299	1900	-440	1918	-321	1936	-475	1954	-338	1972	-466
1883	-481	1901	-373	1919	-326	1937	-819**	1955	-594	1973	-497
1884	-202	1902	-407	1920	-443	1938	-311	1956	-266	1974	-525
1885	-462	1903	-434	1921	-514	1939	-373	1957	-462	1975	-253
1886	-422	1904	-375	1922	-452	1940	-360	1958	-230	1976	-227
1887	-345	1905	-514	1923	-195	1941	-535	1959	-268	1977	-533
1888	-261	1906	-602	1924	-228	1942	-305	1960	-320	1978	-422
1889	-776	1907	-340	1925	-228	1943	-307	1961	-457	1979	-460
1890	-335	1908	-442	1926	-359	1944	-483	1962	-333	1980	-275
1891	-380	1909	-342	1927	-307	1945	-337	1963	-447	1981	-680
1892	-634	1910	-563	1928	-300	1946	-229	1964	-475	1982	-796
1893	-511	1911	-277	1929	-251	1947	-275	1965	-327	1983	-372
1894	-685	1912	-284	1930	-229	1948	-426	1966	-629	1984	-416
1895	-544	1913	-437	1931	-501	1949	-467	1967	-361	1985	(SEE NOTE)

*Snowfall figures are in inches.
**Record

NOTE: Snowfall figures are based on a fiscal year basis. The seasonal snowfall figure shown above for the year 1984 ran from July 1, 1984 through June 30, 1985.

The Streamliner, *City of San Francisco*, refuels on the mainline at Sparks while making its first run west. — J.F. OREM COLLECTION

Appendix C
Selected Timetables

SACRAMENTO DIVISION: Sacramento and Truckee.

TIME TABLE No. 3, May 7, 1893.

FROM SAN FRANCISCO.

Second Class				First Class					Dist. from S.F.	STATIONS
19 Freight Daily	**9** Freight Daily	**7** Through Freight Daily	**5** Freight Daily	**15** Oregon Express Daily	**11** Red Bluff Passenger Daily	**25** Colfax Passenger Daily	**3** Atlantic Express Daily	**1** Atlantic Express Daily		
			PM LV 11.00		AM LV 10.30					
				PM LV 7.00		AM LV 8.00				
							PM LV 8 30	PM LV 5.00	AM LV 7.00	
		AM LV 12.01	AM LV 7.30	PM LV 3.45	PM LV 10.50	PM LV 3.00	PM LV 5.00	9.00	AM LV 10.50	151.19	dn.SAN FRANCISCO dn.SACRAMENTO
		12.15	7.45	4.00	10.58	f 3.09	f 5.08	9.09	11.00	154.55	...Am. River Bridge 3.07
		12.30	8.00	4.15	f11.07	f 3.18	f 5.17	9.18	f11.09	157.62	...Benali 1.49
		12.35	8.05	4.20	11.09	s 3.25	f 5.20	9.20	f11.12	159.11	...Arcade 6.42
		12.55	8.25	4.40	f11.20	s 3.40	f 5.32	9.35	f11.26	165.53	...Antelope 3.90
		1.10	8.45	5.05	11.35 PM AR	3.50 PM AR	s 5.45	s 9.43	s11.35	169.43	d..ROSEVILLE JC 3.91
	AM LV 6.00	1.35) 2.10)	9.15) 10.00)	5.25) 6.00)			s 9.55) 6.00)	s 9.55) 10.00)	s11.45) 11.50) PM	173.34	dn.ROCKLIN 3.04
	6.15	2.25	10.15	6.20			s 6.10	10.15	s12.05	176.38	d..Loomis 2.88
	6.35	2.40	10.30	6.35			f 6.20	10.26	s12.18	179.26	d Penryn 3.18
	7.00	3.00	11.15 PM	7.30			s 6.35	s10.39	f12.32	182.44	d..Newcastle 4.89
	8.30	3.35	1.00	8.15			s 7.00	s11.05	s 1.00	187.33	dn.Auburn 3.31
	8.55	3.55	1.20	8.35			f 7.09	11.14	1.09	190.64	...Bowman 3.40
	9.25	4.15	1.45	8.55			s 7.20	11.24	s 1.20	194.04	d..Clipper Gap 2.97
	9.50	4.45	2.10	9.10			f 7.32	11.35	s 1.35	197.01	...Applegate 3.31
	10.10	5.10	2.40	9.25			s 7.45	11.48	s 1.52	200.32	d..N. E. Mills 5.06
	11.00	5.40	3.10	9.55			8.00 PM AR	AM 12.10	s 2.15	205.38	dn.COLFAX 4.50
	11.30 PM	6.10	3.35	10.25				12.37	f 2.37	209.88	...C. H. Mills 5.94
	12.35	7.10	4.35	11.10				s 1.00) 1.10)	s 2.55) 3.05)	215.84	dn.Gold Run 2.13
	12.50	7.25	4.45	11.25				s 1.26	s 3.18	217.97	d..Dutch Flat 1.87
	1.10	7.50	5.05	11.45				1.35	s 3.27	219.84	n..Alta 0.84
	1.25	8.00	5.10	11.50				f 1.41	s 3.32	220.68	d..Towles 4.00
	1.50	8.25	5.35	AM 12.15				2.02	f 3.50	224.68	...Shady Run 4.72
	2.50	9.10	6.25	1.00				s 2.45	s 4.15	229.40	dn.Blue Canon 3.03
	3.10	9.30	6.45	1.20				3.03	f 4.32	232.43	...27..Wood Shed 2.17
	3.25	10.00	7.05	1.35				s 3.15	f 4.40	234.60	dn.Emigrant Gap 4.26
	3.45	10.20	7.30	2.05				3.32	f 4.54	238.86	...Yuba Pass 4.24
	4.10	10.55	7.55	2.30				s 3.55	s 5.14	243.10	dn.Cisco 3.51
	4.25	11.15	8.10	2.45				4.09	f 5.25	246.61	...Tamarack 4.02
	4.45	11.35	8.30	3.05				4.25	f 5.38	250.63	dn.Cascade 2.81
	4.55	11.45 PM	8.40	3.15				4.35	f 5.45	253.44	...Soda Springs 2.96
	5.10	12.05	9.00	3.40				s 4.50	s 5.55	256.40	dn.Summit 2.70
	5.30	12.25	9.20	4.05				5.01	f 6.06	259.10	...Lake View 3.99
	5.55	12.50	9.40	4.25				5.16	f 6.21	263.09	dn.Tunnel 13 1.10
	6.00	12.55	9.45	4.30				5.20	f 6.25	264.19	...Strong's Canon 2.13
	6.15	1.10	10.00	4.45				5.29	f 6.34	267.16	...Champions 3.55
	6.30 PM AR	1.25 PM AR	10.15 AM AR	5.00 AM AR				5.40 AM AR	6.45 PM AR	270.71	dn.TRUCKEE
		10.00 Daily	4.30 PM AR Daily	1.45 AM AR Daily				5.15 AM AR Daily	4.45 PM AR Daily		...OGDEN

SACRAMENTO DIVISION: Sacramento and Truckee.

TOWARD SAN FRANCISCO.

TIME TABLE No. 3, May 7, 1893.

STATIONS	DIST. FROM TRUCKEE	First Class 2 Pacific Express Daily	First Class 4 Pacific Express Daily	First Class 26 Colfax Passenger Daily	First Class 12 Red Bluff Passenger Daily	First Class 16 Oregon Express Daily	Second Class 6 Through Freight Daily	Second Class 8 Through Freight Daily	Second Class 10 Freight Daily	Second Class 20 Freight Daily
SAN FRANCISCO		PM AR 7.45	AM AR 10.45	PM AR 4.15	PM AR 4.15	AM AR 8.15	AM AR 8.10	AM AR 1.30		
dn.SACRAMENTO..W	119.52	PM AR 3.45	AM AR 6.50	AM AR 10.05	AM AR 10.15	AM AR 4.15	PM AR 10.50	2.00	AM AR 3.00	
Am. River Bridge	116.16	3.37	6.42	9.57	f 10.07	4.07	10.25	1.45	2.45	
Benall	113.09	f 3.28	6.33	f 9.48	f 9.58	3.58	10.10	1.30	2.30	
Arcade	111.60	s 3.23	6.30	f 9.45	f 9.55	3.55	10.05	1.25	2.25	
Antelope	105.18	f 3.15	6.20	s 9.35	f 9.45	3.45	9.35	1.05	2.05	
d.ROSEVILLE JC..W	101.28	s 3.05	s 6.10	s 9.25	9.35 AM LV	3.35 AM LV	9.05	12.50	1.50	PM AR
dn.ROCKLIN......W	97.37	s 2.55	s 6.00	s 9.15			8.30	12.30	1.35	6.00
d..Loomis	94.33	s 2.37	f 5.44	s 9.05			8.05	12.05 PM	1.10	5.35
d..Penryn	91.45	s 2.29	f 5.36	s 8.56			7.50	11.40	1.00	5.15
d..Newcastle....W	88.27	s 2.20	s 5.25	s 8.45			7.30	11.15	12.45	4.50
dn.Auburn......W	83.38	s 2.05	s 5.10	s 8 30			7.00	10.35	12.25	4.10
Bowman	80.07	1.54	5.01	f 8.19			6.35	10.15	12.10 AM	3.35
d..Clipper Gap..W	76.67	s 1.45	4.53	s 8.10			6.20	10.00	11.55	3.15
Applegate	73.70	s 1.35	4.45	f 8.02			6.05	9.50	11.35	2.55
d..N. E. Mills	70.39	s 1.25	4.35	f 7.53			5.50	9.35	11.10	2.40
dn.COLFAX......W	65.33	s 1.05	s 4.20	7.40 AM LV			5.25	9.10	10.50	2.15
C. H. Mills	60.83	f 12.50	4.03				5.00	8.40	10.25	1.15
dn.Gold Run....W	54.87	s 12.35	f 3.47				4.35	8.15	10.00	12.35
d..Dutch Flat	52.74	s 12.29	s 3.40				4.25	8.00	9.45	12.10 PM
n..Alta........W	50.87	s 12.24	3.33				4.15	7.50	9.35	11.55
d..Towles	50.03	s 12.21	f 3.30				4.10	7.35	9.30	11.50
Shady Run	46.03	12.09 PM	3.18				3.50	7.00	9.10	11.25
dn.Blue Canon..W	41.31	s 11.55 s 11.45	2.55 2.45				2.50	6.35	8.40	11.00
27..Wood Shed	38.28	f 11.33	2.32				2.35	6.00	8.00	10.10
dn.Emigrant Gap..W	36.11	s 11.25	s 2.24				2.25	5.50	7.50	10.00
Yuba Pass	31.85	f 11.10	2.05				2.05	5.30	7.30	9.20
dn.Cisco	27.61	s 10.55	s 1.50				1.45	5.10	7.10	9.00
Tamarack	24.10	f 10.41	1.36				1.30	4.50	6.45	8.45
dn.Cascade	20.08	f 10.25	1.20				1.10	4.25	6.25	8.25
Soda Springs	17.27	f 10.16	1.11				1.00	4.00	6.15	8.10
dn.Summit......W	14.31	s 10.05	s 1.00				12.45	3.40	5.55	7.55
Lakeview	11.61	f 9.50	12.45				12.25	3.25	5.30	7.35
dn.Tunnel 13	7.62	f 9.35	12.30				12.05 PM	3.05	5.05	7.15
Strong's Canon	6.52	f 9.31	12.26				11.55	2.55	4.55	7.05
Champions	3.55	f 9.20	12.15				11.35	2.35	4.35	6.50
dn.TRUCKEE....W	0.00	9.05 AM LV	12.01 AM LV				11.15 AM LV	2.15 AM LV	4.15 PM LV	6.30 AM LV
OGDEN		11.15 AM LV	12.45 AM LV				6.30 PM LV	6.45 PM LV	1.20 PM LV	
		Daily	Daily	Daily	Daily	Daily	Daily	Daily	Daily	Daily

TRUCKEE DIVISION: Truckee and Wadsworth.

FROM SAN FRANCISCO.   TIME TABLE No. 1, July 1, 1892.   TOWARD SAN FRANCISCO.

THIRD CLASS 11 Local Freight Lv. Daily	Second Class 9 Freight Lv. Daily	Second Class 7 Through Freight Lv. Daily	Second Class 5 Freight Lv. Daily	First Class 3 Atlantic Express Lv. Daily	First Class 1 Atlantic Express Lv. Daily	DIST. SAN FRAN.	STATIONS	DIST. FROM WADSWORTH	First Class 2 Pacific Express Ar. Daily	First Class 4 Pacific Express Ar. Daily	Second Class 6 Through Freight Ar. Daily	Second Class 8 Freight Ar. Daily	Second Class 10 Freight Ar. Daily	THIRD CLASS 12 Local Freight Ar. Daily
				PM 6.00	AM 8.00	0.00	SAN FRANCISCO	151.19	PM 9.45	AM 9.15				
	AM 12.01	AM 7.40	PM 2.15	PM 10.00	AM 11.55	151.19	SACRAMENTO	119.52	AM 6.05	AM 5.30	AM 12.01	PM 1.45	AM 2.40	
	PM 1.15	PM 10.00	AM 4.20	AM 6.20	PM 8.20	270.71	TRUCKEE	68.81	AM 11.00	PM 10.40	PM 1.15	PM 2.15	PM 4.00	
AM 7.00	PM 2.15	12.01	5.15	AM 6.35	PM 8.35	270.71	dn.TRUCKEE..W	68.81	10.45	10.25	11.59	1.05	2.15	PM 5.30
7.12	2.28	12.10	5.27	6.42	f 8.42	273.47	Winsted	66.05	f 10.37	10.17	11.37	12.48	2.00	5.05
7.32	2.43	12.25	5.44	6.50	8.55	277.57	Prosser Creek	61.95	f 10.25	10.04	11.10	12.25	1.40	4.30
7.40	2.50	12.30	5.50	s 6.53	s 9.00	279.14	dn.Boca......W	60.38	s 10.20	s 10.00	11.00	12.15	1.30	4.15
8.15	3.20	12.51	6.15	7.07	s 9.15	284.84	d..Floriston	54.68	f 10.03	9.40	10.20	11.47	AM 12.40	3.20
8.37	3.35	1.05	6.30	7.15	9.30	288.35	Mystic	50.68	f 9.52	9.30	9.52	11.30	12.40	2.50
9.15	3.53	1.25	6.53	7.28	9.43	293.96	Essex	45.57	f 9.35	9.13	9.15	11.05	12.15	2.10
9.33	3.58	1.30	6.59	s 7.30	s 9.45	295.19	d..Verdi	44.34	s 9.32	f 9.10	9.05	10.55	12.05	2.00
10.22	4.15	1.50	7.22	7.43	9.58	300.67	Lawton	38.85	f 9.15	8.55	8.35	10.31	PM 11.35	1.20
11.10 AM	4.30 5.00	2.10 2.20	7.55 8.40	s 7.55 8.05	s10.10 10.20	305.66	dn.RENO....W	34.86	s 8.40	s 8.30	7.55	10.10 9.30	11.10 10.15	12.40 PM
	5.25	2.45	9.08	8.25	f 10.35	313.39	Vista	26.22	f 8.25	8.14	7.30	9.00	9.47	
	5.40	3.00	9.30	8.33	f 10.43	317.62	Naked	21.90	f 8.16	8.05	7.15	8.45	9.30	
	6.05	3.25	10.00	8.50	f 10.58	325.26	d..Clark's	14.26	f 8.00	7.49	6.51	8.18	8.50	
	6.30	3.52	10.25	9.05	f 11.12	332.81	Salvia	6.71	f 7.44	7.34	6.27	7.50	8.13	
	6.50 PM	4.15 AM	10 50 AM	9.20 AM	11.25 AM	339.52	dn.WADSWORTH W	0.00	7.30 AM	7.20 PM	6.05 PM	7.20 PM	7.45 AM	
Ar. Daily	Ar. Daily	Ar. Daily	Ar. Daily	Ar. Daily	Ar. Daily				Lv. Daily	Lv. Daily	Lv. Daily	Lv. Daily	Lv. Daily	Lv. Daily

Time Table No. 91 — October 5, 1913

Eastward. FROM SAN FRANCISCO

Page 1

THIRD CLASS					SECOND CLASS		FIRST CLASS											Distance from San Francisco	STATIONS
220 Chico Mdse	222 Portland Way Freight	256 Sunset Manifest	308 Way Freight	306 Way Freight	548 Chico MOTOR	254 Ogden Manifest	4 Express	48 El Dorado	2 Overland Limited	34 Colfax Passenger	32 Red Bluff Passenger	20 Pacific Limited	24 Tonopah Express	28 Dunsmuir Passenger	110 The Newsboy	10 California Mail	16 Oregon Express	6 Atlantic Express		
Lv Daily except Sunday	Leave Daily	Leave Daily	Leave Daily Ex.Sunday	Leave Daily Ex.Sunday	Leave Daily	Leave Daily	Leave Daily	Leave Daily	Leave Daily	Leave Daily	Leave Daily	Leave Daily	Leave Daily	Leave Daily	Leave Daily	Leave Daily	Leave Daily	Leave Daily		
8.40PM	6.40AM				8.30AM		10.45PM	8.20AM	7.15AM	4.35AM	4.05PM	1.45PM	12.50PM	11.30AM	7.25AM	3.30AM	12.25AM	12.01AM	88.8	DNR SACRAMENTO
8.50	6.55	6.40AM			f8.40	7.40AM	10.55	8.30	7.25	f4.45	f4.15	1.55	f1.00	f11.40	f7.35	3.40	12.35	12.11	91.8	ELVAS
					f8.46		11.00	8.35	7.30	f4.50	f4.20	2.00	f1.05	f11.45	f7.40	3.45	12.40	12.16	94.9	BENALI
					f9.00		11.10	8.47	7.40	f5.00	f4.33	2.10	f1.15	f11.57AM	f7.50	3.55	12.50	12.26	99.4	WALERGA
					f9.10	8.15	*11.15	*8.53AM	7.50	*5.10	*4.40PM	*2.17	*1.22	*12.05PM	7.58	*4.00	*12.55	*12.31	102.8	ANTELOPE
9.40AM	7.45AM	7.30AM		6.00AM		8.45	*11.18		7.53			*2.20						*12.36	106.6	DNR ROSEVILLE
				6.25			10.00	f11.30	7.58	*5.18		2.30	1.35		*8.07	4.15		*12.46	107.9	ENWOOD
						See Page 5	10.15	f11.41	8.07		See page 5	2.42	See page 5	See page 5	4.30	f12.57	110.6	ROCKLIN
			10.40AM				10.30	*11.55PM	8.16	*5.45		2.54	*2.09		*8.40	4.43	f1.08	115.2	LINCOLN AV. PENRYN
			11.55AM				10.50	f12.10AM	8.24	f5.55		3.03	2.20		*8.50	4.58	*1.23	120.2	DN NEWCASTLE
			1.00PM				11.05	f12.20	8.33	f6.06		3.14	*2.30		f9.01	5.09	1.34	124.2	AUBURN, NEVADA ST.
			1.30				11.20	f12.29	8.38	f6.15		3.23	*2.38		f9.10	5.19	1.44	129.1	DN BOWMAN
			1.55				11.35	12.37	8.45	f6.24		3.32	*2.48		f9.20	5.29	1.52	131.4	CLIPPER GAP
			2.15				11.47	12.46	8.51	f6.32		3.41	2.58		f9.30	5.39	2.00	134.3	APPLEGATE
			2.35				11.55AM	12.53	8.55	f6.40		3.47	3.03		f9.35	5.45	2.05	137.5	N. E. MILLS
			6.15AM	3.00PM			12.30PM	*1.15	*9.07	*6.50AM		*4.00	3.20		*9.45AM	*6.00	*2.20	139.0	LANDER
			6.30				12.45	1.25	9.15			4.10	3.30			6.10	2.31	141.7/142.4	DNR COLFAX
			6.45				12.55	1.40	9.22			4.17	3.38			f6.20	2.48	144.9	WIRT
			7.05				1.10	1.53	9.29			4.25	3.50			f6.30	3.00	146.9	CAPE HORN
			8.00				1.53	2.15	9.40			4.40	4.10			f6.50	3.22	149.6	MAGRA
			8.15				2.05	2.24	9.45			4.48	f4.17			f7.00	3.31	153.2	GOLD RUN
								f					f			f		155.2	DUTCH FLAT
			8.40				2.25	2.32	9.52			4.55	f4.24			f7.12	3.42	157.1	ALTA
			8.55				2.40	2.39	9.58			5.03	f4.31			f7.20	3.50	157.8	DN TOWLE
			9.15				2.55	2.46	10.05			5.08	f4.38			f7.30	4.00	159.7	GORGE
			9.40				3.10	2.55	10.11			5.15	f4.45			f7.42	4.10	161.6	MIDAS
																		164.1	OREL
			10.15AM	3.30PM			*3.05AM	*10.20			*5.30PM	*4.55			7.55AM	*4.25AM	166.6	DN BLUE CANON

Time over District / Average speed per hour

On single track westward trains are superior to trains of the same class in the opposite direction. See Rule 72 and D72.

Track No. 4 between Rocklin and Loomis will be used exclusively by Nos. 110, 24, 34 and 306 and yard engines moving eastward and other trains authorized by train order.

Nos. 24, 110, 34 and 306 will register at Newcastle.

ADDITIONAL STOPS.
No. 110 will stop on signal at County road crossing mile and half west of Benali.
Nos. 6, 10 and 20 will stop on signal at stations west of Colfax to pick up passengers for points east of Ogden.
No. 2 will stop on signal at stations west of Colfax to pick up passengers for points Cheyenne and east.

Page 2 — Eastward. FROM SAN FRANCISCO

THIRD CLASS		SECOND CLASS	FIRST CLASS						Distance from San Francisco	STATIONS
308 Way Freight	310 Way Freight	254 Ogden Manifest	2 Overland Limited	20 Pacific Limited	24 Tonopah Express	10 California Mail	6 Atlantic Express	4 Express		
Leave Daily Ex.Sunday	Leave Daily Ex.Sunday	Leave Daily	Leave Daily	Leave Daily	Leave Daily	Leave Daily	Leave Daily	Leave Daily		
10.30AM		3.50PM	10.25PM	5.35PM	5.00PM	8.00AM	4.30AM	3.10AM	166.6	DN BLUE CANON
10.55		4.10	10.35	5.47	5.13	8.13	4.42	3.22	169.7	FULDA
11.20		4.20	10.41	5.53	f5.19	8.22	4.50	f3.35	171.8	DN EMIGRANT GAP
11.50AM		4.30	10.45	5.57	f5.25	8.27	4.56	f3.40	173.8	DN SMART
12.35PM		4.47	10.53	6.04	5.35	8.37	5.07	f3.48	176.1	YUBA PASS
1.00		5.00	11.00	6.10	5.42	8.47	5.17	f3.59	178.3	CRYSTAL LAKE
1.15		5.14	11.05	6.15	f5.49	8.54	5.25	f4.08	180.3	DN CISCO
1.35		5.33	11.13	6.25	6.00	9.08	5.40	4.20	183.3	DN TAMARACK
1.50		5.45	11.24	6.31	f6.08	9.15	5.48	4.28	185.8	TROY
2.05		6.00	11.30	6.37	6.15	f9.25	5.58	f4.36	187.6	SPRUCE
2.25		6.25	11.38	6.45	*6.25	9.35	6.10	4.45	190.7	SODA SPRINGS
2.45		7.25								
3.00		7.40	11.48	6.55	6.37	*9.50	6.23	5.00	193.0	DN SUMMIT
3.15		7.50	11.57PM	7.06	6.48	f10.02	6.35	5.12	196.2	LAKE VIEW
3.30		8.00	12.03AM	7.13	6.54	f10.09	6.41	5.20	198.2	EDER
			12.08	7.20	7.01	f10.17	6.48	5.30	200.6	DN ANDOVER
									202.7	*STANFORD
									203.6	*ARCTIC
3.50		8.20	12.17	7.30	7.13	f10.30	7.00	5.45	204.1	CHAMPION
									206.8	*DONNER ICE CO.
4.10PM	8.00AM	8.35	*12.28	*7.43	*7.23	*10.50	7.15	6.15	208.0	DNR TRUCKEE
	8.25	9.30	12.33	7.50	7.57	f10.59	7.23	6.23	210.6	WINSTED
									211.2	*POLARIS
	8.45	9.48	12.40	7.58	f8.09	f11.10	7.33	6.35	215.0	PROSSER CREEK
	9.05	9.53	12.44	8.02	*8.14	*11.15	7.38	6.42	216.3	DN BOCA
									218.1	*BURKHALTER
	9.25	10.10	12.51	8.10	8.23	f11.23	7.47	6.53	220.4	HINTON
				f		f			220.9	*ICELAND
									221.5	*WICKES
	10.10	10.18	12.55	8.15	*8.30	*11.30	7.53	7.02	223.5	DN FLORISTON
	10.35	10.30	1.00	8.22	f8.45	f11.37	8.00	7.11	225.5	MYSTIC
	10.55	10.50	1.06	8.29	f8.57	f11.43	8.08	7.20	228.6	CALVADA
	11.55AM	11.10	1.15	8.36	*9.10	*11.55AM	8.18	7.35	232.4	DN VERDI
	12.20PM	11.22	1.25	8.41	9.17	f12.01PM	8.24	7.41	234.6	WARE
					f				235.9	MOGUL
	12.45	11.35PM	1.31	8.46	9.25	f12.10	8.30	7.50	237.9	DNR LAWTON
	2.00	12.15AM	*1.45	*9.05	*9.40	*12.20	*8.45	8.15	242.7	OP RENO
			1.50	9.10	9.55	f12.40	8.55	8.25	245.5	SPARKS (Passenger Depot)
		2.30AM	1.55AM	9.15AM	*10.00AM	*12.45AM	9.00AM	8.35AM	246.2	DNR SPARKS (Depr's Office)

A disc signal, attached to automatic block signal post 2108 at Winsted when displaying blue is to notify Eastward trains to communicate with telegraph office at Truckee by means of telephone located in battery house opposite East Switch—Call, one long ring.
Mystic—Telephone in east end of east car body.
Calvada—Telephone in battery house opposite spur switch.
Prosser Creek—Telephone in battery house east of west switch.
*Frog taken out part of season.

Westward trains are superior to trains of the same class in the opposite direction. See Rule 72 and D72.

ADDITIONAL STOPS.
Nos. 10 and 24 will stop on signal at Union Mills, near mile post 214, Farad and Marmol.
No. 6 Union Mills on flag.
No. 24 stop on signal Summit Hotel.

Time Table No. 91 — October 5, 1913 — TOWARD SAN FRANCISCO (Westward)

Eastward FROM SAN FRANCISCO

306 Way Freight	34 Colfax Passenger	24 Tonopah Express	110 The Newsboy
Lv. Daily Ex. Sun.	Lv. Daily	Lv. Daily	Lv. Daily
6.25AM	5.18PM	1.35PM	8.07AM
6.50	s 5.28	s 1.48	8.17
7.40	s 5.35	s 1.58	8.30
8.00			
9.00	s 5.45	2.09	8.40
10.30			

The above schedules are shown only for information and have no time table superiority between Loomis and Newcastle, but will be known by their numbers and handled only by train orders between Loomis and Newcastle.

First Class / Second Class / Third Class — Stations

Stations	Dist. from Blue Canon	23 Tonopah Express	19 Pacific Limited	1 Overland Limited	9 Fast Mail	3 California Mail	47 El Dorado	33 Colfax Passenger	15 California Express	27 San Francisco Passenger	5 Pacific Express	109 Mountain Express	547 Chico MOTOR	305 Way Freight	253 Ogden Manifest	307 Way Freight	257 Sunset Manifest	221 Portland Fast Freight
DNR SACRAMENTO	77.8	s 4.10AM	s 5.10AM	s 6.00AM	s 6.40AM	7.50AM	8.05AM	9.45AM	9.10AM	3.00PM	4.45PM	6.25PM		6.30PM				7.00PM
ELVAS	74.8	4.00	5.00	5.50	6.30	7.40	7.55	f9.35	9.00	f2.50	4.35	6.15		f6.20		3.25PM		6.00AM 6.45
BENALI	71.7	3.55	4.54	5.45	6.25	7.32	7.50	f9.29	8.52	f2.42	4.28	6.05		f6.13				
WALERGA	67.2							f						f				
ANTELOPE	63.8	3.45	4.42	5.35	6.15	7.20	7.40	f9.19	8.42	f2.27	4.15	5.47		f5.57				
DNR ROSEVILLE	60.0	3.40	4.35	5.30	6.10	s7.15	s7.35	9.12	s8.35	2.20PM	4.10	5.40		s5.50	3.00PM 2.50		5.00PM 6.00PM
ENWOOD	58.7																	
ROCKLIN	56.0	f3.25	4.24	5.15	5.55	f7.00		s9.01			3.55	s5.32			2.45	1.25		
D LOOMIS	52.9	3.16	4.18	5.07	5.48	f6.53		s8.54			3.46	s5.21			2.20	1.10		
D PENRYN	50.1	3.10	4.12	5.00	5.43	6.47		s8.48			3.40	s5.11			1.58	12.55		
DN NEWCASTLE	46.9	3.02	4.05	4.53	5.37	f6.40		s8.40			3.32	s5.01			12.40PM 12.40			
ZETA	44.9	2.55	3.59	4.48	5.30	6.34		f8.35			3.27	f4.50			11.45AM			
FLINT	42.8																	
DN AUBURN	41.9	s 2.48	3.52	4.42	5.25	6.28		8.30		s3.20	4.41			10.45	12.15PM			
DN BOWMAN	38.8	2.40	3.44	4.35	5.19	6.22		f8.20			3.08	f4.31			9.30	11.59AM		
CLIPPER GAP	35.4	2.32	3.36	4.27	5.13	6.15		f8.13			2.59	f4.23						
APPLEGATE	32.4	2.25	3.29	4.20	5.07	6.08		f8.06			2.51	f4.17						
N. E. MILLS	29.2	2.17	3.21	4.13	5.01	6.02		f7.58			2.43	f4.11						
LANDER	27.2	2.13	3.16	4.08	4.56	5.57		f7.52			2.38	f4.07						
DNR COLFAX	24.2	2.05	s3.08	f4.01	4.50	s5.50		7.45AM		s2.30	4.00PM			7.50AM 10.50	5.30PM			
WIRT	21.7	1.50	2.55	3.48	4.40	5.34					2.15				10.30	5.10		
DN CAPE HORN	19.7	1.40	2.48	3.44	4.35	5.29					2.09				10.20	4.50		
MAGRA	17.0	1.28	2.40	3.38	4.29	5.22					2.03				10.10	3.33		
DN GOLD RUN	13.4	1.17	2.32	3.30	4.22	f5.13					f1.53				9.55	3.30		
DUTCH FLAT	11.4	1.10	2.26	3.25	4.18	f5.07					f1.47				9.35	2.30		
ALTA	9.5	s									f							
DN TOWLE	8.8	f 1.00	2.20	3.20	4.13	5.01					1.40				9.23	2.05		
GORGE	6.9	f12.55	2.16	3.15	4.10	4.57					1.35				9.15	1.50		
MIDAS	4.8	12.49	2.10	3.10	4.06	4.52					1.29				9.04	1.29		
OREL	2.5	f12.40	2.03	3.03	4.02	4.45					1.20				8.53	1.00		
DN BLUE CANON	0.0	12.30AM	1.55	2.55AM	3.55AM	4.35AM					1.10PM				8.40AM 12.30PM			

On single track westward trains are superior to trains of the same class in the opposite direction. See Rule 72 and D72.

Westward trains receiving orders east of Newcastle moving an eastward train from Loomis to Newcastle against them, must not pass east cross-over switch at Newcastle until opposing trains on Track No. 1 have arrived.

All westward trains must stop east of east cross-over switch at Newcastle unless they receive a proceed train-order signal.

Nos. 24, 110, 34 and 306 will use track No. 4 Rocklin to Loomis and will register at Newcastle.

ADDITIONAL STOPS.

No. 109 will stop at Antelope, Walerga, Benali and Elvas to discharge passengers from points east of Roseville.

No. 23 will stop at stations between Roseville and Sacramento to discharge passengers from points east of Colfax.

No. 109 will stop at County Road Crossing mile and a half west of Benali on signal.

Nos. 3, 5 and 19 will stop at stations west of Colfax to discharge passengers from points east of Ogden.

No. 1 will stop at stations west of Colfax to discharge passengers from points Cheyenne and east.

Time Table No. 91 — October 5, 1913 — TOWARD SAN FRANCISCO (Westward)

Stations	Dist. from Sparks	9 Fast Mail	3 California Mail	5 Pacific Express	23 Tonopah Express	19 Pacific Limited	1 Overland Limited	253 Ogden Manifest	309 Way Freight	307 Way Freight
		Arrive Daily	Arrive Daily	Arrive Daily	Arrive Daily	Arrive Daily	Arrive Daily	Arrive Daily	Arrive Daily Ex. Sunday	Arrive Daily Ex. Sunday
DN BLUE CANON	79.6	3.50AM	s 4.30AM	1.05PM	12.25AM	1.50AM	2.50AM	8.30AM		12.10PM
FULDA	76.5	3.42	4.19	12.54	12.13	1.38	2.40	8.13		11.45AM
DN EMIGRANT GAP	74.4	3.36	4.14	f12.48	12.06	1.32	2.35	7.45		11.20
DN SMART	72.9	3.32	4.11	f12.44	f12.01AM	1.28	2.31	7.35		11.05
YUBA PASS	70.1	3.25	4.04	12.36	f11.50PM	1.22	2.25	7.20		10.30
CRYSTAL LAKE	67.9	3.20	3.59	12.29	f11.40	1.16	2.19	7.10		10.17
DN CISCO	65.9	3.16	3.53	12.22	s11.30	1.11	2.14	6.55		10.08
DN TAMARACK	62.4	3.09	3.46	12.12	f11.18	1.03	2.06	6.40		9.50
TROY	60.4	3.05	3.41	12.06PM	f11.08	12.58	2.01	6.30		9.38
DN SPRUCE	58.8	3.01	3.36	11.59AM	f10.59	12.52	1.56	6.23		9.25
SODA SPRINGS	55.5	2.55	3.30	11.50	f10.49	12.45	1.49	6.10		9.05
DN SUMMIT	53.2	2.50	3.25	f11.43	f10.40	12.38	1.43	5.55		8.55
LAKE VIEW	50.0	2.40	3.14	11.30	f10.26	12.25	1.32	5.32		8.35
EDER	48.0	2.35	3.09	f11.24	f10.17	12.18	1.27	5.20		8.28
DN ANDOVER	45.6	2.28	3.03	11.18	f10.09	12.08AM	1.20	4.55		8.17
*STANFORD	43.5									
*ARCTIC	42.6									
CHAMPION	42.1	2.20	2.53	11.08	f 9.57	11.52PM	1.12	4.40		8.05
*DONNER ICE CO.	39.9									
DNR TRUCKEE	38.2	s 2.10	2.40	s10.55	9.45	s11.40	1.00	4.20	1.30PM	7.50AM
WINSTED	35.6	1.58	2.25	10.40	s 9.26	11.30	12.50	3.35	1.15	
*POLARIS	35.0									
PROSSER CREEK	31.2	1.49	2.15	10.30	9.16	11.20	12.40	3.10	12.50	
DN BOCA	29.9	1.46	2.11	s10.26	9.12	11.17	12.31	3.05	12.35PM	
*BURKHALTER	28.1									
HINTON	25.8	1.40	2.01	10.15	9.02	11.08	12.24	2.45	11.50AM	
*ICELAND	25.3				s					
*WICKES	24.7									
DN FLORISTON	23.7	1.36	1.56	s10.10	8.57	11.04	12.20	2.35	11.30	
MYSTIC	20.7	1.31	1.48	9.59	8.45	10.57	12.14	2.20	10.35	
CALVADA	17.6	1.25	1.41	9.50	8.29	10.50	12.08	2.05	9.50	
DN VERDI	13.8	1.15	f 1.31	9.40	8.10	10.42	12.02AM	1.45	9.15	
WARE	11.4	1.08	1.25	9.32	8.01	10.36	11.56PM	1.35	8.50	
MOGUL	10.3				f					
DNR LAWTON	8.3	1.02	1.10	9.25	f 7.55	10.29	11.50	12.45	8.30	
D RENO	3.3	s12.50	s12.58	9.15	7.45	10.19	11.40	12 30	7.50	
SPARKS (Passenger Depot)	0.7	12.43	12.49	9.03	7.28	10.08	11.33			
DNR SPARKS (Dspr'sOffice)	0.0	12.40AM	12.45AM	9.00AM	7.25AM	10.05AM	11.30AM	12.15AM	7.30AM	

Westward trains are superior to trains of the same class in the opposite direction. See Rule 72 and D-72.

*Frog taken out part of the season.

ADDITIONAL STOPS.
No. 23 will stop on signal at Union Mills, near mile post 214, Farad, Marmol and Summit Hotel.

No. 3 stop Verdi, Floriston and Boca to discharge passengers from points east of Sparks.

SACRAMENTO SUBDIVISION

Time Table No. 166 — June 7, 1942

EASTWARD

			THIRD CLASS				SECOND CLASS					FIRST CLASS						
Capacity of Sidings in Car Length	488 Freight	486 Freight	484 Freight	482 Freight	478 Freight	470 Portland Freight	606 Mixed	423 Freight	442 Mdse.	421 Freight	STATIONS	Distance from San Francisco	88 Challenger	102 Streamliner City of San Francisco	22 Pacific Limited	202 Passenger	10 Passenger	28 San Francisco Overland Limited
	Leave Daily	Leave Daily	Leave Daily	Leave Daily	Leave Daily	Leave Daily Ex. Monday	Leave Daily Ex. Sundays	Leave Daily	Leave Daily Ex. Sunday and Monday	Leave Daily			Leave Daily	Leave *See Note	Leave Daily	Leave Daily	Leave Daily	Leave Daily
BKWO TIP											TO-R SACRAMENTO 2.9	89.0 / 88.9	11.10 PM	5.53 AM	3.10 PM	10.00 AM	1.25 AM	12.10 AM
IYP					8.20 AM	6.00 AM			1.00 AM		ELVAS 1.7	91.8	11.17	6.00	3.17	10.07	1.32	12.17
WP								11.20 AM			SWANSTON 1.4	93.5						
South 92 M 66											BENALI 7.9	94.9	11.23	6.04	3.23	10.13	1.38	12.23
90 P											ANTELOPE 3.8	102.8	11.31	6.11	3.31	10.21	1.46	12.31
BKWO TYP	7.00 PM	4.00 PM	12.30 PM	12.30 PM	9.05 AM	6.45 AM		11.50 AM	1.40 AM	1.30 AM	TO-R ROSEVILLE 4.0	106.6	s 11.40 / 11.48 PM	6.18	s 3.39 / 3.50	s 10.30 AM	s 1.55 / 2.05	s 12.40 / 12.48
P											ROCKLIN 9.8	110.6					2.15	
Yard Limits E 73 WP	7.35	4.35	1.05	1.05							TO NEWCASTLE 4.0	120.2	12.13 AM	6.39	f 4.17		2.35	1.13
E 67 WP											AUBURN, NEVADA ST. 4.9	124.2	12.20	6.46	4.28		2.55	1.20
E 90 P				1.28							BOWMAN 5.2	129.1	12.28	6.54	4.37		3.03	1.28
E 62 W											EAST APPLEGATE 3.3	134.3	12.36	7.01	4.45		3.11	1.36
63 P											N. E. MILLS 4.1	137.6	12.41	7.06	4.52		3.18	1.41
Yard Limits BKWYP	8.40	5.40	2.10	2.20							TO-R COLFAX 4.4	141.7	s 1.00	7.17	5.15		s 3.30 / 3.50	s 2.00
M 46 P											CAPE HORN 4.3	145.1 / 146.0	1.11	7.26	5.27		4.02	2.12
E 119 WOYP	9.25	6.25	2.55	3.05							TO GOLD RUN 4.8	152.2	1.26	7.39	5.41		4.17	2.28
6 Spur											TOWLE 3.9	156.8	1.37	7.49	5.53		f 5.38	2.40
M 90 P											MIDAS 4.1	160.7	1.47	7.58	6.02		4.40	2.51
M 63 WP											KNAPP 0.7	164.8	1.57	8.07	6.11		4.49	3.02
WP											BLUE CANON 5.2	165.5 / 165.6					4.52	
Yard Limits M 90 WTP	11.20 PM	8.19	4.55	5.15							TO EMIGRANT GAP 6.1	171.8	2.15	8.19	f 6.30		s 5.15	3.21
M 69 WP											CRYSTAL LAKE 2.4	177.9	2.30	8.31	6.45		5.31	3.37
WP											OISO 5.2	180.3			f 6.51		f 5.38	
M 55 WP											TROY 5.5	185.5	2.48	8.47	7.03		5.51	3.56
E 102 BKWITP	1.10 AM	10.10	6.35	6.40							TO NORDEN 3.8	192.0	3.03	9.02	7.20		6.10	4.15
											EDER 5.7	195.8 / 197.2						
M 63 WP	2.15	11.15 PM	7.40	7.40							STANFORD 5.1	202.9	3.23	9.21	7.40		6.30	4.35
Yard Limits BKWOYP											TO-R TRUCKEE 10.1	208.0	s 3.40	9.30	s 8.00		s 6.55	s 5.00
M 97 P											HINTON 4.3	213.1	3.57	9.44	8.17		7.15	5.17
64 P											FLORISTON 10.0	222.4	4.04	9.51	8.24		f 7.25	5.24
M 122 P	3.15	12.15 PM	8.40	8.45							VERDI 10.5	232.4	4.20	10.04	8.40		f 7.50	5.40
P											RENO 2.6	242.9	s 4.40 / 4.50	s 10.25	9.15		s 8.15 / 8.40	s 6.00 / 6.10
BKWOYP	4.00 AM	1.00 AM	9.35 PM	9.30 PM							SPARKS (PSGR. STA.) 0.7	245.5	f		9.25		8.50	
							6.50 PM f 6.58											
							8 7.02 PM				TO-R SPARKS (DSP.OFF.)	246.2	5.05 AM	s 10.35 AM	9.28 AM		8.55 AM	6.25 AM
	Arrive Daily	Arrive Daily	Arrive Daily	Arrive Daily	Arrive Daily	Arrive Daily Ex. Monday	Arrive Daily Ex. Sunday	Arrive Daily	Arrive Daily Ex. Sunday and Monday	Arrive Daily	(154.9)		Arrive Daily	Arrive *See Note	Arrive Daily	Arrive Daily	Arrive Daily	Arrive Daily
	(9.00) 15.24	(9.00) 15.24	(9.05) 15.10	(9.00) 15.24	(0.45) 23.60	(0.45) 23.60	(0.12) 16.50	(0.30) 29.60	(0.40) 26.55	(0.30) 29.60	Time over District. Average Speed per Hour.		(5.55) 26.18	(4.42) 32.96	(6.18) 24.59	(0.30) 35.40	(7.30) 20.65	(6.15) 24.78

RULES S-71, D-71, 72, S-72, 85, 86, 87, and 93: No. 101 is superior to ALL trains except No. 101. No. 102 is superior to ALL trains.

First-class trains must clear the time of Nos. 101 and 102 not less than 10 minutes. Second and inferior class trains, extra trains and engines must clear the time of Nos. 101 and 102 not less than 15 minutes.

No. 606 may run ahead of first-class trains from Reno.

RULE 6. At Emigrant Gap—Time of first-class schedules applies at Passenger Station and time in train orders applies at siding.

No. 10 stop at Soda Springs to receive or discharge passengers and at Boca to exchange mail by locker.

Additional Stations:
Planehaven......M.P. 97.5
Walerga.........M.P. 99.4
Lincoln Ave.,
 Penryn.........M.P. 115.5
Clipper Gap.....M.P. 131.4
Magra...........M.P. 148.5
Dutch Flat......M.P. 154.1
Alta............M.P. 156.0

Smart...........M.P. 173.3
Yuba Pass.......M.P. 176.1
Soda Springs....M.P. 190.4
Mystic..........M.P. 225.5
Eder Cross-over M.P. 197.7
Andover.........M.P. 200.6
Andover.........M.P. 235.7
Cross-over......M.P. 237.1

Boca............M.P. 216.3
Wickes..........M.P. 221.9
Calvada.........M.P. 228.5
Mogul...........M.P. 231.5
Lawton..........M.P. 201.3

*Note—No. 102 leave and arrive 2nd, 6th, 8th, 11th, 14th, 17th, 20th, 23rd, 26th and 29th of each month.

ADDITIONAL FLAG STOPS TO RECEIVE OR DISCHARGE PASSENGERS

Train	At	Passengers (to or beyond) / Passengers from (or beyond)
10	Dutch Flat	Receive or Discharge
10	Troy	Tuesdays
10	Eder	Tuesdays and Saturdays
10	Andover	Sundays and Saturdays
22	Alta	Discharge Rev. Passenger
28	Soda Springs	Receive and Discharge
88	Any Station	Receive Revenue Passengers
88	Auburn, Nev. St.	Discharge

Sacramento .... Ogden .... Sparks

Berkeley

SACRAMENTO SUBDIVISION — WESTWARD

Time Table No. 166 — June 7, 1942

Notes

★No. 101 leave and arrive 4th, 7th, 10th, 13th, 16th, 19th, 22nd, 25th, 28th, 31st and 1st. Rules S-71, D-71, 72, S-72, 85, 86, 87, and 93: No. 101 is superior to ALL trains; No. 102 is superior to ALL trains except No. 101.

First-class trains must clear the time of Nos. 101 and 102 not less than 10 minutes. Second and inferior class trains, extra trains and engines must clear the time of Nos. 101 and 102 not less than 15 minutes.

RULE 5. At Loomis—Time applies at Passenger station.

At Emigrant Gap—Time of first-class schedules applies at Passenger Station and time in train orders applies at siding.

Westward trains receiving orders moving eastward trains from Loomis to Newcastle on No. 1 track, must not pass east crossover switch at Newcastle until opposing trains on No. 1 track have arrived, and eastward trains authorized to use No. 1 track to Newcastle, proceed on No. 1 track to first crossover switch, east of station at Newcastle.

Westward trains must stop east of east crossover switch at Newcastle unless train-order signal indicates "proceed."

No. 27 stop at the following stations to exchange mail by locker: Norden, Soda Springs, Emigrant Gap, Blue Canon, Towle, Alta, Dutch Flat, Gold Run, N. E. Mills, West Applegate, Clipper Gap, Bowman, Auburn, Newcastle, Penryn, Loomis and Rocklin.

No. 21 stop at Boca when requested by postal clerk to dispatch registered postal supplies and reduce speed, or stop if necessary, at Norden for mail exchange, stop Alta for express and Penryn, daily except Sundays and holidays to receive parcel post.

ADDITIONAL STATIONS

Station	M.P.
Lawton	237.1
Mogul	235.7
Calvada	228.5
Mystic	225.5
Wickes	221.9
Andover cross-over	201.3
Andover	200.6
Eder cross-over	197.7
Soda Springs	190.4
Smart	173.3
Blue Canon	165.5
Alta	156.6
Dutch Flat	154.1
Magra	148.5
Clipper Gap	131.6
Walerga	99.4
Planehaven	97.5

ADDITIONAL FLAG STOPS TO RECEIVE OR DISCHARGE PASSENGERS

Train	At	Receive or Discharge	Passengers to (or from or beyond)
21	Any Station	Discharge Revenue Passengers except between Truckee and Soda Springs	Sparks
21	Soda Springs, Alta, Dutch Flat, Blue Canon		
87	Alta, Dutch Flat	Discharge	Sacramento
87	Any Station	Discharge Revenue	Sparks
27	Any Station	Receive Revenue	Reno
27	Any Station	Discharge	

Timetable — Westward

First Class

Distance from Sparks	STATIONS	101 Streamliner City of San Francisco *See Note Arrive	7 Passenger Arrive Daily	21 Pacific Limited Arrive Daily	9 Fast Mail Arrive Daily	27 San Francisco Overland Limited Arrive Daily	87 Challenger Arrive Daily
156.4	TO-R SACRAMENTO	s 7.10 AM	s 7.10 AM	s 7.20 PM	s 1.50 AM	s 3.55 AM	s 4.15 AM
153.5	ELVAS	7.00	6.59	7.10	1.42	3.44	4.04
151.8	SWANSTON		f				
150.4	BENALI	6.57	6.53	7.04	1.36	3.38	3.58
142.5	ANTELOPE	6.50	6.45	6.56	1.28	3.30	3.50
138.7	TO-R ROSEVILLE	6.44	s 6.35 PM	s 6.48	s 1.10	s 3.20 / 3.30	s 3.30 / 3.40
134.7	ROCKLIN	6.34		6.17	12.56	2.52	3.14
131.4	LOOMIS	6.34		s 6.17	12.56	2.44	s 3.08
128.7	PENRYN			f 6.07		2.36	f 3.02
125.7	NEWCASTLE	6.24		s 5.59	12.45	2.27	f 2.55
121.7	FLINT						
120.8	TO AUBURN	6.15		5.45	12.35	2.12	2.40
116.9	BOWMAN	6.08		5.31	12.27	2.00	f 2.28
111.4	WEST APPLEGATE	5.59		5.20	12.16	1.44	f 2.16
108.2	N. E. MILLS	5.53		f 5.13	12.09 AM	1.35	f 2.08
103.2	TO-R COLFAX	5.45		s 5.00	s 11.59 PM	s 1.20	s 1.55
98.9	CAPE HORN	5.36		4.43	11.45	1.05	f 1.38
92.7	TO GOLD RUN	5.24		4.30	11.32	12.52	f 1.25
88.1	TOWLE	5.13		4.16	11.23	12.39	f 1.14
84.2	MIDAS	5.06		4.08	11.15	12.31	f 1.06
80.1	KNAPP	4.59		3.59	11.07	12.22	12.58
74.1	TO EMIGRANT GAP	4.48		f 3.45	10.55	12.08 AM	f 12.46
69.8	YUBA PASS			3.35	10.47	11.58 PM	12.37
68.0	CRYSTAL LAKE	4.36		3.31	10.43	11.54	12.33
65.6	CISCO			f 3.26			f 12.28
60.3	TROY	4.22		3.12	10.28	11.35	12.16
53.6	TO NORDEN	4.11		f 2.55	10.15	11.20	s 12.01 AM
52.9	SUMMIT						
49.6	DONNER	4.01		2.43	10.05	11.05	11.47 PM
47.7	EDER						
43.0	STANFORD	3.48		2.27	9.51	10.45	11.32
37.9	TO-R TRUCKEE	3.39		s 2.15	9.40	s 10.30	s 11.20
29.7	BOCA	3.27		1.53	9.18	9.53	f 10.54
27.9	HINTON	3.24		1.49	9.11	9.48	10.50
23.6	FLORISTON	3.17		1.42	9.11	9.38	f 10.43
13.7	VERDI	3.02		1.27	8.56	9.18	f 10.27
3.3	RENO	2.46		s 1.10	s 8.30	s 8.53 / 8.43	s 10.03 / 9.53
0.7	SPARKS (PSGR. STA.)			s 12.53	8.30	8.43	s 9.45
0.0	TO-R SPARKS(DSP.OFF.)	2.40 AM		12.50 PM	8.20 PM	8.30 PM	9.40 PM
(156.4)		Leave *See Note	Leave Daily	Leave Daily	Leave Daily	Leave Daily	Leave Daily
	Time over District / Average Speed Per Hour	(4.30) 34.76	(0.35) 30.34	(6.30) 24.06	(5.30) 28.44	(7.25) 21.09	(6.35) 23.76

Second Class / Third Class

STATIONS	605 Mixed Arrive Daily Ex. Sunday	420 Freight Arrive Daily	481 Freight Arrive Daily	483 Freight Arrive Daily	471 Oakland Freight Arrive Daily
SACRAMENTO		9.10 PM			2.45 PM
ELVAS					2.30
ROSEVILLE		8.30 PM	11.00 AM	3.20 AM	2.00 PM
NEWCASTLE			10.10	2.35	
COLFAX			8.45	1.20	
GOLD RUN			8.10	12.40 AM	
EMIGRANT GAP			6.30	10.55 PM	
NORDEN			5.00	9.30	
TRUCKEE			3.39	8.00	
RENO	s 6.50 PM / f 6.40				
SPARKS	6.30 PM		1.30 AM	6.00 PM	
Leave	Leave Daily Ex. Sunday	Leave Daily	Leave Daily	Leave Daily	Leave Daily
Time/Avg	(0.20) 9.90	(0.40) 22.20	(9.30) 14.51	(9.20) 14.86	(0.45) 23.60

Capacity of Sidings in Car Lengths

BKWO ITP — IYP — WP — South 92 / M 86 — BKWO TYP / Roseville yd. P — 85 P — 44 P — Yard Limits 54 WP — 62 P — 47 WP — W 83 P — 46 P — Spur P 60 — BKWYP P — C 52 P — 61 WOYP — P Spur 8 — M 95 — Yard Limits M 95 WITP — Summer 73 — M 78 WP — M 54 WP / Summer 71 — E. BKWITP — P(Upper) 77 / (Lower) 59 — 81 P — M 61 WP — Yard Limits BKWOYP — 42 P — M 98 P — WP — M 122 P — BKW OTP — Sparks yard

(No. 1 Track — A.B.S. — A.T.O. — A.B.S.)

SACRAMENTO DIVISION TIMETABLE No. 8, OCTOBER 30, 1977

ROSEVILLE SUBDIVISION

EASTWARD — No. 2 Track

FIRST CLASS 6 Passenger Leave Daily	Mile Post Location	Station Number	STATIONS SIDING CAPACITIES AND FACILITIES	Distance from Sacramento
PM 3.50	89.0 / 88.9	23050	TO-R **SACRAMENTO** — BKIYPQ	0.0
	90.0	23040	1.1 **SACRAMENTO** (15th St.) — P	1.1
	91.8	23037	1.8 **ELVAS** — IYPQ	2.9
	94.9	23021	3.1 **BENALI** — P	6.0
4.08	102.8	23008	7.9 **ANTELOPE** — BKIPQ	13.9
4.15	106.6	23000	TO-R 3.8 **ROSEVILLE** — BKIYPQ	17.7
	110.6	16480	4.0 **ROCKLIN** — P	21.7
4.31	120.2	16450	Yd. Lmts. 9.6 **NEWCASTLE**	31.3
4.36	124.2	16440	4.0 **AUBURN, NEVADA ST.**	35.3
4.42	129.1	16425	E-4200 4.9 **BOWMAN**	40.2
s 5.00	141.7	16300	E-6400 Yd. Lmts. 12.6 TO **COLFAX** — BKYPQ	52.8
5.09	146.1 / 146.0	16270	4.4 **CAPE HORN**	57.2
5.21	152.2	16259	E-6400 6.2 **GOLD RUN**	63.4
5.38	160.7	16242	8.5 **MIDAS**	71.9
5.48	165.5 / 166.6	16234	4.8 **BLUE CANON**	76.7
5.58	171.4	16229	M-5400 Yd. Lmts. 4.8 **EMIGRANT GAP** — IYPQ	81.5
	179.0	16220	7.6 **SHED 10** — IP	89.1
	180.3	16217	1.3 **CISCO** — P	90.4
	185.5	16211	5.2 **TROY** — P	95.6
6.39	192.0	16190	E-6336 6.5 TO **NORDEN** — BKIYPQ	102.1
	197.3 / 198.7	16175	5.3 **SHED 47** — IP	107.4
s 7.14	208.0	16160	E-4850 Yd. Lmts. 9.3 TO **TRUCKEE** — BKIYPQ	116.7
7.35	222.4	16148	14.4 **FLORISTON** — P	131.1
7.47	231.8	16133	9.4 **VERDI** — P	140.5
s 8.05	242.9	16110	Yd. Lmts. 11.1 **RENO** — P	151.6
s 8.14 PM	246.2	16105	TO-R 3.3 **SPARKS** — BKYPQ	154.9
Arrive Daily			(154.9)	

6

WESTWARD — No. 1 Track

Mile Post Location	STATIONS SIDING CAPACITIES AND FACILITIES	Station Number	Distance from Sparks	FIRST CLASS 5 Passenger Arrive Daily
89.0 / 88.9	TO-R **SACRAMENTO** — BKIYPQ	23050	156.4	PM s 12.08
90.0	1.1 **SACRAMENTO** (15th St.) — P	23040	155.3	
91.8	1.8 **ELVAS** — IYPQ	23037	153.5	
94.9	3.1 **BENALI** — P	23021	150.4	
102.8	7.9 **ANTELOPE** — BKIPQ	23008	142.5	AM 11.37
106.6	TO-R 3.8 **ROSEVILLE** — BKIYPQ	23000	138.7	11.31
110.6	4.0 **ROCKLIN** — P	16480	134.7	
113.9	W-6032 3.3 **LOOMIS** — P	16370	131.4	
116.6	2.7 **PENRYN** — P	16360	128.7	
119.6	Yd. Lmts. 3.0 **NEWCASTLE** — P	16350	125.7	11.10
124.5	Yd. Lmts. 4.9 **AUBURN**	16340	120.8	
128.4	3.9 **BOWMAN**	16330	116.9	10.52
142.1	W-5000 Yd. Lmts. 13.7 TO **COLFAX** — BKYPQ	16300	103.2	s 10.24
146.4	4.3 **CAPE HORN** — P	16270	98.9	10.11
152.6	6.2 **GOLD RUN** — P	16259	92.7	9.58
161.1	8.5 **MIDAS** — P	16242	84.2	9.40
166.0	4.9 **BLUE CANON** — P	16234	79.3	9.30
170.7 / 171.4	M-5400 Yd. Lmts. 4.7 **EMIGRANT GAP** — IYPQ	16229	74.6	9.20
179.0	7.6 **SHED 10** — IP	16220	67.0	
180.3	1.3 **CISCO** — P	16217	65.7	
185.6	5.3 **TROY** — P	16211	60.4	
192.1	6.5 TO **NORDEN** — BKIYPQ	16190	53.9	8.38
197.3 / 198.7	6.6 **SHED 47** — IP	16175	47.3	
208.0	W-6023 Yd. Lmts. 9.3 TO **TRUCKEE** — BKIYPQ	16160	38.0	s 8.04
222.4	14.3 **FLORISTON** — P	16148	23.7	7.39
231.7	9.2 **VERDI** — P	16133	14.5	7.26
242.8 / 242.9	Yd. Lmts. 11.2 **RENO** — P	16110	3.3	s 7.10
246.2	TO-R 3.3 **SPARKS** — BKYPQ	16105	0.0	6.57 AM
	(156.4)			Leave Daily

5

ADDITIONAL STATIONS — Roseville-Sparks No. 2 Track

Capacity and Direction of entry into Spurs	Mile Post	NAME	Station Number
540W	126.5	Foothill..........(Spur)	16430
.. P	148.5	Magra................	16265
.. P	156.8	Towle................	16247
.. ..	177.9	Crystal Lake........	16221
.. ..	197.7	Eder.................	16176
.. ..	200.9	Andover.............	16172
.. P	216.3	Boca.................	16154
.. P	238.0	Lawton..............	16125
.. P	241.0	West Reno...........	16122

RULE 5: Time applies at station signs between Sparks and Sacramento.

ADDITIONAL STATIONS — Sparks-Roseville No. 1 Track

Capacity and Direction of entry into Spurs	Mile Post	NAME	Station Number
490E ..	241.0	West Reno........(Spur)	16122
1125E P	238.0	Lawton..........(Spur)	16125
835W P	216.2	Boca............(Spur)	16154
.. ..	200.9	Andover.............	16172
.. ..	197.7	Eder................	16176
880E P	193.4	Summit..........(Spur)	16181
.. ..	177.9	Crystal Lake........	16221
880E P	157.2	Towle...........(Spur)	16247
.. P	148.9	Magra...............	16265

Bibliography

BOOKS

Best, Gerald M. *Snowplow, Clearing Mountain Rails*. Berkeley: Howell-North, 1966.

Church, Robert J. *Cab Forward*. Wilton: Central Valley Railroad Publications, 1982.

Davis, Leonard M. *History of the City of Roseville California*. Roseville: Roseville Community Projects Inc., 1964.

_____ *Rocklin, Past, Present, Future*. Roseville: Rocklin Friends of the Library, 1981.

Farquhar, Francis P. *History of the Sierra Nevada*. Berkeley: University of California Press, 1965.

Fulton, Robert Lardin *Epic of the Overland*. San Francisco: A.M. Robertson, 1924.

Hinckley, Helen *Rails From the West*. San Marino: Golden West Books, 1969.

Kraus, George *High Road To Promontory*. Palo Alto: American West Publishing Co., 1969.

Lee, Willis T. and others. *Guide Book To The Western United States-Part B The Overland Route*. Washington D.C.: U.S. Government Printing Office, 1916.

Lewis, Oscar *The Big Four*. New York: Alfred Knopf, 1946.

Mescherr, Joanne *Truckee*. Truckee: Rockingstone Press, 1978.

McGlashan, C.F. *History of the Donner Party, A Tragedy of the Sierra*. Stanford, CA: Stanford University Press, 1977.

Myrick, David F. *Railroads of Nevada & Eastern California Vol. 1*. Berkeley, CA: Howell-North Books, 1962.

Nadeau, Remi *Ghost Towns and Mining Camps of California*. Los Angeles: Ward Ritchie Press, 1965.

Shearer, _____ *The Pacific Tourist*. New York: Adams & Bishop, 1884.

Stewart, G.R. *Donner Pass — and Those Who Crossed It*. San Francisco: California Historical Society, 1960.

PERIODICALS

Bull, Howard "Big One at Shed 27." *Trains,* Nov. 1951: pp 20-23.

_____ "Right Hand Man in the Cab." *Trains,* May 1948: pp 40-48.

Everywhere West. Berkeley, CA.

Hack, W.L. "Operating a Mountain Division." *Railroad,* Vol. 28 No. 1. (June 1940): pp 24-33.

Haughton, Lee. "Link and Pin Days." *Railroad,* Vol. 28 No. 6. (Nov. 1940): pp 55-63.

Hecox, Arthur "A Staff Operators Story." *Railroad,* Vol. 27 No. 4. (Mar. 1943): pp 24-33.

Morgan, David P. "How to Hoist 5000 tons 1¼ Miles." *Trains,* Aug. 1958: pp 40-47.

Railway Age. New York.

Railway Age Gazette. New York.

Rasmussen, Christ "Hoodoo Number." *Railroad,* Vol. 29 No. 5. (April 1941): pp 86-89.

Sanders, Dale "SP's Rotary Snow Plows." *CTC Board,* No. 82 April 1982.

Southern Pacific Bulletin. San Francisco.

NEWSPAPERS

Colfax Record, Colfax, California.

Placer County Herald, Auburn, California.

Placer County Republican, Auburn, California.

Roseville Press Tribune, Roseville, California.

Roseville Register, Roseville, California.

Sacramento Union, Sacramento, California.

San Francisco Chronicle, San Francisco, California.

Truckee Republican, Truckee, California.

DOCUMENTS

Department of the Interior Special Commissioners Report — Conditions and Equipment of Central Pacific Railroad of California Item B Sacramento to Rose Creek. February 1869.

History and Function of the Pacific Fruit Express Co. Office of the Vice president and General Manager, San Francisco, 1967.

Prospectus — Relocation and Electrification Roseville — Sparks District Sacramento Division Southern Pacific Company. Kaiser Company Inc. L.H. Nishkian, Consulting Engineer. October 1945.

Snowsheds of the Central Pacific Across the Sierra Nevada. Office of the Division Engineer SP Co. Sacramento July 1913.

Storm of January 1952 in Sierra Nevada. Office of the Chief Dispatcher Sacramento, March 1952.

Through Manifest and Perishable Freight Schedules. Southern Pacific Company. Office of the General Superintendent of Transportation. San Francisco, March 1962.

PAMPHLETS

Wayside Notes on the Ogden Route. Southern Pacific Co. San Francisco, 1915.

The Overland Route to the Road of a Thousand Wonders. Union Pacific and Southern Pacific Passenger Departments, 1908.

The Tahoe Country. Southern Pacific Co. San Francisco, 1916.

UNPUBLISHED MATERIALS

Buike, R.E. *Southern Pacific (Pacific Lines) McKeen Cars.* San Francisco 1976.

Knowles, Constance Darrow. *A History of Lumbering in the Truckee Basin from 1856-1936.* 1942.

Miller, R.A. Papers On The 1952 Storm.

Waddell, James, Papers gathered while Trainmaster at Rocklin. 1903-1916.

---

*picture reference

Index

†map reference

Advance Challenger, 152
Alta, 21, 38, 42, 57, 61, 95*, 152
American, 98*, 231*
American Railway Union, 37
AMTRAK, 213, 215, 221, 223*, 252*, 254*, 257*
Andover, 67, 70, 71, 117*, 118*, 210*, 212, 243*-246*, 269*
Angel's Camp (Pullman), 152
Antelope, 74*, 145, 150*
Applegate, 24, 59, 61, 65, 183*
Aransas (Pullman), 146*, 147
Arcade Creek, 10*, 19
Arcade Station (Sacramento), 72*, 73*
Arctic, 36
Atlantic & Pacific Express, 35, 37
Atlantic Express, 35, 62, 139*
Auburn, 19, 34, 59, 64, 69, 85*, 211, 212
Auto ferry service, 146
Automatic Train Stop, 149, 151, 209, 219

Babcock, Alan H., 58, 65
BAESF (Freight Train), 220
BAEST (Freight Train), 220
Barclay, A.J., 58
BAX (Freight Train), 215
Baxter, 261*
BCW (Freight Train), 215, 252*, 253*
Beal, E.F., 19
Bear Flag (Pullman), 152
Bechtal Engineers, 108*
Ben-Ali, 56

Big Four, 14, 16, 17, 19, 26
Big Jack Davis, 37
Bigler, Gov. John, 57
Birce & Smart, 64
Bliss, D. B., 125
Bloomer Cut, 18*, 19, 21
Blue Cañon, 30, 34, 36-38, 42, 47*, 48, 53, 61, 62, 64, 67-71, 100*-103*†, 149, 156, 188*, 196*, 207, 212, 226*
Boca, 30*, 31, 36, 64, 67, 132*, 134-135*, 273*
Boca & Loyalton RR, 64
Boca Brewing Co., 36, 132*
Boca Mill & Ice Co., 35
Bowman, 59, 60*, 221
Bucker plow, 40, 42, 44*, 45*

California & Oregon RR, 26
California Cental RR, 16, 26
California Mail, 62
California Pacific RR, 26
California Republic (Pullman), 152
California Zephyr, 175*, 202, 213, 230*, 254*
Canadian Pacific Ry, 158
Cape Horn, 12, 20*, 21, 35, 36, 61, 93*, 231*
Cape Horn Mills, 42
Caporn, 61
Capt. John Sutter, (Pullman), 152
Carson, Kit, 12
Carson Pass, 12, 13†

Cascade, 24*, 42, 43*, 46*, 48, 69, 70, 194*
Cascade Tunnel, 57, 70, 158
Central Pacific RR (Ry), 12, 14, 15, 19, 21, 22, 27, 31, 33-37, 41, 48, 51, 61, 64, 69, 220
Challenger, 149, 151, 152, 153, 158, 174*
Champion, 55*
Chicago & North Western RR, 149, 151
China & Japan Fast Mail, 62
Chinatown (Dining car), 207
Chinese, 19, 21, 33, 34, 212, 248*
CHOAT (Freight Train), 220
Cisco, 21, 23*, 30, 38, 42, 44*, 48, 61, 70, 71, 153, 197*, 213, 221, 256*, 257*
City of San Francisco, 62, 149, 150*-153, 155, 157, 158, 182*, 200*-205*, 207-209, 213, 214, 227*-229*, 233*, 241*, 242*, 247*, 263, 271*
Civil defense precautions, 153
Clement, L.M., 19
Clipper (Locomotive), 33*
Clipper Gap, 19, 21, 24
Coburn's station, 21, 22
Colfax, 19, 21, 30, 35, 38, 42, 57, 58, 59, 61, 64, 66-69, 86*-91*†, 145, 147, 151, 155, 156, 158, 184*, 185*, 201, 207, 209, 211, 212, 216, 221, 230*, 254*, 262*
Comstock Lode, 26
Contract & Finance Company, 26
CPEFF (Freight Train), 220
CPWFF (Freight Train), 220

288

Crocker, Charles, 14, 15*, 19, 21
Crocker, Charles Fredrick, 41
Crown Willamette Paper Co., 64, 137*
Crystal Lake, 55*, 69, 70, 109*, 192*, 198*, 200, 201, 211, 221, 233*
CS (Freight Train), 215
Cutting, E.M., 53
Cutting Disk Signal, 53, 54*
Cyclone steam plow, 42, 46*

Dane, Timothy, 26
Debs, Eugene V., 37
Deer Park, 163*
Denver & Rio Grande Western RR., 219, 220, 253*, 275
Derby, Lt. George H., 12
Detours, 175*, 207, 222, 230*
Dieselization, 208, 209
Dietz lights, 68*
Donahue, Peter, 26
Donner, 36, 53, 122*, 211
Donner Lake (Pullman), 152
Donner Party, 12, 207
Donner Pass, 12, 13†, 25*, 208
Double-track program, 57, 58, 59†, 60*, 61, 70, 71*, 108*
Dutch Flat, 14, 15, 19, 20, 21, 42, 57, 227*
Dutch Flat & Donner Lake Wagon Road, 12*, 17
Dutch Flat Swindle, 16

Eagle (Bark), 33
East Applegate, 183*, 211
Eastern Express, 62
Ebbetts Pass, 12†
Eder, 116*, 146*, 147, 168*, 169*, 270*, 271*, 275*
Electrification, 57, 58, 65, 157
Elvas (Tower), 52, 54
Emigrant Gap, 22*, 30, 38, 42, 57, 64, 70, 71, 105*, 151, 155, 156, 188*, 189*, 190-191†*, 200, 201, 202*, 206*, 207-209, 212, 221, 223*, 232*, 259*, 261*
Enwood, 178*, 179*, 229*
Erickson & Peterson, 58
ESBAA (Freight Train), 220
ESBAF (Freight Train), 220
Essex, 36
European Mail, 35
Excess miles, 155
Express, 34, 87*

Farad, 133*
Fast Mail, 62, 109*, 149, 153, 158, 206*, 213, 221*, 239*
Feather River Canyon, 16, 26, 222
Fire Train, 48, 49*, 70, 71, 101*, 129*, 153, 154, 171*, 172*, 173*, 190*, 211
Flanger, 40, 130*, 133*, 166*, 200, 221, 222, 258*, 259*, 268*, 269*
Flint, 64, 152, 156
Floriston, 22, 36, 61, 64, 67, 136*, 137*, 145, 160*, 200
FMS-RG-UP-ADV (Freight Train), 215, 216, 232*
Font, Pedro, 11
Ford Motor Co., 216
Forebay, 64
Forty Niner, 151, 152, 181*, 183*

Fremont, Col. John C., 12
Fulda, 57, 64, 104*, 189*, 208
Full crew law, 156
Furloughee Challenger, 152

General Motors, 216
Gerry Machine, 49, 171*
GOAD (Freight Train), 152-154
Gold Coast (Limited), 62, 158, 213
Golden Gate Special, 35
Golden State Route, 219, 220
Gold Run, 21, 30, 37, 42, 57, 61, 66, 69, 94*, 95*, 151, 156, 173*, 200, 201, 211, 212, 255*
Gold Run (Pullman), 152
Gorge, 61, 99*
Governor Stanford (Locomotive), 36, 48
Great Northern Railway, 57, 65, 70, 158
Grey Eagle (Locomotive), 48
Gunter, 53

Harold's Club, 213, 214, 239*
Harrah, William Fisk, 213
Harriman, E.H., 51, 52*, 54, 57, 61-64, 69, 70, 208, 275
Heath, Erle, 39
Henness Pass, 12†, 13, 14
Hinton, 133*, 161*, 211
Hobard Southern RR., 64
Hood, William, 52, 57, 58, 61
Hopkins, Mark, 14, 15*
Hot Springs grade, 36, 52
Houghton, J.F., 19
Hours of service, 67
Humboldt Division, 31
Huntington, Collis, 14, 15*, 16, 26

Ice harvesting, 35, 64
Ice Land, 36, 136*
Illinoistown, 19
Interstate Commerce Commission, 70

James Marshall (Pullman), 152
Jiboom St., 31
Joaquin Miller (Pullman), 152
Judah, T.D., 13, 14*, 15-17, 19, 26, 38, 54, 56, 223, 275
Junction (Roseville), 16*, 30

Kaiser Engineers proposal, 156, 157†
KCBAY (Freight Train), 220
Keefe Time Saving Device, 54, 121*
Keene, 53
Kerr-McGee Chemical Co., 221
Knapp, 53, 100*, 156, 211, 212
Kraus-Maffei, 216, 217*, 218
Kruttschnitt, Julius, 52, 58, 61

Lake Tahoe, 125, 126*, 127*
Lake Tahoe Branch, 64, 125*†, 126*, 127*, 146, 163*
Lake Tahoe Railway & Navigation Co., 64
Lake View, 117*
Lander, 61
Lawton, 61
Lincoln Highway, 146
Lincoln, Abraham, 15, 19
Long Ravine, 18*, 61, 69, 92*, 187*
Loomis, 54, 56, 61, 64, 149, 156

Magra, 61
Main Trains, 152, 153, 154, 167, 174*, 175*
McGlashin, C.F., 147
McGranttans (Pullman), 146*, 147
McKeen cars, 62, 78*, 87*, 208
Merced (Locomotive), 48
Midas, 61, 156, 201*, 207, 211
Military Challenger, 152
MJRGN (Freight Train), 221, 255*
Montague, S.S., 19, 38, 39, 52, 54
Motive power developments, 36, 64, 65, 66, 155, 156, 216
Mountain Quarries RR, 64, 96*†
Mountain Special, 62
Mystic, 22, 59

National Ice Co., 36
Nevada (Steamer), 125
Nevada County Narrow-Gauge Ry., 64, 89*†
Nevada Merchandise, 215
Newcastle, 16*, 21, 34, 59, 64, 69, 85*, 181*, 211, 212, 230*
New England Mills, 42
Newsboy, 62
Nitroglycerin, 21
Noble Pass, 13†, 15
Norden, 70, 71, 114*, 115*†, 147, 148*, 152, 153, 155, 156, 158, 170*-173*, 200, 201, 207, 211, 212, 221, 235*, 247*-251*†, 262*, 264*-269*
Norden fire, 212
Nyack Lodge, 207

OACHT (Freight Train), 263*, 273*
OAOGF (Freight Train), 220
Ogden Route, 63, 220
OGFRL (Freight Train), 220
OGPIL (Freight Train), 220
Oilville, 186*
OMW (Freight Train), 254*
Operations in the sheds, 54, 64, 68
Oregon Division, 30
Oregon Railway & Navigation Co., 41
Orel, 61, 64
Oriental Mail, 35
OVE (Freight Train), 215, 254*
Overland (Limited), 62, 65, 66*, 87*, 104*, 123*, 145, 152, 153, 166*, 213
Overland Route, 11, 12, 35, 52, 62, 145, 152, 157, 158, 207, 213, 215, 219, 220, 275
OVW (Freight Train), 215

Pacific Express, 35, 62, 92*, 102*, 109*
Pacific Fruit Express Co., 63, 64, 69, 76*, 77*, 145, 176*, 177*, 215, 220, 270, 271, 275
Pacific Gas & Electric Co., 64, 105*, 207
Pacific Limited, 61, 62, 85*, 146*, 147, 149, 154, 161*, 167*, 170*, 186*, 187*, 188*
Pacific Portland Cement Co., 64, 96*
Pacific Railroad, 12, 13†, 14, 15, 19, 27, 34
Palace Car Express, 35
Panama Canal, 61, 93*
Parker, G.M., 30
Penryn, 35, 61, 84*, 180*

289

Perishable business, 62-64, 76*, 77*, 176*-179*, 182*, 215, 220
PIOGN (Freight Train), 220
Placerville, 26
Polaris, 36
Prosser Creek, 31, 36
Pullman Co., 35, 37, 149
Pullman Strike, 37

Quong, Fong, 248*

Rasmussen, Christ, 37
Raton Pass, 53
R Block (Freight Train), 63, 153, 154, 159*, 166*, 176*-180*, 189*, 274*
Read Timber & Lumber Co., 64, 104*
Red Light district, 31
Red Mountain Lookout, 48, 49, 106-107*
Reno, 22, 31, 32*-33*, 35, 37, 42, 52, 139*-141*, 146, 159*, 213-215, 239*
Reno Fun Train, 214*, 215, 232*, 238*, 269*
Reno Passenger, 62
RFRS (Freight Train), 215
RGBAT (Freight Train), 220
RGMJL (Freight Train), 221
RGOAF (Freight Train), 220
Rio Grande Division, 208, 209
Robinson, L.L., 16
Rocklin, 18*, 19, 30, 31, 35, 36, 52-59, 61, 64, 67-69, 82*, 83*†, 84*, 180*, 228*, 229*, 252*
Rogers Pass, 158
Roseville, 16*, 19, 30, 31, 35, 36, 52-59, 61, 64, 67-69, 71, 74-75†*, 76*-81*, 145, 147, 149, 151*-157, 174*-177*, 200, 208, 209, 211, 212, 215-217*, 220-222, 224*, 225*, 275
Rotary snowplow, 40, 41, 46*, 81*, 103*, 130*, 132*, 133*, 163*, 196*, 197*, 200, 203*, 204*, 206*, 208, 221, 222, 261-263*
Run-throughs, 219
RVCHT (Freight Train), 220
RVKCP (Freight Train), 220
RVNPP (Freight Train), 220
RVNPY (Freight Train), 222
RVOGP (Freight Train), 220, 270*, 271*
RVRGT (Freight Train), 220

Sacramento, 17*, 22, 26, 27, 30, 34-37, 52, 54, 62, 67, 73*, 146, 147, 149, 202, 209, 212
Sacramento Division, 12, 30, 31, 36, 37, 48, 53, 63, 67, 149, 200, 209, 222
Sacramento Valley RR, 13, 16, 26
Salt Lake, 62, 122*
Salt Lake Division, 31, 208
San Francisco & San Jose RR, 26
San Francisco Limited, 62, 145
San Francisco Zephyr, 213, 252*
Santa Fe Ry, 220
Sargent, Aaron, 19
Secret Town, 21
S.F. Overland, 153, 158, 169*, 174*, 183*, 209, 213, 214, 239*, 240*
Shady Run, 40
Sierra, 61, 85, 98*, 145, 146, 149, 152, 184*

Sierra Express, 209
Signalling, 54, 61, 86*, 108*, 211
Shed 47, 270*
601 Committee, 31
Six Companies, 33
Ski Hut, 148*, 149, 152
SKRVY (Freight Train), 221
SKSQL (Freight Train), 221
Smart, 64, 67, 198*
Smart Ridge, 39, 147, 200, 202, 203*
Smith, Harold, 213
Smith, Jedediah, 11
Snowball Specials, 147-149, 152, 163*
Snowsheds, 38-39*, 40-41†, 43*, 48, 49, 69-71, 106-107*, 110*-113*, 115*-117*, 158, 171*, 172*, 189*, 190*, 208, 212, 235*
Soda Springs, 152, 199*, 234*, 235*, 258*, 262*
Southern Pacific Co., 27, 51, 64, 65
Southern Pacific RR, 26, 27, 37, 61, 62, 69, 125, 149, 158, 207, 216, 220, 275
Sparks, 36, 57, 58, 61-63, 67, 69-71, 142*, 149, 152, 153, 155, 157, 159*, 200, 207, 209, 211, 214, 216, 220, 221, 236*-238*, 273*
Sprague, Frank J., 58
Sproule, W.M., 69
Spruce, 69, 193*
Staff system, 52, 53*, 54, 55*, 120*, 121*
Standard Oil Co., 216
Stanford, 43, 69, 70, 118*-121*, 156, 167*, 242*
Stanford, Leland, 14, 15*
Stevens, A.J., 32
Stevens, Elisha, 12
St. Louis Express, 62
St. Marcy (Pullman), 146*, 147
Strobridge, James H., 19, 21
Strong, D.W., 12
Strong's Cañon, 42
Suez Canal, 26
Sugar Bowl, 148, 149, 201*
Summit, 25*, 27*†, 30, 35, 36, 38, 42, 48, 53, 65, 67-71, 110*, 111*, 113*, 156, 216
Summit Tunnel, 21, 22, 25*, 53, 57, 70, 116*, 212
Sunset Route, 27, 216
Superliner, 213
Sutter, John A., 27
Switch 9, 211

Tahoe (Steamer), 125
Tahoe, 62, 145
Tahoe Ice Co., 36
Tahoe Sugarpine Co., 188*
Tamarack, 31, 53
Tehachapi Pass, 12, 207, 220, 222
Telescoping shed, 49, 106*
Test trains, 65, 69, 149, 216, 217*, 218*, 225*
Tonnage ratings, 65, 208, 219
Towle, 62, 64, 97*
Towle Brothers Lumber Co., 64, 97*
Towne, A.N., 42
Treasure Island Special, 152
Troy, 57, 70, 156, 192*, 196*, 200, 201, 211, 212, 232*, 263*
Truckee, 21, 28*, 29*-31, 34-37, 42, 47*-50*, 52, 53, 57, 61, 62, 64, 67-71, 123*, 124*, 129*, 130*, 147, 155, 156, 158, 162-166*, 200, 207-209*, 211-213, 216, 221, 241*, 259*
Truckee Division, 31, 32
Tucker Snowcat, 197*
Tunnel Chart, 24
Tunnel Motor, 219*, 222
Tunnel No. 6, 53, 112*, 113*
Tunnel No. 13, 42

Unicorn (Locomotive), 48
Union Ice Company, 36
Union Pacific RR, 12, 19, 22, 41, 51, 61, 62, 149, 207, 219, 220, 222, 255, 275,
Union Switch & Signal Co., 52, 61, 70, 149
Unit trains, 216
United States Railway Administration, 63, 69
UP-SP case, 61, 69
UPOAM (Freight Train), 220
UPMIA (Freight Train), 216, 220
UPRML (Freight Train), 272*
UPSFF (Freight Train), 220
UPWSA (Freight Train), 216
U.S. Steel, 216
Utah Construction Co., 58

Verdi, 31, 35-37, 64, 69, 138*, 150*, 153, 157, 160*, 211
Virginia & Truckee Ry, 32, 33, 37
Virginia City, 22, 31, 34

Wadsworth, 22, 24, 30-33*, 35, 36, 52, 67, 143*
Walker, Joseph, 12
Western Division, 151, 209, 216
Western Express, 62
Western Pacific RR, 16, 26, 63, 175*, 201, 207, 220, 222, 230, 275
Whitney, Josiah, 19
Wickes, 36
Winstead, 61
Winter of 1865-66, 21
   1866-67, 21, 38
   1889-90, 41, 42, 46*, 47*, 200
   1935-36, 146, 147
   1937-38, 147, 200, 222
   1951-52, 200-208*, 221
   1966-67, 221
   1974-75, 221
   1981-82, 221
Wirt, 55*, 61
Wreck of: No. 210, 69
  the *Fast Mail,* 109*
  the *Pacific Limited,* 146*, 147
  the *Overland,* 65, 66*
  first No. 87, 151

XAP (Freight Train), 216

Yuba (Locomotive), 36
Yuba Pass, 64, 70, 156, 193*, 195*, 200*-205*, 211, 232*, 260*

Zeta, 69

DONNER PASS
THE EAST SLOPE

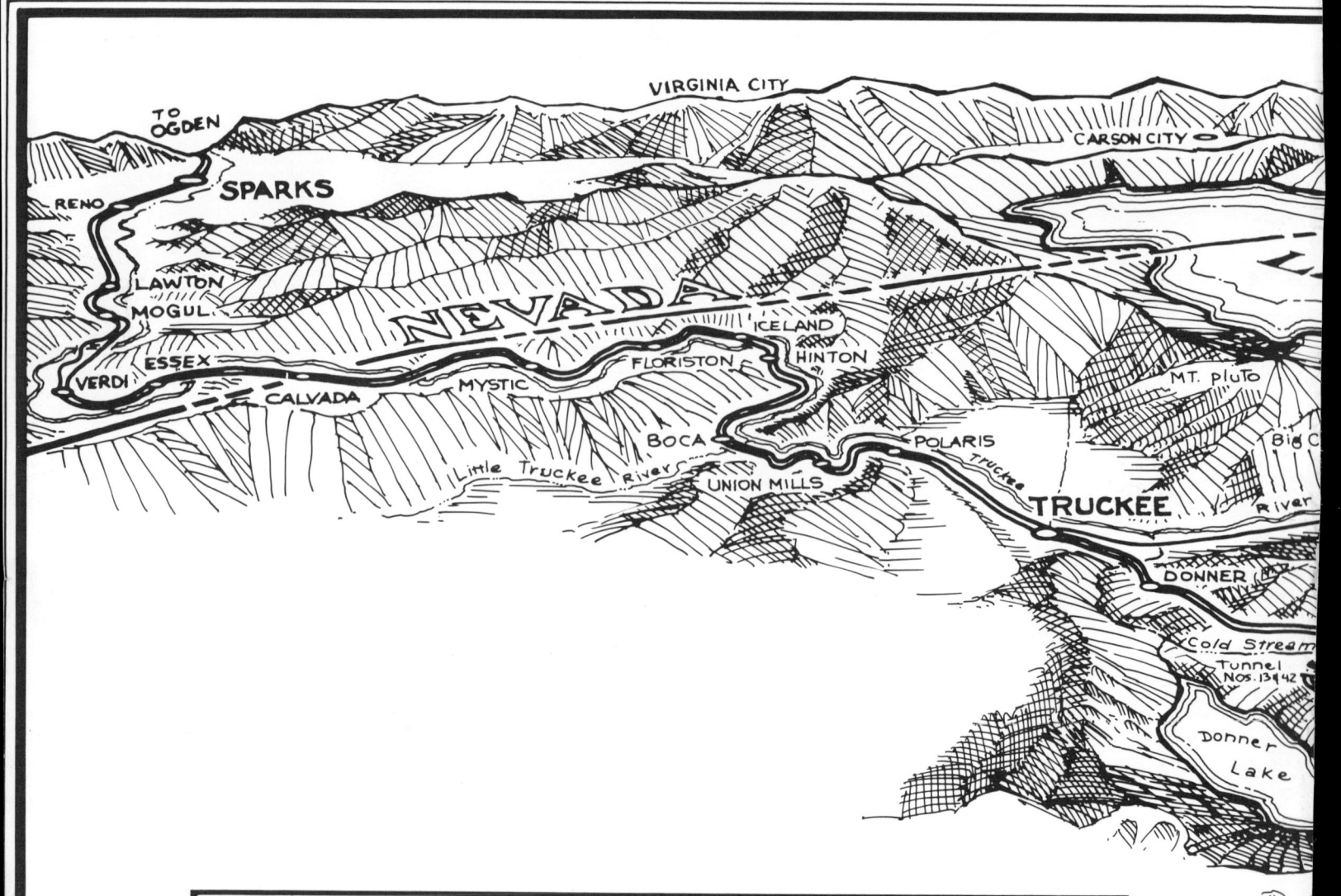